Arctic National Wildlife Refuge

ARCTIC NATIONAL WILDLIFE REFUGE

MATHEW T. COGWELL (EDITOR)

nova Science Publishers, Inc.
New York

Senior Editors: Susan Boriotti and Donna Dennis
Coordinating Editor: Tatiana Shohov
Office Manager: Annette Hellinger
Graphics: Wanda Serrano
Editorial Production: Jennifer Vogt, Matthew Kozlowski, Jonathan Rose, Alexandra Columbus and Maya Columbus
Circulation: Ave Maria Gonzalez, Vera Popovich, Luis Aviles, Melissa Diaz, Vladimir Klestov, Nicolas Miro and Jeannie Pappas
Communications and Acquisitions: Serge P. Shohov
Marketing: Cathy DeGregory

Library of Congress Cataloging-in-Publication Data
Available Upon Request

ISBN 1-59033-327-6.

Copyright © 2002 by Nova Science Publishers, Inc.
400 Oser Ave, Suite 1600
Hauppauge, New York 11788-3619
Tele. 631-231-7269   Fax 631-231-8175
e-mail: Novascience@earthlink.net
Web Site: http://www.novapublishers.com

All rights reserved. No part of this book may be reproduced, stored in a retrieval system or transmitted in any form or by any means: electronic, electrostatic, magnetic, tape, mechanical photocopying, recording or otherwise without permission from the publishers.

The authors and publisher have taken care in preparation of this book, but make no expressed or implied warranty of any kind and assume no responsibility for any errors or omissions. No liability is assumed for incidental or consequential damages in connection with or arising out of information contained in this book.

This publication is designed to provide accurate and authoritative information with regard to the subject matter covered herein. It is sold with the clear understanding that the publisher is not engaged in rendering legal or any other professional services. If legal or any other expert assistance is required, the services of a competent person should be sought. FROM A DECLARATION OF PARTICIPANTS JOINTLY ADOPTED BY A COMMITTEE OF THE AMERICAN BAR ASSOCIATION AND A COMMITTEE OF PUBLISHERS.

Printed in the United States of America

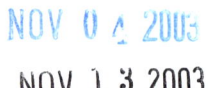

NOV 1 3 2003

CONTENTS

Preface	vii
Arctic National Wildlife Refuge: Background and Issues	1
M. Lynne Corn (Coordinator)	
Arctic National Wildlife Refuge: Legislative Issues	101
M. Lynne Corn, Bernard A. Gelb and Pamela Baldwin	
Legal Issues Related to Proposed Drilling for Oil and Gas in the Arctic National Wildlife Refuge	117
Pamela Baldwin	
Index	145

PREFACE

One important element of the energy debate in the 107th Congress is whether to approve development in the Arctic National Wildlife Refuge (ANWR) and, if so, under what restrictions or whether to continue to prohibit energy development in order to protect the area's biological resource values. This book discusses legal issues that relate to possible development of the Refuge and the current provisions in bills before Congress are discussed as well.

Corn begins the book with a chapter giving a brief overview of ANWR. She notes the rich biological resources and wilderness values of northeastern Alaska have been widely known for about 50 years, and the rich energy resource potential for much of that time. The future of these resources has been debated in Congress for over 40 years. The issue for Congress is whether to open a portion of what is now the Arctic National Wildlife Refuge (ANWR) to allow the development of potentially the richest on-shore source of oil remaining in the United States, and if so under what restrictions. Alternatively, Congress might choose to provide further protection for the Refuge's biological and wilderness resources through statutory wilderness designation or to maintain the current status of the area. Under current law, if Congress chooses not to act, the entire Refuge will remain closed to development under provisions of the 1980 Alaska National Interest Lands Conservation Act.

The coastal northern plain of the Refuge is the focus of debate. This remote and largely untouched area is an example of an arctic ecosystem that, by virtue of being essentially intact, is increasingly rare. The area also is an immensely promising oil prospect, which some feel could be as productive as Prudhoe Bay. For over 20 years, the debate over energy development in the Refuge has been highly polarized and remains so. President George W. Bush is committed to opening the Refuge to development, citing unrest in the Middle East among his reasons. And opposition to development remains strong, as opponents point to other means of achieving national energy goals.

In the next chapter Corn joins Gelb and Baldwin in discussing whether Congress will approve energy development in the ANWR, and if so, under what restrictions, or whether to continue to prohibit development in order to protect the area's biological resource values. Shortages of gasoline and natural gas and resulting increased prices from late 2000 to early 2001, followed by terrorist attacks, renewed the ANWR debate for the first time in 5 years. Six bills have been introduced in Congress that would directly affect the future of ANWR.

Four of these would open the refuge to development; they share many overlapping provisions. Two would designate the coast of ANWR as wilderness.

Development proponents argue that ANWR oil would reduce U.S. energy markets' exposure to recurring crises in the Middle East; boost North Slope oil production and extend the economic viability of the TransAlaska Pipeline System; and create numerous jobs in Alaska and elsewhere. They maintain that ANWR oil could be developed with minimal environmental harm, with a footprint limited to 2000 acres out of a 19 million acre Refuge. Opponents argue that intrusion on this ecosystem cannot be justified on any terms; that it should be designated as wilderness; that oil found (if any) would provide little energy security and could be replaced by cost-effective alternatives; and that job claims are overstated.

Baldwin continues with a chapter analyzing legal issues around ANWR. If the current prohibition against production of oil and gas anywhere in the Refuge is repealed, then oil and gas development and related activities could occur not only on the federal lands, but also on Native lands within the Refuge. Although H.R. 4 contains a 2,000 acreage limitation on the development "footprint" in the coastal plain, this limitation would not apply to some, and possibly not to any, of the Native lands, in which case some or all of the more than 100,000 acres of such lands in the Refuge (inside and outside the officially designated coastal plain) could be developed. Absent statutory clarification, development on these lands could occur under existing standards, which many observers contend are lenient. In additional to current regulations, the terms and environmental stipulations of a 1983 Agreement with the Arctic Slope Regional Corporation (ASRC), a Native Regional Corporation, would govern oil development on ASRC subsurface holdings in the Refuge. This Agreement contains environmental stipulations that, while originally intended as beneficial requirements, may permit practices now regarded as undesirable. In addition, unless the relevant provisions of the Agreement were superseded by statutory language, it appears that the United States would have to obtain a court order to change an ASRC leasing plan whenever the United States and ASRC disagreed as to environmental harm.

More generally, it appears that under the Senate bill the Bureau of Land Management would be in charge of the federal leasing program in the Refuge *and* the development of environmental constraints to protect the Refuge wildlife. Therefore, under the Senate bill, the scope of authority of the Fish and Wildlife Service (FWS) to protect Refuge resources from the effects of drilling appears to be less than under current law and regulations; the status of FWS under the House bill is less clear. The environmental standard used in both the House and Senate bills – "no significant adverse effect" – has been used in the past, but could allow a range of effects before protection would be triggered compared to other standards that have also been used. New leasing and environmental regulations would be developed and mineral leases sold on an accelerated schedule without new environmental impact studies. Many of the environmental constraints that would be imposed on leases in ANWR would be left to the discretion of the Secretary, whose discretionary acts would be more difficult to challenge under the strict standard of review in H.R. 4.

Both bills would share leasing revenues with Alaska, and both would establish new Funds with the federal share that would benefit energy research and mitigate coastal impacts. However, the provisions on disposition of leasing revenues in the House bill present issues related to the Alaska Statehood Act. If the disposition provisions were enacted and later held by a court to be invalid, the revenues from leasing could be divided 90% to the State of

Alaska and 10% into the federal Treasury, with no revenues going to be conservation purposes.

The Senate bill would leave in place current authority permitting the export of oil coming from the Refuge via the Trans-Alaska Pipeline. H.R. 4 would direct the Secretary to prohibit export as one of the terms and conditions of leases.

Chapter 1

ARCTIC NATIONAL WILDLIFE REFUGE: BACKGROUND AND ISSUES[*]

M. Lynne Corn (Coordinator)

OVERVIEW

From Alaska's Prudhoe Bay eastward 200 miles to the Canadian border is an area of unique natural wealth. An area teeming with wildlife, it has been called the "Serengeti of the Arctic." The eastern part of the region also contains America's best remaining onshore oil prospect, beneath the coastal plain of the Arctic National Wildlife Refuge (ANWR). (See Figure 1.)

This remote and largely untouched area is an example of an arctic ecosystem that, by virtue of being essentially intact, is increasingly rare. It is an important habitat for musk oxen, migratory waterfowl, vast numbers of caribou, and predators such as grizzly bears, polar bears, wolves, and golden eagles.

Moreover, the coastal plain is immensely promising for oil and natural gas, possibly on the scale of Prudhoe Bay's resources. Its development could help reduce America's energy dependence to some degree and keep the Alaska pipeline in use for decades — benefiting the national economy, the oil industry, and people in Alaska.

The Purpose of the Report

When Congress expanded the boundary of ANWR in the Alaska National Interest Lands Conservation Act (ANILCA) in 1980, it designated about 8 million acres within the earlier boundaries of the refuge as wilderness — off-limits to any form of development. However, in two sections of ANILCA, Congress postponed a decision on wilderness designation of 1.5 million acres of the coastal plain (called the *1002 area*) — a portion of ANWR thought to be

---

[*] The following authors contributed to this chapter: Pamela Baldwin, Claudia Copeland, M. Lynne Corn, Bernard Gelb, James McCarthy, Wayne Morrissey, Mark Reisch and Roger Walke

rich in oil and gas resources — and required the Department of the Interior (DOT, or Interior) to prepare a detailed study of the area and to recommend how it should be managed.

Interior finished its detailed analysis of oil potential, wildlife resources, impacts, and mitigation measures in April 1987. In its report to Congress, DOI estimated then that the chance of recovering economic quantities of oil at 19%, a figure that is very high by industry standards. The report recommended that the entire area be made available for leasing. The report and its recommendation generated controversy, as have virtually all subsequent reports on this topic. In intervening years, estimates of oil potential have varied, but enthusiasm for ANWR oil development remains strong, particularly in Alaska. Likewise, opposition to energy development continues to be strong, based on concern for the area's wilderness values and wildlife.

Figure 1. Shaded Relief Map of Northeastern Alaska

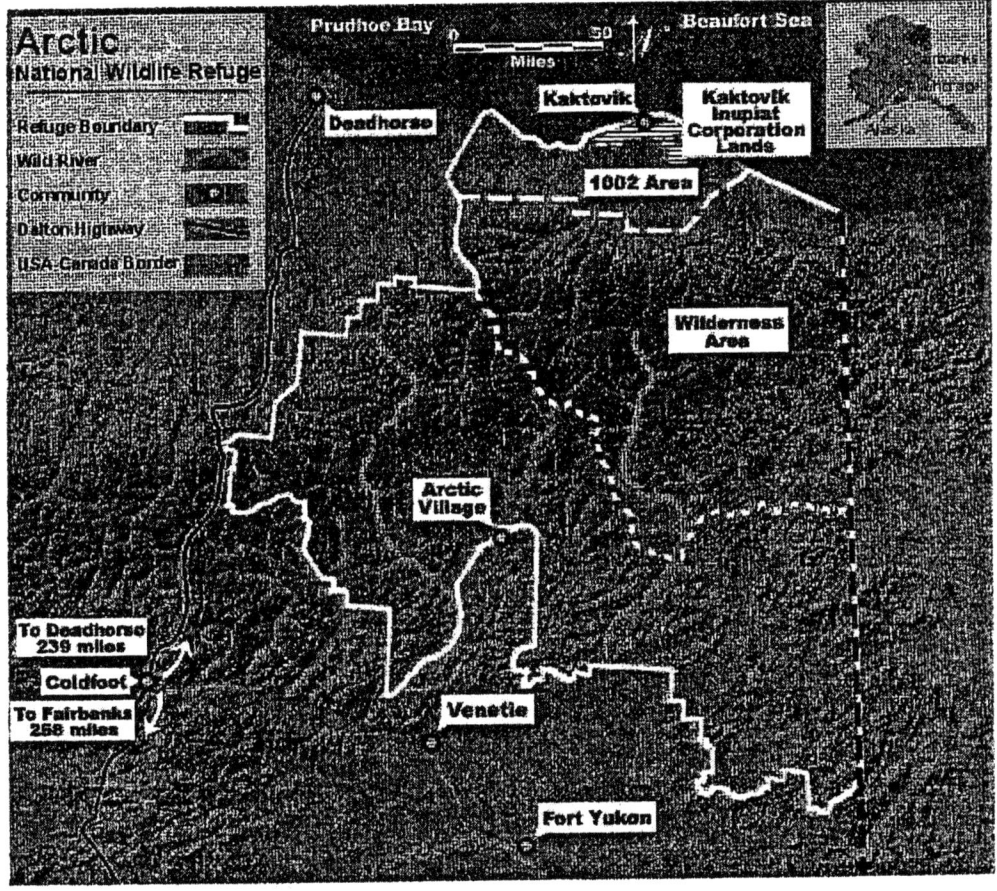

Source: U.S. Dept. of the Interior, Fish and Wildlife Service [http://www.r7.fws.gov/nwr/ arctic/shademap.html], Nov. 9, 2001. Minor modifications made to enhance clarity in monochrome.

This chapter goes beyond reporting the opposing views of development versus protection. Rather, it provides background and basic material for analyzing possibilities and implications of emerging options.

The Tradeoffs and Possible Alternatives

Much is at stake in the ANWR decision, for U.S. energy interests, for proponents of unspoiled wilderness, and for the State of Alaska. On the one side, if oil were found and developed, the additional domestic supply would be seen as enhancing national security (although some opponents of opening ANWR argue that the vulnerability of the TAPS pipeline to sabotage diminishes the national security argument). Further, oil development would create several thousand short-term jobs in Alaska and elsewhere, and a substantial number of long-term jobs as well. The State would benefit from additional royalty income, and many of Alaska's Native groups would benefit as well (though some would face threats to important subsistence resources).

On the other side, many believe developing oil would irrevocably compromise the area's wilderness values — defined as an area "untrammeled by *man.*" Some counter that the area has already been affected by man: there are a few remains of DEWLine construction and a capped oil well in the 1002 area. Some argue, too, that the coastal plain itself is not of a wilderness quality most would expect. The area is bounded on the south by the spectacular Brooks Range, but is itself mostly flat or rolling — a treeless tundra laced with shallow streams, most of which flow only during the brief arctic summer.

However, the apparently hostile nature of the area belies its national and international significance as an ecological reserve. It protects a virtually undisturbed, nearly complete spectrum of arctic ecosystems, and is one of the last places north of the Brooks Range that remains legally closed to development. Those who favor preservation argue that when the United States is serving as an international leader in the protection of vanishing ecosystems, development of the 1002 area would not set a good international example. Thus, if oil development occurred, the issue would become how to ensure that development would be compatible, as far as possible, with the purposes of the wildlife refuge.

Developing oil in the harsh, fragile arctic environment is expensive and risky. Since oil was discovered at Prudhoe Bay in 1968, oil companies and government agencies have done much to reduce environmental impacts, *e.g.,* through reducing the size of drill pads, numbers of roads, and size and location of support facilities; and through improving waste management. Depending on statutory and regulatory requirements, and with proper investment, monitoring, and enforcement, energy companies could develop the 1002 area in ways that continue to reduce effects on plants and animals.

The Choices Before Congress

In the context of these tradeoffs, the spectrum of alternatives before Congress includes:

- No action, which would maintain the status quo, which prohibits drilling for oil and gas throughout the refuge.
- Authorize leasing in the coastal plain of ANWR to proceed under the current regulatory requirements and capabilities of DOI

- Allow leasing in the coastal plain of ANWR to proceed, but with special statutory and regulatory conditions, (which could be greater or less than currently required). Among a variety of possibilities or proposals, these conditions might include:
  1. Limiting surface occupancy in the 1002 area to reduce environmental impacts (recognizing evolving technology).
  2. Requiring environmental controls, phasing, special area protection, or enforcement mechanisms.
  3. Requiring various measures for site restoration or removal of infrastructure upon completion of oil operations and/or establishing bonding mechanisms to ensure accomplishing these goals.
  4. Reducing requirements for environmental review under the National Environmental Policy Act or limiting judicial review of executive actions.
  5. Allowing different standards for environmental protection or reclamation to prevail on Native lands than on the remainder of the coastal plain.

- Designate the coastal plain as wilderness, thereby foregoing any energy development and associated economic benefits, but maintaining existing natural values and employment and subsistence opportunities.

Exploring and Developing the Oil Resource

Exploration does not necessarily mean that the coastal plain immediately would be spread with drilling pads, service facilities, and pipelines. Companies may not discover economic quantities of oil — or any oil at all. If they do find economic quantities and development occurs, oil facilities likely would occupy only a small, though dispersed, portion of the total area; and it is unlikely that oil would be produced until 7 to 12 years after any congressional approval of exploration. Drilling proponents argue that this long lead time is a reason for making a decision now.

Assessing the Potential

Parts of Alaska's North Slope coastal plain have proved abundant in oil reserves, and its geology holds further promise.[1] The oil-bearing strata extend eastward from the National Petroleum Reserve-Alaska (NPRA), past the prolific Prudhoe Bay field and a few smaller fields, and may continue into and through ANWR's 1002 area. Clearly, a key step in making a decision on ANWR is estimating how much oil might be there. Drilling (both exploration and confirmation), now prohibited, is the only method by which the 1002 area's petroleum potential can be ascertained with reasonable assuredness in the context of the uncertainties of oil discovery.

On its part, the Department of the Interior, without drilling, has issued assessments in 1987, 1991, 1995, and 1998 of the amount of oil and gas that might be present in ANWR.

---

[1] For maps of existing discoveries along the North Slope, see .the website of the Division of Oil and Gas, Alaska Department of Natural Resources, at:
[http://www.dog.dnr.state.ak.us/oil/products/maps/northslope/northslope.htm]

Those prepared after 1987 have been based upon progressively newer geological data from outside ANWR and upon reinterpretation of previous information using improving techniques, and have changed estimates of ANWR's oil potential.

Two considerations might be noted at this point. One is that the projected price of oil is a key factor in estimating the amount of oil that might be economically recoverable. The second is that the larger the area open to leasing and resultant oil company participation, the more likely that company bidding will give the government (the people of the United States) a larger return for making resources accessible to private entities.

ANWR Oil, U.S. Oil Consumption, and ANWR Gas

Based upon the results of the 1998 Interior Department assessment, the 1002 area contains some of the most promising undrilled onshore geologic structures with petroleum potential known in the United States. The U.S. Geological Survey (USGS) estimated that, at $24/barrel (in 1996 dollars), there is a *95%* chance that 2.0 billion barrels or more could be recovered, and a *5%* chance of *9.4* billion barrels or more. In comparison, the Prudhoe Bay field originally was estimated at 11-13 billion barrels of economically recoverable oil.

Many argue that this large potential should be explored and developed to offset the decline in domestic oil production. Domestic production without ANWR is projected by the U.S. Energy Information Administration (EIA) in its base case to be down to 5.6 million barrels per day (bbl/d) by 2020 (from 5.8 million bbl/d in 2000), while consumption is projected to rise from 19.7 million bbl/d to 26.7 million bbl/d. Other things being equal, domestic output without ANWR would supply only about one-fifth of U.S. consumption, with the rest coming from imports. Assuming a higher price of $30 per barrel, it appears that potential peak output from USGS's "low" and "high" ANWR volumes of economically recoverable oil at 300,000 and 1,575,000 bbl/d, respectively. These would represent a 5% and a 28% rise in U.S. output, respectively, at peak production.

Possibly of greater importance, are the gathering and transportation economics of both existing and prospective fields, which include the cost of shipment through the TAPS pipeline. Combined production at Prudhoe Bay and other North Slope fields is now at only about half of its peak and is projected to rise only slightly between 2000 and 2020. Development of and production from ANWR would improve the commercial viability of currently producing North Slope fields by spreading the per barrel cost (maintenance and capital charges) of operating the pipeline over a larger number of barrels.

The possibility of large amounts of natural gas in ANWR together with huge amounts of proven gas reserves in the Prudhoe Bay area (not being produced presently) may increase the appeal of oil and gas development of ANWR to energy companies. For economic reasons, natural gas generally has not been emphasized, but becomes more attractive as demand grows and prices rise. Construction of a pipeline to transport natural gas to North American markets and/or a warm water port for shipping liquefied natural gas would be a necessary element.

Controlling Impacts

If Congress decided to authorize development, then the issue would become whether and how to minimize effects on wildlife and the coastal arctic ecosystem, and — through them —

on Native cultures. Changes in the ecosystem could result from several facets of oil development. Major intrusions would include large requirements for water and gravel; and the displacement and disturbance of land, animals, and plants by pipelines, roads, airstrips, and other infrastructure. There is particular concern for caribou migration routes; calving and insect relief areas; migratory bird nesting and staging; effects of air and water pollutants; and direct and indirect effects of human presence. In addition, because of mixed ownership in the area, problems arise in how to establish and enforce controls on development.

Infrastructure

The trend in North Slope energy development is toward compactness, reduction in numbers and mileage of roads, centralization or reduction of support facilities, reduction of hazardous wastes, and concentration of exploration and early development activities in winter (when the frozen tundra makes cross-tundra travel possible, and when roads can be built from ice). Industry representatives now argue that the entire ANWR area can be developed with only a 2,000 acre "footprint." Opponents argue that the 2,000 acres would be spread across the entire 1002 area, is achievable only if one fails to count some major facilities, and is misleading in any case, since effects of the area covered by gravel may extend well beyond even a broadly defined footprint. Limitation of the footprint has begun to be a major point of congressional debate.

Physical Environment

Much of the controversy over development of the 1002 area has focused on potential impacts on biological resources in the area. However, if development occurs, there also would be impacts on the physical environment and resources of the area — land, air, and water — as a result of construction, operations, and human habitation. Currently, because the area is uninhabited (except for Kaktovik), the condition of the physical environment has been characterized as pristine and nearly unaffected by human activity.

Exploration and development activities would alter the existing physical environment. For example, oil field operations would result in air pollution emissions. There would be need for large amounts of water for drilling and ancillary activities, including construction of roads, drill pads, and airstrips. There likely would be impacts from both the mining and use of gravel as part of some of these activities. Exploration and development also would result in the generation of several types of waste streams, both from industrial operations and domestic wastes, requiring disposal. At issue are the individual and cumulative effects of such alterations and the ability of the natural environment to recover and be reclaimed when oil-related activities have ceased.

Industry points out that companies use improved technology in the arctic today (compared with that used in the past for development of existing sites in the arctic region), which greatly reduces the "footprint" of operations and relies on practices that minimize and provide for better disposal of wastes. The result is less direct and indirect impact in terms of habitat loss and environmental contamination. Moreover, numerous environmental protection requirements administered by federal and state authorities are intended to govern and regulate activities that might take place. Critics, however, are concerned about environmental effects of routine operations in the fragile 1002 environment, as well as the possibility of leaks and spills of various contaminating substances, and whether adequate safeguards would be adopted and enforced by regulators. Moreover, critics argue that even careful development would lead to lasting changes in the fragile arctic environment.

Alaska Native Ownership

Over 100,000 acres in ANWR are owned by Alaska Natives. The surface of 90,000 acres is owned by the Kaktovik Inupiat Corporation (MC) and the subsurface of these acres is owned by the Arctic Slope Regional Corporation (ASRC). The remaining 10,000 acres are owned by individual Natives. Some of the 100,000 acres are within the legal description of the 1002 area; some also lie along the coast but are legally described as outside the 1002 area, and all 100,000 acres are within the Refuge as a whole. Regulation of development on these lands is problematic and is often not considered explicitly in legislative proposals.

Special Areas

Wildlife experts are particularly interested in threats of development to several sensitive or special areas. For example, on the southern edge of the coastal plain, Sadlerochit Spring is of great biological importance because it never freezes. Other areas include the southeast portion of the coastal plain, where caribou calving is particularly likely to occur; certain staging areas for snow geese; riparian areas important to musk oxen; deep rivers and lakes important to overwintering fish; and denning or nesting sites of bears and raptors, to name a few.

Secondary Development

Also of concern are the effects of possible spinoff development both in Kaktovik, an Alaska Native settlement and Distant Early Warning Line (DEWLine) station on Barter Island just off the coast, and on other Native lands within the Refuge. Kaktovik could be a staging area for oil operations. Such development could compromise wildlife and other environmental values. Currently, Deadhorse (at Prudhoe Bay, the oldest support center), the Kuparuk Industrial Center (west of Prudhoe Bay), and to some extent Alpine (a very modern oil development west of the Kuparuk oil field, with much of its support activities reduced or taking place elsewhere) offer alternate examples of how service support areas might be handled. Deadhorse was left mostly to private decisions, and its sprawl and contamination problems led to the more compact, controlled approach at the Kuparuk Facility. Still later, the Alpine field essentially eliminated the need for some kinds of additional support facilities, reduced the physical size of some of the remaining facilities, and shifted still other operations to other sites by flying material in and out or carrying other equipment in on winter ice roads. In the 1002 area, facility reduction might continue, and some needs might be shifted to Native lands within and near the 1002 area.

Future Recovery

Whether strict statutory and regulatory controls and strong government enforcement could protect wildlife values to the satisfaction of those opposing development is open to question. (Wilderness values, by definition, would be compromised if full development occurred.) But for the long term, an equally important question is whether, after oil production ceased, the area could be and should be restored as nearly as possible to pre-development conditions.

If major oil reserves were found, energy companies might operate on the coastal plain for decades. If natural gas were also found, it too might be developed. (There is currently no means to send natural gas to market, either from the 1002 area or from Prudhoe Bay.) Offshore oil fields might also be found, and might be developed with onshore support in ANWR. Any of these outcomes could lead to significant human activity in the area for a century or more.

Assuming eventual dissipation of industrial presence, would the area eventually revert to something of its former condition? New data exist to show that such an intensive presence could last many decades after activity ceases. Complete removal of all infrastructure seems unlikely, and resulting water flow patterns might not even make it desirable. The short growing season and low precipitation make complete revegetation of disturbed areas uncertain. Recovery of animal populations and species diversity would depend on viable populations close enough to restock the area or site, and possibly explicit controls limiting future presence so that the site or area can recover. If Congress decides to open ANWR, it may include rehabilitation requirements.

INTRODUCTION

The debate over whether to open the coastal plain of the Arctic National Wildlife Refuge (ANWR) to energy leasing has raged for decades, with the main periods of controversy occurring in the late 1950s before the refuge was established; the period 1977-1980 at the passage of the Alaska National Interest Lands Conservation Act; 1987 when the Final Legislative Environmental Impact Statement (FLEIS) was released; the early 1990s during the Persian Gulf War; and the current debate, which began months before the attacks on New York and Washington, but was certainly heated by those events.

This chapter is a collection of the background information and new developments that have arisen since the 1987 FLEIS, and it discusses the possibilities and implications of emerging approaches to development. It does not focus on any particular legislation.[2] Rather, it provides background and basic material for analyzing proposals and ideas about developing or not developing the 1002 area.

---

[2] For a discussion of current legislative proposals on ANWR, see CRS Issue Brief IB10094 *Arctic National Wildlife Refuge: Legislative Issues,* updated regularly.

The Decision Before Congress

The portion of Alaska's North Slope between Prudhoe Bay and the Canadian border represents this country's largest, most diverse remaining example of a largely untouched arctic ecosystem.[3] All major arctic species are relatively abundant in the area. The coastal plain and adjacent areas are important habitat for caribou, migratory waterfowl, and such predators as wolves, polar bears, and grizzly bears. However, the coastal area is also very likely one of the nation's best remaining oil prospects, possibly containing quantities nearly as great as the fields at Prudhoe Bay.[4]

Congress recognized this conflict in values in 1980 when *it* expanded the existing Arctic National Wildlife Range, and renamed it the Arctic National Wildlife Refuge in the Alaska National Interest Lands Conservation Act (ANILCA, P.L. 98-487). The major portion of the pre-existing Range was designated as wilderness, and the remainder, which constituted most of the Range's coastal plain, was hotly contested because of its high biological value and potential oil resources. The compromise reached in §1002 of ANJLCA required that DOI intensively evaluate the oil potential, environmental impacts, and alternative policies for future disposition of 1.5 million acres of the coastal plain of ANWR. This "1002 area" is approximately 100 miles wide, and is 10 to 25 miles from north to south, roughly to the margin of the Brooks Range. (See Figure 2.) DOI was to provide the report with its findings and recommendations to Congress, so that decisions relating to development could be made with more information and with the full participation of Congress. In the meantime, §1003 of ANILCA explicitly forbids energy development throughout the Refuge until Congress acts.

The issue has been debated several times since 1980. The round in the 107th Congress was stimulated by rising energy prices (though these have since fallen), and by a predicted favorable environment in Congress and a strongly supportive President. Subsequent drops in oil prices shift in control of the Senate, and concern over terrorism have all complicated the outlook in recent months.

Congressional options can be divided into categories. A decision could be postponed, thereby continuing the development prohibitions of §1003; the area could be made permanent wilderness; development could be permitted under current laws applicable to other federal lands; or development could be allowed subject to specified restrictions.

---

[3] Outside of Kaktovik, only a few physical artifacts reflect modern human presence. See *Use of Resources by Non-Natives: Status and Effects,* below.

[4] *National Energy Policy: Reliable, Affordable, and Environmentally Sound Energy for America's Future,* Report of the national Energy Policy Development Group, May 2001. p. *5-9.*

Figure 2. Petroleum Accumulations in Northern Alaska and Nearby Parts of Canada (1998)

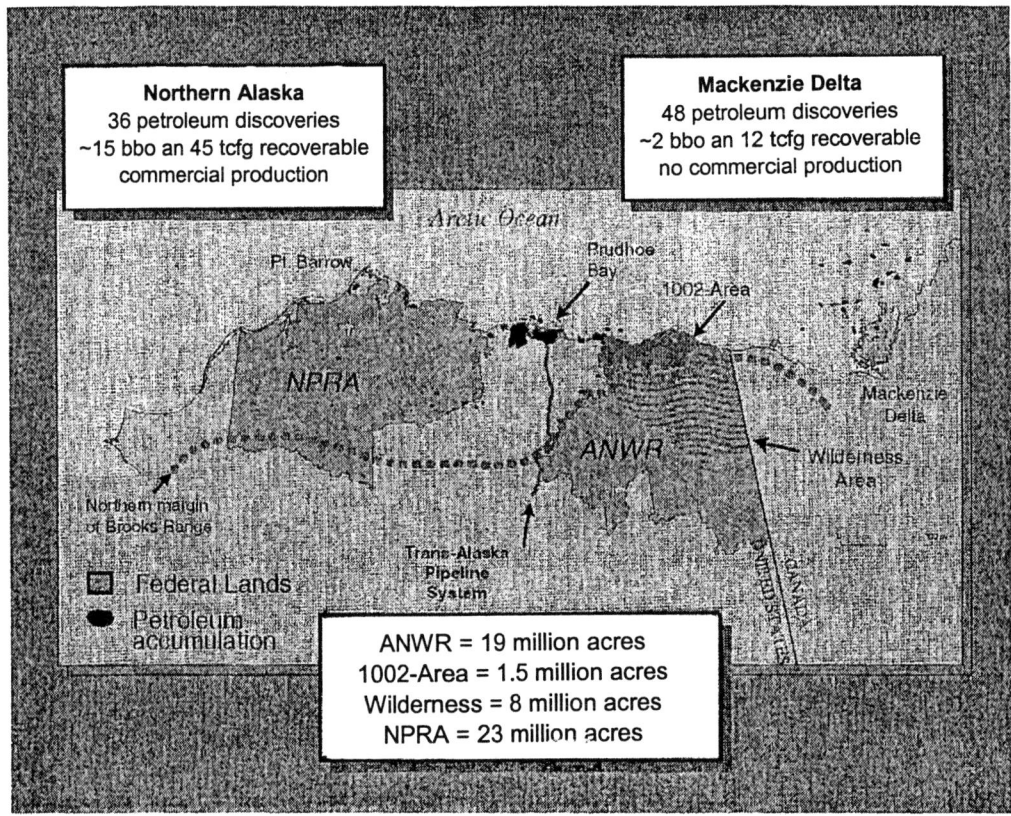

Notes: "Locations of known petroleum accumulations and the TransAlaska Pipeline System (TAPS) are shown as well as summaries of known petroleum volumes in northern Alaska and the Mackenzie delta of Canada. Bbo = billion barrels of oil, included cumulative production plus recoverable reserves; tcfg = trillion cubic feet of gas recoverable resources." **Source:** Figure A01, USGS, *Oil and Gas Potential of ANWR*.

Scope of the Chapter

Although it is unclear whether Congress will present the President with ANWR legislation, the House passed a bill in the 1st session of the 107th Congress, and the Senate seems likely to take up energy legislation early in the 2nd session. This is therefore an appropriate time to review the history of the debate and what has been learned about the complex issues surrounding this decision.

This chapter provides the background for such analysis. It summarizes and integrates relevant information and points of view on the economic, legal, environmental, management, and national energy concerns surrounding any decision on ANWR. The chapter does not attempt to focus on specific legislative issues, bills, or provisions, but rather attempts to provide a baseline for analyzing such proposals.

Congress faces several difficult questions in deciding whether to open the area to energy development, and if so, under what conditions to do so. These include:

- How much oil might be recovered, and how quickly might it begin to supply the country?
- What would be the economic benefits and Costs of development to the nation? To Alaska specifically?
- What role do Native lands on the coastal plain play in the development of any energy resources and what environmental restrictions might apply to those lands specifically in the event of development?
- What environmental impacts are likely to occur if the area is opened and how might these impacts be avoided, reduced, or mitigated?
- Is it possible for industry to limit the "footprint" of development, and if so how widely scattered must the footprint be, in order to permit full development?
- After completion of several decades of energy production, could the coastal plain ever be restored to an approximation of its current condition?
- How should revenues be shared between the federal and the Alaska state governments?

The following sections provide background and analysis on the questions raised above. Besides extensive information in the 1987 two volume FLEIS, other information is now available in scientific reports, economic analyses, position papers, and testimony. Many of these tend to be focused at one extreme or the other, but not all. Wherever possible, additional materials or references are noted which treat the issues in more depth than is possible in this report.

The chapter begins with background on the geography or setting of the refuge, and Continues with its history. The next portion is on the history of related energy development issues. To set the scene, the likely development sequence if Congress opens ANWR is presented next, followed by an extensive review of the resources of the 1002 area, including the current status, regulations, and potential effects of development of those resources. Finally, the report ends with a presentation of the legislative issues, which have arisen most frequently in recent years. A glossary is included to define the key terms and acronyms.

Although the sections of this chapter are not entirely independent, readers may find it useful to consult them selectively as background, in order to follow the evolving debate about the possible opening of the 1002 area to development.

THE SETTING: THE GEOGRAPHY OF ALASKA'S NORTH SLOPE

Physically, what is called the *North Slope* of Alaska consists of those lands north of the Brooks Range where waters drain into the Beaufort and Chukchi Seas. Its area exceeds 100,000 square miles (64,000,000 acres), and includes the northern side of the mountains, foothills, and a relatively flat coast plain. The western part of the North Slope is very broad, with the crest of the Brooks Range being as much as *250* miles from the coast. The eastern part of the North Slope, which includes part of the Refuge, is relatively narrow, with the crest of the range lying as little as 30 miles from the coast. (See Figures 1 and 2.)

The foothills of the Brooks Range merge gradually into the *coastal plain* of the North Slope. The western portion of the plain is extremely flat, and much of it is covered in small lakes. In the narrower eastern coastal plain, the topography is sufficiently rolling that lakes are much less common in the Refuge.

Lying north of the Arctic Circle, darkness and extreme cold prevail much of the year. The area is underlain by permafrost — a permanently frozen layer 1,000 to 2,000 feet thick. During the brief summer, about 3 feet of soil thaws, supporting lichens, mosses, grasses, forbs, and other low shrubby plants that make up the *tundra*. Although precipitation is low, flat areas become wetlands in summer. Most streams and rivers are frozen in winter, flood in spring breakup, and meander in braided channels of gravel until freeze-up. Because the 1002 area has more topographic relief, its drainage is better established, and its vegetation is more woody than the wetland grasses that dominate Prudhoe Bay and other developed areas. Foothills and the hilly portions constitute 45% and 22%, respectively, of the ANWR coastal plain. The foothills reach 1,250 ft, while the hills are mostly less than 100 ft above their surroundings (FLEIS, p. 18-19).

HISTORY OF THE REFUGE

A chronology of the Refuge's history might begin in 1956, with the visit to northeastern Alaska by naturalists Olaus and Margaret Murie, who reported the vast migrating herd of caribou that winter in the United States and Canada around the Porcupine River. Upon their return, the Murie's worked with other scientists to set aside the area to protect the caribou herd and the whole relatively intact arctic ecosystem of which they were a central part. However, the first group actually to propose that the area become a national wildlife range, in recognition of the many game species found in the area, was the Tanana Valley (Alaska) Sportsmen's Association.[5] The following is a description, in chronological order, of major events concerning the Refuge, and related energy development in northern Alaska since the 1950s.

Land Order

In November 1957, an application for the withdrawal of lands to create an Arctic Wildlife Range was filed. Under the regulations in effect at the time, this application "segregated" the lands in question, removing them from disposal. This fact was important because on July 7, 1958, the Alaska Statehood Act was signed and on January 3, 1959, Alaska was formally admitted to the Union. On December 6, 1960, after statehood, the Secretary of the Interior issued Public Land Order 2214 reserving the area as the Arctic National Wildlife Range. (In Figure 1, the outer boundaries of the "1002 area", plus the wilderness boundaries, were the boundaries of the Range.) The Supreme Court has held that the initial segregation of lands

---

[5] *U.S.* Congress, Senate, Committee on Interstate and Foreign Commerce. *Arctic National Wildlife Range - Alaska,* Hearing, Part I. June 30, 1959. (Washington, DC, *1959).* Also see: U.S. Congress, House of Representatives, Committee on Merchant Marine and Fisheries. *Miscellaneous Fish and Wildlife Legislation,* Hearing, July 1, 1959. (Washington, DC, *1959).*

was sufficient to prevent the passage of ownership of certain submerged lands within the Refuge to the State of Alaska at statehood.[6]

Alaska National Interest Lands Conservation Act

In 1980, Congress enacted the Alaska National Interest Lands Conservation Act (ANILCA, P.L. 96-487, 94 Stat. 2371), which included several sections about ANWR. The Arctic Range was renamed the Arctic National Wildlife Refuge, and was expanded, mostly southward and westward, to include an additional 9.2 million acres. Section 702(3) of ANILCA designated much of the original Refuge as a wilderness area, but not the coastal plain.[7] Instead, Congress postponed decisions on the development or further protection of the coastal plain. ANILCA defined the "coastal plain" as the lands on a specified map.[8] A later legal description of the boundaries excludes most Alaska Native lands, even though these lands are *geographically part* of the coastal plain. Three key sections of ANILCA are discussed below.

Section 1002 Study

Section 1002 of ANILCA directed a study of the "coastal plain" (which therefore is often referred to as the "1002 area") and its resources be completed within 5 years and 9 months of enactment. The executive branch was to conduct a comprehensive baseline study of the fish and wildlife resources of the coastal plain of the Refuge; to develop guidelines for, initiate, and monitor an oil and gas exploration program; to prepare a report to the Congress on the biological resources, the extent of hydrocarbon resources, the impacts of development, transportation of oil and gas, and the need for them; and to make a recommendation on whether exploration, development, and production should proceed. The resulting "1002 report" or Final Legislative Environmental Impact Statement (FLEIS)[9] was issued in April 1987.

The FLEIS recommended full development of the 1002 area. It described the 1002 area as "the most outstanding petroleum exploration target in the onshore United States" (FLEIS, p. vii), and estimated a 19% chance of finding economically recoverable oil. Its mean estimate of economically recoverable oil was 3.2 billion barrels, and the report predicted the area could supply about 4% of total U.S. demand in 2005, and reduce imports by nearly 9%. (See *Oil Potential*, below, for updates of these figures.) It estimated total national economic benefits of $79.4 billion and federal revenues of $38.0 billion. It assumed that oil would be selling at $33/barrel in 1984 dollars by 2000. (In actuality, West Texas Intermediate, a

---

[6] United States v. Alaska, 521 U.S. 1 (1997). If this ruling had been in favor of Alaska, certain lands beneath the rivers in the coastal plain might have belonged to the state, which could have developed the oil and gravel in or under them.
[7] Newer portions of the Refuge were not included in the wilderness system.
[8] This map apparently does not exist. See *Legal Definition of the 1002 Area*, below.
[9] U.S. Dept. of the Interior, Fish and Wildlife Service, U.S. Geological Survey, and Bureau of Land Management, *Arctic National Wildlife Refuge, Alaska, Coastal Plain Resource Assessment*, Report and Recommendation to the Congress of the United States and Final Legislative Environmental Impact Statement, (Washington, DC, 1987). 208 p. (Hereafter referred to as the "FLEIS.")

benchmark crude oil, sold from about $25.50 per barrel to about $34.50 per barrel in 2000, which was about $20.30 to $27.50 in 1984 dollars.)

The FLEJS also said the "1002 area is the most biologically productive part of the Arctic Refuge for wildlife and is the center of wildlife activity.... The area presents many opportunities for scientific study of a relatively undisturbed ecosystem." It analyzed the effects of the various development alternatives on the plants and animals, and especially on the calving grounds of the Porcupine Caribou Herd (PCH). It stated that "major effects on the PCHI could result if the entire 1002 area were leased and all prospects contained economically recoverable oil" (p. 123). It concluded that full leasing would lead to reductions in bird nesting habitat, loss of over-wintering fish habitat, and loss of polar bear denning habitat. It also predicted moderate effects on polar and grizzly (brown) bears due to direct. mortality related to human encounters; and recommended buffer zones of at least 0.5 miles around known polar bear dens. It also noted the special sensitivity of snow geese to aircraft disturbance.

Legal Definition of the 1002 Area

Section 1002 of ANILCA defines the *coastal plain* as the area shown on a map dated August, 1980. However, the Bureau of Land Management informs us that no such official map or maps with that date depicting the coastal plain exist. The official 1980 maps of the Refuge as a whole, less the area of designated wilderness might be said to indicate the coastal plain. These maps show the Native lands in the Refuge with boundaries crossed out presumably to indicate they are included within the Refuge. However, the legal description of the boundaries of the coastal plain that were published pursuant to §103 of ANILCA (48 Fed. Reg. 16838, 16869 (April 19, 1983)) exclude the Native lands as of that date from inclusion in the 1002 coastal plain.

Section 1003 Prohibition

In ANILCA, Congress also included §1003, which prevents further development of energy resources, until Congress acts:

> Production of oil and gas from the Arctic National Wildlife Refuge is prohibited and no leasing or other development leading to production of oil and gas from the range shall be undertaken until authorized by an Act of Congress.

Development opponents are well satisfied with the *status quo* under §1003. While many development bills have been introduced since 1987, very few have been reported out of a committee, despite considerable interest by various Members. In the Senate, for example, a willingness to filibuster against development bills has prevented such bills from coming to the floor; the sole exception (see *ANWR Consideration in the 101 – 106th Congresses,* below) was in a reconciliation bill which was later vetoed. Consequently, development continues to be prohibited.

ANILCA and Native Claims

ANILCA also contained provisions in §1431 that followed up on the previously enacted Alaska Native Claims Settlement Act (ANCSA, P.L. 92-203), and gave the Native village corporation of Kaktovik rights to make certain selections and to enter into certain land exchanges. The result is that Kaktovik has surface rights to some lands inside and some lands outside the 1002 area. However, all of the Kaktovik lands are within the *Refuge* and are subject to the current restrictions on oil and gas development of §1003 of ANILCA and to §22(g) of ANCSA, which made Native lands selected in a refuge subject to the regulations of the refuge. If Congress were to lift the restriction of § 1003 on oil and gas development in the Refuge, development of Native lands would be allowed to occur. (See discussion of ANCSA provisions in *Use of Resources by Alaska Natives,* below.)

ANWR Consideration in the 101st to 106th Congresses

After the FLEIS of 1987, and the *Exxon Valdez* oil spill of 1989 (see below), congressional interest in the energy potential of the 1002 area has waxed and waned. Bills to open the 1002 area to development or to designate it as wilderness have been introduced repeatedly in both House and Senate. In the House, these bills were referred to the Merchant Marine and Fisheries Committee or (beginning with the 104th Congress) to the Committee on Resources. In the Senate they have been referred to the Committee on Environment and Natural Resources or the Committee on Environment and Public Works. Whether they were development bills or wilderness bills, they have rarely been reported from committees, much less received floor consideration. From 1989 to 1994 (101St to lO4tlt Congresses), no ANWR bill received floor consideration.

In 1995, Congress passed the FY1996 budget reconciliation bill (H.R. 2491) in which §5312-5344 authorized the opening of ANWR, but the measure was vetoed. President Clinton cited the ANWR sections as one of his reasons for vetoing the measure.[10] Key Senate votes occurred on May 24 and October 27, 1995, on motions to table amendments that would have stripped ANWR development provisions from the Senate version of the bill (Roll Call #190 and #525, respectively). Both motions succeeded.

While bills were introduced, the ANWR issue was not debated in the 105th Congress. In the 106th Congress, bills to designate the key northern portion of the Refuge as wilderness, and others to open the 1002 area to energy development, were introduced. The FY2001 budget resolution (S.Con.Res. 101) reported by the Senate Budget Committee on March 31, 2000 included assumptions about federal revenues that would be obtained if ANWR leasing were approved. An amendment to remove the language was tabled (51-49) on April 6,2000 (Roll Call #58); however, conferees rejected the language. The conference report on budget reconciliation did not contain this assumption, and the report was passed by both Houses on April 13.[11] These three roll call votes in two Congresses were all in the Senate, and were the only recorded votes on Refuge development from the 101st through the 106th Congress.

---

[10] For key provisions of that legislation, see archived CRS Issue Brief 1B95071, *The Arctic National Wildlife Refuge.* 16 p.

[11] Budget resolutions do not require the signature of the President.

HISTORY OF RELATED ENERGY DEVELOPMENT

In 1967, oil was discovered on the North Slope of Alaska at Prudhoe Bay, about 50 miles west of ANWR. (See Figure 2.) Since that time, developments following from that discovery have affected the economics, potential support facilities, and understanding of proposed development of the Refuge. This section provides a short history of related energy development on the North Slope and describes how that development has influenced the ANWR debate.

TransAlaska Pipeline System (TAPS) Authorization

The Prudhoe Bay discovery was a great distance from markets and/or a warm water port from which to transport oil to markets. Development of the resource was thwarted for several years by lack of agreement on how and by which route the crude oil would be transported out of the area.

Alternative Routes Considered

Transporting the oil directly from the area by tanker was considered briefly, but an experiment failed. Pipeline routes were seen as the only viable option. Initially, three general pipeline routes were conceptualized. Two never reached the stage of serious study: one was an easterly route into Canada, to the McKenzie River Delta, then south to a Chicago-area destination, and the other was a southeasterly route along the Alaskan Highway into Canada and then south into the United States. The third was overland, south to the port of Valdez.

Proponents of the first two routes argued that the oil was needed most in the Midwest, because it has no indigenous source of crude oil. Midwestern interests favored it because of the prospective economic gain. Opponents contended that such routes were very long, and therefore would cost more and take longer to build. Oil prices had not reached levels sufficient to justify further investigation.

The third route was ultimately chosen: oil is shipped via TAPS south to the seaport of Valdez on Prince William Sound, then loaded on tankers destined for other ports. Proponents cited its shorter length, and therefore lower total cost and shorter construction period. Some opponents were concerned that the proximity of Valdez to Pacific Rim countries such as Japan and Korea presented too great a temptation to export the oil; others were concerned about possible oil spills along the West Coast.

Export Restrictions in Original TAPS Law

Much of the pipeline's route between the North Slope and Valdez is on federal lands, for which rights-of-way were needed. The Mineral Leasing Act of 1920 prohibits export of oil transported through pipelines granted rights-of-way over federal lands (30 U.S.C. 185(u)). There was considerable opposition to the export of North Slope oil and many saw a growing domestic need for the oil in late 1973 as a result of the Arab oil embargo (imposed during the Arab-Israeli War of October 1973), and of the gasoline shortages (resulting from petroleum allocation regulations). The increased concern over U.S. dependency on foreign oil brought urgency to the pipeline debate. A compromise was soon reached over whether to exempt North Slope oil from this prohibition.

The compromise was the Trans-Alaska Pipeline Authorization Act (P.L. 93-153, 87 Stat. 584,43 U.S.C. 1651 *et seq.),* signed November 16, 1973. It specified among its many provisions that oil shipped through the pipeline could be exported only under certain restrictions.[12] Subsequent legislation strengthened the export restrictions further.[13] The restrictions proved to be, in effect, a complete ban on exports of North Slope oil. However, the restriction was not to last, as market forces created pressure to change the law. (See *Export Restrictions Loosened,* below.)

Exxon Valdez Oil Spill

The grounding of the *Exxon Valdez* on March 24, 1989, near the southern terminal of the TAPS in Prince William Sound played a major role in placing the development debate on hold. Environmental damage at the time included an estimated 300,000 to 645,000 dead seabirds; 4,000 to 6,000 dead marine mammals; and $100 million in other losses, including commercial fishing impacts. Some cleanup methods were criticized as doing more harm than good. Lawsuits were abundant.

Today, there is still disagreement over the impact of the spill. Some scientists note the lack of toxicity of the water, and a visitor in the area would still see rugged beauty on most beaches. But other observers stress the accumulation of oil in some species, such as mussels (which filter sea water), and the effects on species that consume contaminated organisms. For example, a 2001 study of seabirds in the area showed that of the 17 groups (containing a total of 33 species) "most [groups] for which injury was previously demonstrated are not recovering and others continue to show potential population effects nine years after the spill."[14] The affected birds included species of sea ducks, grebes, terns, murres, and gulls. Exxon Mobil responded that bird populations may not be recovering due to a variety of other environmental changes in the area, *e.g.,* higher water temperatures.[15]

---

[12] Many opponents of the pipeline (or at least of its presence on federal lands) argued that potential environmental damage was unjustified if the primary beneficiaries would be Pacific Rim nations receiving the oil. Therefore, they wished to prevent export of the oil, even though the oil would fetch higher prices if it could be sold on world markets.

[13] These restrictions included the Energy Policy and Conservation Act of 1975 (P.L. 94-163), the 1977 amendments to the Export Administration Act (P.L. 95-52 and P.L. 95-223*),* and the Export Administration Act of 1979 (P.L. 96-72), which replaced the Export Administration Act of 1969.

[14] Brian K. Lance, *et al.,* "An Evaluation of Marine Bird Population Trends Following the *Exxon Valdez* Oil Spill, Prince William sound, Alaska," *Marine Pollution Bulletin,* Vol. 42: p. 298-3 09. Elsevier Science, Ltd. (April 2001). Species were considered to be recovering if either (a) the populations in the oiled areas were increasing, or (b) if their trend was similar to that of populations of the same species in areas without oil.

[15] Unnamed ExxonMobil spokesperson, cited in Pearce, Fred." Alaska's oil spill may still be hitting wildlife hard." *New Scientist.* May 2, 2001. [http://www.newscientist.com].

Export Restrictions Loosened

The TransAlaska Pipeline System was completed in 1977, and oil was being shipped through by the end of the year. Continued oilfield development on the North Slope resulted in a 10-year increase in production to a peak of 2.0 million barrels per day (bbl/d) in 1988.

With exports effectively banned, much of North Slope oil went to West Coast destinations. The rest was shipped to the Gulf Coast via the Panama Canal or overland across the Panamanian isthmus. Such Gulf Coast shipments reduce average effective wellhead prices on the North Slope, which must absorb at least the cost of transportation through the pipeline and by tanker, and therefore always are a few to several dollars below Lower-48 wellhead prices.

In the early and mid-1990s, California — the nation's third largest oil producing state -.- was producing about 800,000 bbl/d on average. Another 150,000 bbl/d were being produced in federal waters off the West Coast, and about 100,000 bbl/d of crude oil were being imported. At the same time, total consumption of petroleum in California was falling—8% between 1989 and 1995. The combination of Californian and federal offshore production, North Slope oil,[16] and imports, resulted in such large quantities relative to demand that prices of crude oil in California fell below those elsewhere in the United States. Prices obtained by producers — from California and North Slope — naturally suffered as well, and elicited concern and complaints from those producers.

Attempts to obtain help were unsuccessful until 1995 despite arguments that the gains of exporting would outweigh the losses. For example, a June 1994 Department of Energy (DOE) study found that exporting Alaskan crude oil would increase prices for both Californian and Alaskan producers and result in up to 100,000 bbl/d more production in California and Alaska (combined) than would be the case with continued export restrictions.[17] As a result of avoiding the trip through Panama, Alaskan oil would gain higher prices (net of transportation costs) if sold in Japan. DOE predicted that higher resulting prices on the West Coast would spur additional production. In addition, the study found, exporting North Slope oil would stimulate imports of crude oil better suited to California's petroleum product demand mix. However, the study acknowledged, exporting Alaskan oil would divert cargoes away from the U.S. domestic merchant marine fleet and workforce.[18]

These expected benefits and costs, less concern about petroleum in 1995 (after three or four years of low world oil prices), relative calm in the Mideast, and continued pleadings from West Coast producers (after two years of wellhead prices averaging below $12 per barrel) helped open the way to repeal of the export restrictions. The Clinton Administration was supportive, and bills in the House and Senate (FLR. 70 and S. 395) passed by large margins. On November 28, 1995, the President signed P.L. 104-58 (109 Stat. 557), Title If of which amended the Mineral Leasing Act to provide that any oil transported through the Trans-Alaska Pipeline may be exported unless the President finds, after considering stated

---

[16] North Slope oil production had fallen by *0.5* million bbl/d, to 1.5 million bbl/d by 1995 — still a very large quantity.

[17] U.S. Department of Energy. *Exporting Alaskan North Slope Crude Oil Benefits and Costs, DOEIPO-0025* (Washington, DC, June 1994).

[18] The Jones Act of the Merchant Marine Act of 1920 (P.L 66-261; 46 U.S.C. 883) requires that cargoes transported from one U.S. port to another be carried in U.S.-flag ships; export cargoes (from a U.S. port to a foreign port) may be transported in foreign-flag ships.

criteria, that it is not in the national interest (30 U.S.C. 185(s)). The President may impose terms and conditions; and authority to export oil may be modified or revoked. Beginning with 36,000 bbl/d in 1996, ANS exports rose to a peak of 74,000 bbl/d in 1999. The latter represented 7% of North Slope production. Exports of ANS oil ceased voluntarily in May 2000.

Opening of NPR-A to Leasing

Almost concurrent with the push to allow export of North Slope oil, production of North Slope oil began to fall, reducing if not eliminating the California oil surplus, but also spurring discovery and development of other North Slope fields. The successful exploration, although not sufficient to stop the production decline, increased geological information and strengthened belief that there are commercial quantities of oil in the National Petroleum Reserve-Alaska (NPR-A). (See Figure 2.)

Established in 1923 by President Harding as Naval Petroleum Reserve Number 4, the 33 million acre Reserve, together with other government petroleum reserves, was intended to help assure availability of fuels for the Navy. Rationale for the Reserves faded over time, however, as the likelihood of a sustained interruption in oil supply declined, and markets showed a capacity to allocate and price petroleum when supply was uncertain. In 1981, stewardship of the Reserve passed from the Navy to the Department of the Interior (DOI), and its designation was changed to National Petroleum Reserve-Alaska. Public Law 96-5 14 authorizes the Secretary of the Interior to conduct oil and gas leasing and development in the NPR-A. Four lease sales were held between 1981 and 1984. An exploratory well drilled in 1985 was dry; but none of these leases was developed and all have expired. The area actually has been explored (including drilling) and/or mapped by various federal government agencies or on their behalf on and off from 1901 through 1998.

By 1996, total Alaskan oil output had fallen below 1.4 million barrels per day. Many Alaskans supported exploration of NPR-A, hoping that output from there would help offset the drop in royalty payments from reduced Prudhoe Bay production. Some argued that NPR-A might assure sufficient throughput to keep the Trans-Alaskan Pipeline running. In addition, lease sales provide bonus bid revenue to the U.S. Treasury; and the government collects royalties if there is production.

In early 1997, the Department of the Interior (DOI) initiated a study of potential drilling areas in a 4.6 million acre portion of the northeast part of the Reserve, and of the steps that would be needed to protect wildlife. The discovery of the large and soon to be commercially successful Alpine Field (discussed later in this report) adjacent to the eastern boundary of NPR-A was important in spurring development of a leasing proposal for NPR-A. On August 6, 1998, DOT released its Final Integrated Activity Plan and Environmental Impact Statement (EIS), making 4 million acres available for leasing, with surface pipelines banned on 20% of that area. The EIS was prepared to meet National Environmental Policy Act requirements and to serve as the basis for managing the area; its preferred option provided for a number of restrictions intended to strike a balance between permitting exploration and protecting the environment.[19] DOJ officials estimated that the quadrant under review for leasing could hold 500 million to 2.2 billion barrels on an assumption of a crude oil price of $18-30/barrel.[20]

A lease sale held in May 1999 drew 174 bids from six companies on 3.9 million acres. More than 130 bids were accepted, totaling $105 million. ARGO initially picked up the leases and then sold these holdings to Phillips Alaska Inc. as required by the Federal Trade Commission for the takeover of ARGO by British Petroleum (BP). In the spring of 2001, Phillips Alaska and minority partner Anadarko Petroleum Corporation reported findings of oil and gas, and indicated the find might be commercial.[21] Additional lease sales are anticipated in NPR-A in 2002.

POSSIBLE DEVELOPMENT SEQUENCE

There are five phases of oil development on federal lands: the leasing process, exploration, development, production, and reclamation. If economic quantities of oil are not found, only three phases — leasing, exploration and reclamation — would occur. In a large area with numerous tracts, all of these phases could be occurring simultaneously: exploration in some fields, development in others and production in still other fields. Exploration specialists might move from prospect to prospect for several years, followed by construction and other workers carrying out development where discoveries occurred, and so on. The following section describes these five phases.[22]

Where newer technologies are used, they may reduce not only environmental damage or risk, but also costs. Cost-effective technologies would likely be used whether specified in legislation or not. Where savings are less likely, legislation could be required to ensure use of advanced technologies or to ensure environmental standards (with the latter perhaps driving development of still newer technologies). However, any federal requirements to use advanced or environmentally friendly technology may not necessarily apply to Native lands unless Congress explicitly applies them.

Leasing Phase

Through §1003 of ANILCA, Congress has clearly reserved to itself the decision on whether to lease the coastal plain. If it passes development legislation, it may choose to deviate from the typical pattern of leasing on other federal lands or other national wildlife refuges. This section highlights how the leasing process would normally work, and some of the leasing issues that might be considered by Congress in legislation to open ANWR.

---

[19] U.S. Department of the Interior. Bureau of Land Management. *Northeast National Petroleum Reserve-Alaska. Final Integrated Activity Plan/Environmental Impact Statement.* August 1988.

[20] Gee, Robert W., Asst. Secretary for Fossil Energy, U.S. Department of Energy. Testimony before the U.S. House of Representatives, Committee on Energy. April 12,2000.

[21] *Oil & Gas Journal,* Phillips Makes Own Mark on North Slope with Alpine Start-up, NPRA Strikes. August 6, 2001. p. 68 et seq.

[22] Aspects relating to the technology of ANWR petroleum development are treated more extensively in CR8 Report RL31022, *Arctic Petroleum Development: Implications of Advances in Technology,* by Terry R. Twyman. June 19, 2001. 29 p. (Hereafter referred to as CRS Report RL31022.)

In the leasing phase as it is carried out under the Mineral Leasing Act of 1920,[23] BLM gathers information about an area of federal land, based on data from federal agencies and industry submissions. The leasing phase involves a series of decisions and actions by the federal government and by oil corporations, with each decision or action influencing the next. Then BLM determines how much, and what specific lands would be offered. Generally, BLM offers federal leases on a competitive basis, though non-competitive leases may be offered in some circumstances. BLM solicits bids on the tracts, selecting the winning companies based on these bids. Competitive leases would probably be the norm in the 1002 area. The entire process, from initial public notice, to sales, and to any production, with public input along the way, generally requires several years. Broadly speaking, Congress may choose to pass legislation, which entirely replaces the normal processes for leasing on other federal lands, or may selectively override, or substitute for, some of those processes. The following is an abbreviated outline of the steps in a competitive oil or gas lease sale. It indicates as well the areas in past bills where there were proposed changes from current practices.

Leasing must be in accordance with relevant land management plans, such as those for National Forests or for BLM lands, but an analogous plan does not exist for ANWR, though the 1987 FLEIS carried out some of the same functions. These plans are developed with public input and information, as did the FLEIS. Even if the federal lands in question are not subject to general land management planning, the NEPA processes or special statutory provisions may provide opportunity for public participation. If ANWR were opened to leasing, Congress might choose to specify that some of these planning steps, or measures for public participation, be included in the ANWR leasing process. Alternatively, given past reviews such as the FLEIS, it might override some or all of the NEPA process. (See *Compliance with NEPA*, below.)

The Director of BLM may elect to accept formal or informal nominations of lands to be leased. If nominations are to be accepted, a company would normally nominate more land than those areas it felt most promising, in order to conceal its intentions and avoid excessive attention by future competitors on what it believes are the best prospects. In the case of ANWR, it seems highly likely that formal nominations would be part of any leasing process, and measures to provide for formal nominations have been included in bills in previous Congresses. In deciding which (if any) nominations to make, companies would already be considering factors such as likely operating costs, future oil prices, and alternative or perhaps more attractive prospects in the United States or elsewhere. In Alaska, the North Slope's generally high operating costs would tend to be an especially important consideration as companies decided which tracts to nominate. Those companies with past experience elsewhere on the North Slope might be more interested in participating than those lacking such experience.

BLM would use the nominations and other information to determine how much land to offer (if this is not set in legislation) and in what tract sizes.[24] For example, the geology of the area is markedly different on either side of the Marsh Creek anticline (see Figure 4), and the agency might wish to recognize that in some way in its selection of tracts. In previous Congresses, bills have often directed a particular schedule usually setting a fairly fast pace for

---

[23] For a slightly more detailed guide, see U.S. Department of the Interior. Bureau of Land Management. *The Federal Onshore Oil and Gas Leasing System.* Washington, DC. September, 1994. BLM/WO/GI-92/001+4110+REV94, 7p. (Hereafter referred to as *The Federal Onshore Oil and Gas Leasing System.*)

[24] The Mineral Leasing Act sets a maximum of 5,760 acres for tracts in competitive sales in Alaska.

the initial and subsequent lease offerings. BLM would not normally choose to offer millions of acres for bidding at once, but instead offer portions over a number of years, using previous discoveries and geologic information to determine future offerings.

At the time of any offering, BLM would also specify terms or conditions that may apply to particular tracts. These conditions might include, in the case of ANWR, limits on surface occupancy, size of footprint, seasonal availability to exploration, wildlife protection measures, reclamation standards, and the like. Congress could also specify particular terms or conditions in legislation to open the 1002 area to development, and these terms and conditions could be a major vehicle for environmental protection measures in the 1002 area. (Though these terms and conditions might not necessarily apply to Native lands; *see Alaska Native Lands and Rights,* below.) It would be essential for industry to have a firm idea of the terms and conditions of a lease, since these provisions would likely affect the cost of operating the lease, and therefore the amount a company might be willing to bid for the tract. Leases under the Mineral Leasing Act are for 10 years and continue as long afterwards as oil and gas is being produced commercially; Congress could choose any length for the leases.

Under current law, on the date of a competitive sale, oral bidding takes place at a specified location. Competition among companies is based on the size of their up-front offer, called the *bonus bid.* A bonus bid is required to be at least $2 per acre, but bonus bids can be many millions of dollars for some tracts, while others may receive no bid at all. Payment of the bonus bid will occur at a point when the winning bidder cannot yet be certain that oil will be present. As a result, even an ANWR utterly devoid of commercial oil deposits might still earn millions of dollars for...the federal government, whether oil is ever produced or not. According to BLM, leases on other federal lands are granted "on the condition that the lessee will have to obtain BLM approval before conducting any surface-disturbing activities."[25] Congress may choose to specify certain conditions or modifications on the requirement for this final step after a lease is sold and before construction of roads or drilling platforms.

In a typical lease under the MLA, a successful bidder must pay $1.50/acre in rent for its tract(s) in the first 5 years, and $2.00/acre thereafter. The first year's rental payment, plus the minimum bonus bid and a $75 administrative fee is due on the date of the sale. The remainder of the bonus bid must be received within 10 workdays. Subsequent *rental payments* are due on the anniversary date of the lease. In addition, once production starts, companies pay a standard 12.5% *royalty* on the sale of the oil they produce. Leases expire after 10 years unless production or specified steps toward production are occurring. Lessees may also voluntarily surrender the lease, subject to requirements concerning abandonment of wells, clean up, and any final payments that may be owed. Generally speaking, few bills in previous Congresses have treated an ANWR leasing program in this level of detail (save for a willingness to specify a 12.5% royalty rate). Instead, development bills usually direct the Interior Secretary to promulgate rules and regulations to carry out the leasing program in order to carry out the provisions of the legislation.

---

[25] See p. *5, The Federal Onshore Oil and Gas Leasing System,* previously cited.

Frontier Variations

In a typical frontier area, where energy leases have been rare to non-existent, and geological knowledge is sparse, BLM might allow companies to conduct seismic exploration in the general area before specific tracts are designated. (ANWR is not typical, however, because ANILCA bad specific exploration provisions for the 1002 area.) Once the sale tracts have been named, further exploration might take place. Congress might specify whether additional exploration could occur before nominations were required. However, due to the seasonality of North Slope exploration, this choice could lengthen the time required to make a first lease offering. In the NPR-A (which has its own distinct regulations), this exploration occurred for the first lease sale; exploration took place during the arctic winter, and companies focused on data analysis once melted tundra made the area inaccessible. Far more exploration then took place on leased tracts, in order to help the companies select specific drill sites.

In addition, in frontier areas such as NPR-A and elsewhere, the NEPA impact assessment process is occurring both before and during preparation for the sales. A full EIS can add substantially to the time required to carry out a sale, even if it occurs concurrently. Congress has, in several ANWR development bills, shown a willingness to modify or eliminate NEPA requirements, on the basis that the 1987 FLEIS fulfilled that function.

Thus, a leasing phase may overlap substantially with an exploration phase. In the 1002 area, while both of these phases might be shortened by reducing requirements for environmental review, for example, there is a limit to how much the process might be truncated. Furthermore, in the arctic, current technology limits exploration to the winter season only. Since BLM would wish to consider the views of industry in selecting the tracts to be offered — views that will take time and further exploration to develop — this too could lengthen the leasing process.

Leasing on National Wildlife Refuges

A factor which Congress might consider, should it decide to open ANWR, would be the special circumstances that apply to leasing part of a National Wildlife Refuge, since leasing would normally have to be determined to be "compatible" with the major purposes of the National Wildlife Refuge System and with the purposes of the particular unit of that System. (See *Compatibility with Refuge Purposes,* below.) While energy leasing does occur in the National Wildlife Refuge System, it occurs in less than 10% of refuges, and in virtually no instance has leasing occurred after a compatibility determination. (See Box for examples.) If Congress wished ANWR development to occur as expeditiously as possible, it could override the compatibility test. In previous Congresses, bills have expressly addressed the potential conflict by stating that Congress has determined energy leasing to be compatible with the purposes for which ANWR was designated.

Energy Leasing in National Wildlife Refuges

A survey by the General Accounting Office in 2000 found that of the 567 refuge system units, 45 units had producing oil or gas wells, of which 19 units were in Texas or Louisiana. (See *Wildlife Refuge Oil and Gas Activity,* Oct. 31, 2001.16 p. GAO Report GAO-02-64R.) In only eight of the units did the federal government own the oil and gas rights. (Due to an apparent miscommunication with FWS, Kenai NWR (see below) was not included among the eight, but should have been.) Where there are preexisting rights, FWS has little control over the determination to develop energy or minerals, though it may determine its timing or manner. The refuges with energy development had special features that make comparison with proposals to develop ANWR difficult. However, there appear to be no instances to date in which FWS has had full control of surface and subsurface rights, formally determined leasing to be compatible with refuge purposes, and then allowed new leasing to proceed. The examples below illustrate refuges in which leasing occurs.

In Medicine Lake (MT) and J. Clark Salyer and Upper Souris (ND) NWRs, BLM offered leases because of "drainage" in which oil was being extracted on adjacent land from oil field, which extended into the refuge. If no leases had been given, then adjacent leases would have drained the (federally owned) oil underlaying the refuges. Oil drainage from adjacent development is not occurring around ANWR at this time.

In one refuge (Delta, LA), some activity occurred due to privately owned subsurface rights; and some federal government leases had been issued before the refuge was created in 1935. In the 1002 area, while private subsurface rights are held by Alaska Native corporations, their activities are governed by laws that do not apply at Delta NWR.

At Hagerman NWR (TX), FWS has secondary jurisdiction on land owned by the Army Corps of Engineers. As a result, FWS does not have control of leasing decisions there, in ANWR, FWS has primary jurisdiction.

Bitter Lake NWR (NM) has several leases that were granted when the land was owned by BLM. The lands were gained by FWS in an exchange of outlying FWS lands for inholdings or adjacent parcels owned by BLM. The purpose of the exchange was to increase administrative efficiency.

Kenai NWR (AK) has 12,000 acres under federal leases, with the refuge zoned into leasing and non-leasing areas. The first oil leases were in 1956 under the Mineral Leasing Act; no formal compatibility determination was required at that time, but the Secretary of the Interior determined that leasing could proceed. As a result of a lawsuit, FWS in 1994 determined that leasing was compatible. After passage of the National Wildlife Refuge System Improvement Act (1997), this informal determination was rescinded, with the approval of the Regional Administrator. While the decision does not affect pre-existing leases, nor subsurface rights not owned by the federal government, it would prevent future development where the federal government owns the mineral rights.

Exploration Phase

As the previous section makes clear, the leasing and exploration phases overlap the exploration phase is the time at which industry and the federal government accumulate data about the area that will be, or has already been leased. Exploration activity is most intense after leases have been purchased. Preliminary seismic exploration, using two-dimensional (2-D) imaging technology, continues to be used in early exploration in new areas. It is carried out directly across frozen tundra (without special ice roads) in widely spaced grid lines. Seismic exploration uses trains of rolligons (large vehicles with enormous soft tires that spread their weight evenly across the surface) for vibrating the surface and recording the result, plus vehicles for carrying fuel, mechanical repair facilities, and a crew of 80 to 120 people. Damage in the area around Prudhoe is prevented by waiting until the tundra is well frozen, though tractors with heavy rubber treads are required to pull some of the heavier equipment. For the much-less expensive, but less precise 2-D surveys, lines may be several miles apart, but for the high accuracy of 3-D seismic, lines are about 1100 feet apart. More exploration using 3-D seismic technology becomes economic in defining more precisely the boundaries of potential structures, though drilling may occur based on 2-D alone. Under the more advanced 3-D technology, finer grid lines are also run directly across the tundra. The better data resulting from 3-D increase the chance that a given well will be successful from 1 in 10 to perhaps 3 or 4 in 10.

Modern arctic exploration on the state-owned lands of the North Slope is carried out in winter; while early phases involve travel across frozen open tundra, subsequent exploration drilling uses a combination of ice roads, and ice pads. Each mile of ice road uses an estimated one million gallons of liquid water, and road builders typically transport liquid water no more than 10 miles, since it may freeze before it is used. Technical solutions to water shortages could involve greater use of chipped ice scraped from lakes to supplement liquid water, and/or development of new technologies using a desalination plant and a heated elevated pipeline.[26] Though such technologies could prove feasible and some are already in use on the North Slope, they could also change the economics of exploration and later development.

If data indicate economic quantities of oil may be present, a bole is drilled entirely in winter, on thick insulated pads of frozen water. These pads melt in summer, leaving the tundra in relatively good condition.[27] If no commercial quantity of oil is found, the pipe is plugged and temporarily or even permanently abandoned, covered by a small cube-shaped building. Use of these methods, in comparison to the technology available in 1987, can substantially reduce impacts of exploration on the landscape.[28]

---

[26] W. Wayt Gibbs, "The Arctic Oil and Wildlife Refuge", *Scientific American* (May 2001) pp. 62-69. (Hereafter referred to as Gibbs, "The Arctic Oil and Wildlife Refuse.")

[27] With insulating panels, ice pads can be maintained over the summer, allowing the drilling rig to remain in place for additional drilling in the early winter, thereby eliminating the need to remove the rig in spring and replace it in the next winter. Such a practice can increase the drilling season 50 to 70 days. (See CRS Report 31022, p. 17, previously cited.)

[28] For more information on exploration technology, see CRS Report RL31022, previously cited.

Development Phase

In the development phase, companies construct the infrastructure needed to go from a find to actual production; employment peaks in this phase. If economic quantities of oil are found, a gravel drill pad is built and multiple wells are drilled from the pad. The newest arctic development technology is demonstrated in the Alpine field, at the extreme western edge of current oilfield development, on state lands near the NPR-A. (See Figure 3, showing the Alpine field.) Two gravel pads, linked by a 3-mile long combined road and runway, support 112 wells. Heavy equipment to be used in the field was delivered to the nearest staging area in summer via gravel road. Once winter ice roads were built, the equipment was transported to the field. In summer, access to Alpine is by aircraft only. While no gravel roads link Alpine with other North Slope development, pipelines connect the Alpine field to collection lines from several fields and these in turn connect to TAPS to carry the oil south.

Since the 1987 FLEIS, considerable advances have been made in the technologies surrounding the development phase. These advances contribute to efficiency and often to reduced environmental impacts, and some would likely be used, required or not, due to Cost savings. Others might be used if required by the federal government or the state; such requirements could change the economics of development. One clear improvement, as a result of data analysis at the exploration phase, is that development can be more efficient, since fewer "dry holes" are likely to be drilled. Other improvements are as follows.

Advanced Drilling

Drilling technology has evolved from a single hole straight down into a prospect, to directional, extended reach, horizontal, multilateral, and designer wells. All of these designs permit more efficient production of hydrocarbon reserves, and allow easier connection to production facilities, with fewer pipelines. They also reduce the number of wellheads. Drill bit technology has improved, allowing wells to be drilled faster. Drilling muds are less toxic; cuttings generated during drilling can be stored in temporary reserve pits and then used in construction, or re-injected into special wells for waste disposal.[29] Efforts are made to avoid any surface discharge of wastes. Savings make it likely that these technologies would be used if ANWR were opened; legislative provisions might push further requirements.

Drill Pads

With this advanced drilling technology, more of the oil-bearing structure can be tapped from a well head, and drill pads can be located, under very favorable conditions, up to 7 miles in horizontal distance from a target. These technologies reduce development's footprint, as well as allow greater protection of surface features. Since each drill pad can develop a greater area, fewer drill pads are needed than in the past. Technologies developed largely in the 1990s also permit closer spacing of wells, and more wellheads can be placed on a smaller drill pad. Drill pads in the 1970s were about 44 acres. In contrast, Alpine's 2 drill pads are 36

---

[29] For more extensive discussion of these technologies, and for illustrations of types of drilling methods, see CRS Report RL31022, previously cited.

acres and 10 acres.[30] The larger pad is the main production pad, and includes a central processing facility, housing, and storage area, along with wellheads. The secondary pad contains only drilling facilities and wellheads; workers there commute from the main pad. If the Prudhoe Bay oilfield and surrounding fields had been developed using this technology, only 4,000 acres, instead of the present 12,000 acres, would be needed.[31] Production facilities (like those at Alpine) would be scattered in a network over producing fields, due to the 7-mile maximum reach of horizontal drilling, and multiple pads could be needed for producing fields. (Pipelines would carry oil from the pads to a collection line; see *Production Phase.*)

Figure 3. Alpine Oil Field

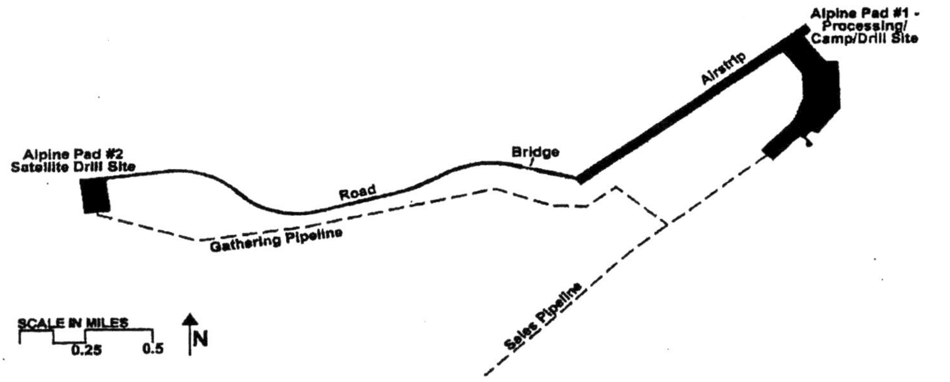

Source: ARCO Alaska, Incorporated. Permit Application to U.S. Army District Engineer, Alaska, Permit No. 2-960874, Colville River 18. Jan. 22 and 24, 1998. Map somewhat simplified for clarity in monochrome.

Roads

If a development phase followed the model at Alpine, heavy equipment would be carried to a staging area as near as possible to the drill site and accessible to the gravel road network that services the currently developed areas. As soon as ice roads could be built, the equipment would be moved to the drill site, where a gravel pad would have been constructed previously. All heavy equipment would be transported to the site during the winter; equipment needed in the summer would be flown in along with personnel to an adjacent airstrip. As at Alpine, gravel roads might be constructed to link pads within the same field.

If this model were followed, the mileage of roads constructed in the 1002 area would be far smaller than was expected in the 1987 FLEIS (for a given size and location of discovery).

---

[30] U.S. Army Corps of Engineers Alaska District, Permit Evaluation and Decision Document, Alpine Development Project, Colville River 18 (2-960874), p. 2 (Feb. 13, 1998).

[31] Stephan Taylor, retired director of environmental policy, BP Exploration (Alaska). Cited by Janet Pelley, "Will Drilling for Oil Disrupt the Arctic National Wildlife Refuge?" *Environmental Science and Technology* (June 1, 2001).

Heavy reliance on ice roads could mean high demands for water if the staging area were just to the west of the 1002 area and discoveries were in the eastern portion of the 1002 area — a distance of roughly 100 miles. Alternatively, staging areas could be located farther east, perhaps by off-loading barged equipment at Kaktovik. Water demands might be further reduced, perhaps by developing new technologies, or by placing gravel roads to transport heavy equipment on Native lands. The feasibility of these options would also depend on the extent to which Congress regulated development on Native lands (as opposed to federally-owned land).

The Meaning of Footprints

The *footprint* of development infrastructure is the area within the outline of any structures on the surface of the land as these features might be shown on an ordinary two dimensional map. In the case of arctic energy development, most observers appear to include drill pads, runways, and roads in the total footprint of development. However, in the case of elevated pipelines, some might choose to count only the base of the support arms holding aloft the pipelines (footprint in the narrow sense), rather than the entire length and width of the pipeline (footprint in the broad sense).[32] Some would also count the surface covered by gravel mines, ports, water impoundments, water treatment facilities and the like (footprint in the broadest sense).

Arctic Power (a consortium of development proponents that includes industry) has estimated that the 1.5 million acre 1002 area could be developed with a maximum footprint of 2,000 acres.[33] Some have assumed that the footprint would be a single compact unit of 2,000 acres (equivalent to 3.125 square miles — about 0.13% of the 1002 area). However, full development would be impossible if the footprint were a single compact unit. With advanced drilling technology (extended reach drilling), under favorable circumstances, lateral drilling can reach 5 to 7 miles from a drill site. Thus, if development were confined to a compact box of 3.125 mi^2 (equivalent to a square 1.77 miles by 1.77 miles) and optimum conditions obtained, up to 10.5% of the 1002 area could be developed. In contrast, full development of the 1002 area would require the strategic placement of pads, connector roads (the type of road at Alpine), and pipeline supports to be scattered about the 1002 area in a network.

Most development advocates do not oppose a surface occupancy, or footprint, limitation to 2,000 acres, apparently feeling that such a limit based on a definition covering pads, airstrips and pipe supports would not hinder full development. Even if the term *footprint* were expanded to include connector roads like that at Alpine (where the road represents about 15% of the gravel surfaces), they do not appear to consider a 2000-acre limit to be overly confining. If, however, gravel mines, water catch basins, water treatment plants, ports, causeways, and other possible features (FLEIS, p. 99), were to be built and included in a 2,000-acre limit on footprint (the broadest definition of the term), and if geology of the fields required more numerous or widespread wells, there appear to be three possible responses to the problem: (1) facilities might be modified (perhaps through improved technology) in order

---

[32] The difference could be likened to the choice between counting the actual area touched by the supports of a highway overpass or the outline of the whole overpass, as the footprint.

[33] For example, Arctic Power's website [http://www.anwr.org/features/pdfs/tech-facts.pdf] for January 9, 2002 makes this claim.

to stay within a 2,000 –acre limit; (2) some otherwise economic prospects might be missed; or (3) the footprint limitation might be modified in some way. Finally, if legislation did not apply limitations to Native lands, some additional prospects on federal l eases might be developed from pads within these Native lands, some additional prospects on federal leases might be developed from pads within these Native lands by using advanced drilling technologies. Support facilities also could be located on the Native lands within the Refuge and as a result avoid an acreage limitation, if legislation did not specifically include such lands.

Production Phase

In a production phase, drilling equipment would be removed, and small buildings (housing oil pumps) would be installed and connected to pipelines and, for the 1002 area, ultimately to TAPS. Fewer employees are necessary during the production phase. Production facilities to extract hydrocarbons consist of drilling equipment and rigs, central processing facilities (which include oil and gas separation units, power plants, flowlines, and crew offices and living quarters), access roads, gravel mines, airstrips and possibly ports and desalination facilities. Should commercial quantities of oil be discovered in ANWR, it is likely that the most advanced production facilities would be used in order to contain costs and minimize physical size and effect on the environment.

With current technologies, permanent drill sites would be constructed of gravel or recycled cuttings from the exploration wells. Compact factory-manufactured production facilities would be transported to the site instead of built on site. Depending upon conditions, slim-hole or coiled tubing drilling would be used.[34] Multilateral wells (wells with additional boreholes branching from a common hole) might be used in restricted spaces and/or to share the same surface facility. When wells not accessible to conventional rigs became old, the life of the reservoir may be extended by using through-tubing rotary drilled wells, that go through existing production tubing. Unmanned production facilities might be installed to exploit accumulations in remote sites, precluding the need for crew facilities at those locations. Together, these techniques reduce the amount of support facilities needed and the amount of waste.

The Alpine development, at the far western edge of North Slope development, uses these technologies, the most advanced currently available. The total Alpine development, according to the U.S. Army Corps of Engineers, is permitted at 98.4 acres of gravel fill. The permit provides for 1 large drill pad (36.3 acres), 1 satellite pad (10.1 acres), 1 airstrip (35.7 acres), 1 connector road of 3 miles (14.6 acres), and other features (culverts, etc., 1.7 acres).[35]

---

[34] See CRS Report RL31022, previously cited, for a description of these technologies.
[35] It appears that somewhat less acreage was actually occupied than called for in the permit: the size of the Alpine complex is variously cited as 93, 94, 97, and 98 acres, depending on the source. It is unclear exactly what portion of the development is reduced relative to the permitted size.

Reclamation Phase

In the reclamation phase, lessees would remove the traces of their activities to whatever standard was specified. Any authorization to develop the 1002 area could include reclamation provisions.[36] If oil production were to occur, industrial activity would probably last decades, especially if natural gas resources could also be developed, so reclamation would be decades in the future. Removal of gravel pads, roads, and runways; pipelines; support centers; water treatment plants; etc., would come as production (and therefore revenue) was declining. To ensure financial resources to support this final industrial phase, some have suggested that companies be required to post bonds. Even with consistent use of the best available technologies, decades of disturbance could require more decades for the disappearance of human intrusion in the slow-growing environment.[37] It is unclear whether local residents or Refuge managers would even wish to have roads or other facilities removed once energy production ceases.

However, as noted above, new developments in production field facility construction and maintenance and in drilling and production have reduced the size of oil and gas field operations. And, since modern technology attempts to avoid any surface discharge, the technical aspects of reclamation could be somewhat less demanding than for older fields.

RESOURCES: STATUS, CURRENT REGULATION, AND POTENTIAL EFFECTS OF DEVELOPMENT

While much is still unknown regarding both the biological and geological resources of the 1002 area, much has also been learned during 40 years of debate over the Refuge. Among the areas with improved information are estimates of the oil and gas potential of the area and the ecology of several of the species that frequent the area. Some of the specific resources are discussed below.[38] This report will first give background information, and then discuss potential effects of development on Alaska Natives, the economy, and the Refuge.

---

[36] If commercial quantities were not found, reclamation would occur after some years of exploration. FWS or BLM (Or other agencies given such responsibility) might condition development permits on mitigation, reclamation, or rehabilitation of affected lands. If no commercial quantities of oil were found, cleanup needs might be fairly minimal — although with the slow growth rate of vegetation in the arctic, even minimal disturbance can take decades to recover. See *Reclamation Issues After Development*, below.)

[37] The response of arctic vegetation to disturbance is complex. Factors that tend to lengthen recovery include greater dryness, changes in moisture conditions, and soil compaction. Recovery is hastened by re-planting with native plants and careful, selective use of appropriate fertilizers. Recovery is slower than in temperate habitats. See Jay D. McKendrick, "Vegetative Responses to Disturbance," in *The Natural History of an Arctic Oil Field*, pp. 35-36.

[38] As noted above, many opponents of Refuge energy development focus less on the specific resources (discussed below) that might be at risk if oil development is allowed, and more on wilderness protection, or integrity of the ecosystem as a whole.

Energy: Status and Effects

Potential energy resources are the attraction that drives the ANWR question. From a long term and basic perspective, U.S. oil production has been declining for three decades, petroleum consumption has been increasing, and oil imports fill the growing gap. During 2001, the nation's attention was drawn to energy issues by successive jumps in the pump price of gasoline and by California's serious electric power problems.[39] The potential for oil in the 1002 area has been a focus of that attention.

Oil Potential

Parts of Alaska's North Slope (ANS) coastal plain have proved abundant in oil reserves, and its geology holds further promise. The oil-bearing strata extend eastward from structures in the National Petroleum Reserve-Alaska (NPR-A), to the 2 billion barrel Kuparuk River field, past the Prudhoe Bay field (originally 11-13 billion barrels, now down to about 4 billion barrels), and a few smaller fields, and may continue into and through ANWR's 1002 area. Further east in Canada's Mackenzie River delta, once promising structures have not produced significant amounts of oil. These smaller accumulations include some fields that have produced intermittently and others that currently are noncommercial due mainly to lack of transportation infrastructure. The 1002 area contains some of the most promising undrilled onshore geologic structures with petroleum potential known in the United States.

Geology and Potential Petroleum Resources

Estimates of ANWR oil potential, both old and new, depend on limited data and numerous assumptions about geology and economies. New geological data from outside ANWR and reinterpretation (using new techniques) of the limited old FLEJS information have changed estimates of ANWR's oil potential. Another factor affecting resource and recovery estimates is the projected price of oil, which the Bureau of Land Management (BLM) in 1987 assumed would increase steadily (excluding inflation) over coming decades. In actuality, except for short intervals of spiking, the price of oil has not risen to the extent assumed by BLM until recently. A third factor is falling production costs. As technology improves, once unprofitable structures may become profitable; this has occurred repeatedly on the North Slope. (See Box, *What the Numbers Mean,* for discussion of terms used below.) Three major studies are reviewed below; due to changes in methods, assumptions, and goals of the studies, comparisons among them must be done with caution.

---

[39] As discussed later, oil and gas development of ANWR essentially would not address these current issues.

> **What the Numbers Mean**
>
> There are many widely varying estimates of oil quantities in the 1002 area. Here is a guide to these estimates and their meaning.
>
> *How much oil might be present?* The amount that might be present or "in place" is just a starting point, since it is not possible to extract all of the oil in a field. Estimates are almost always given as a range of numbers. First, petroleum geologists ask "what quantity of oil are we confident of finding?" There is a good chance of finding a small amount (ore more), and a small chance of finding a large amount (or more). The probability levels used are fixed (by tradition) at 95% (chance of at least a certain small amount), and 5% (chance of at least a certain large amount). The third number is the mean estimate – the average of all of the estimated amounts. The numbers could change with better data or better technology.
>
> *How much oil is technically recoverable?* This set of estimates does not take into account the cost of recovery and price of oil, and assumes that only current technology is used to recover the oil. Like the previous set of estimates, it states the large (95%) chance that a certain small amount (or more) of oil is present, the small chance (5%) that a large amount (or more) is present, and the mean estimate. These numbers always are smaller than the estimates of oil that might be present. As technology advances, this number also could change.
>
> *How much oil is economically recoverable?* These numbers are often the most useful. They reflect assumptions about oil prices, cost of production, etc. They also are given as 95%, mean, and 5% estimates (of small or more, mean, and large or more amounts). If technology later advances, costs decrease, or prices rise, then these numbers could increase, and vice-versa. Estimates of economically recoverable oil tend to increase over time.
>
> *Minimum field size* is the smallest amount of oil that must be present in a prospect for it to be commercial. Embedded in this concept are assumptions about future oil prices, technology development, and costs of production and transportation; if these change, this threshold will change. At ANWR, the minimum field size usually is estimated at a few hundred million barrels. Many smaller fields very close together might serve as well as a larger one in terms of potential profitability.
>
> *What area is being measured?* Some estimates of oil in ANWR include the inholdings of the Kaktovik Inupiat Corporation and those of the Arctic Slope Regional Corporation, as well as state owned lands offshore. This report refers to estimates on federal lands only, unless otherwise noted.

1991 and 1995 Studies

In 1991, BLM reviewed its 1987 estimate of ANWR's recoverable petroleum resource, based on reprocessed geophysical data, newly-acquired information on four wells drilled near ANWR, additional seismic data from offshore areas near the coastal plain, and the characteristics of new applicable technology (used in the development of the Endicott and Mime Point fields on the ANS frontier). This review gave BLM a greater level of confidence that ANWR is part of the North Slope oil province, and increased its estimates of the probability of economic success. BLM reduced its estimate of the smallest field that could be developed economically from 440 million to 400 million barrels,[40] thereby increasing the marginal probability of economic success from 19% to 46%; if such a field is found, the mean estimate of economically recoverable oil would be 3.57 billion barrels — 0.37 billion bbl more than in 1987.

In June 1995, the U.S. Geological Survey (USGS) revisited the Bureau of Land Management's 1991 estimates, relying upon several new geologic studies and data from a new well, the Tenneco Aurora, a federal offshore lease north of the 1002 area. The USGS reduced its estimates of technically recoverable oil reserves in the 1002 area to between 148 million and 5.15 billion barrels. (The draft study, which was never finalized, did not give a mean estimate.[41] See Box *What the Numbers Mean,* for the difference between "technically recoverable" and "economically recoverable.")

1998 Study

The most recent government study of oil and natural gas prospects in ANWR, also by the USGS, was completed in 1998.[42]

Table 1. Probability of the Presence of Given Quantities of Oil and the Recoverability of the Oil in the 1002 Area
(billions of barrels)

Crude Oil	95% Chance This Much or More	Mean Estimate	5% Chance This Much or More
In place	11.59	20.73	31.52
Technically recoverable	4.25	7.69	11.80
Economically recoverable at			
... a market price of $30/bbl	2.98	6.30	10.47
... a market price of $24/bbl	2.03	5.24	9.37
... a market price of $18/bbl	-0-	2.40	6.15

Note: All calculations to estimate economically recoverable resources and the prices used are in 1996 dollars.
Source: U.S. Dept. of the Interior, Geological Survey. *The Oil and Gas Potential of the Artic National Wildlife Refuge 1002 Area, Alaska.* U.S.G.S. Open File Report 93-34 (Washington, DC: 1999) Summary, and Table EA4. (Report available on 2-disk CD-ROM.)

According to USGS, there is an excellent chance (95%) that at least 11.6 billion barrels are present on federal lands in the 1002 area. There also is a small chance (5%) that 31.52 billion barrels or more are present. If cost were no object, USGS estimates there is an excellent chance (95%) that 4.25 billion barrels or more are technically recoverable. And

---

[40] The seeming paradox of reduction constituting an improvement is analogous to taking two tests, in which a passing score on the first is 70, while the passing score on the second is 60. The probability of passing the test (finding an economic field) increases if the minimum passing score (minimum economic field) decreases. This particular figure for field size was applicable to western prospects in the 1002 area. The minimum field size for eastern prospects, needing a longer pipeline to hook up with TAPS, was reduced from 600 million to *550* million barrels.
[41] U.S. Dept. of the Interior, Geological Survey. Implications of U.S. Geological Survey Region Hydrocarbon Assessment of Northern Alaska to Oil Resource Potential of Arctic *National Wildlife Refuge 1002 Area.* June 2, 1995. 6 p. (Issued in draft form only; unnumbered report.)

there is a small chance (5%) that 11.80 billion barrels or more are technically recoverable.[43] (If state offshore lands and Native corporation lands are included, these numbers become 5.7 and 16.0 billion barrels, respectively.) It appears that natural gas is likely to be present as well. USGS estimates that there is a *95% chance that 2.28 trillion cubic feet (tcf) associated with crude oil are technically recoverable, and a 5% chance that 5.16 tcf are technically recoverable.

Technically or Economically Recoverable?
However, cost inevitably comes into play, whether in the extreme conditions of the North Slope or elsewhere. Thus, the primary question is *how much oil can be extracted profitably?* Each company has its own internal criteria for this. The higher the price of crude oil, the greater the proportion that would be economically recoverable. High prices also could provide incentives to improve extraction technology thereby reducing extraction costs. The USGS estimated that, at $24/barrel (in 1996 dollars), there is a 95% chance that 2.03 billion barrels or more could be recovered, and a 5% chance of 9.37 billion barrels or more. For comparison, the spot price of West Texas crude oil ranged from an average of $11.35 per barrel in December 1998, to $34.34 per barrel in November 2000, according to the Energy Information Administration (EIA). It was estimated at $20 in November 2001. (In 1996 dollars, these were $10.95, $32.00, and $18.10, respectively.)

The projected price of oil is only one of many factors entering into the decision on bidding for a lease. Efforts to reduce exploration and production costs through new technologies play a key role, for example. Each prospective bidder would do its own analysis of the economic and physical factors of the areas offered for lease, and company analyses historically have differed from one another and from government analyses. With geological evidence pointing to the presence of recoverable oil and gas, developers are expected to be interested in bidding on ANWR leases.

Possible Production Levels
It is difficult to estimate the development rates or production levels over time that would be associated with given volumes of economically recoverable oil resources. Some of the various factors considered by prospective bidders also would come into play in determining the rate of development and levels of production. Oil prices (current and projected), geologic characteristics such as permeability and porosity, cash flow, and any transportation constraints would be among the most important.

The EIA estimated production "schedules" that would be associated with several different volumes of *technically* recoverable resources at two development rates.[44] At the faster development rate, a production peak would occur 15 to 20 years after the start of

---

[42] U.S. Dept. of the Interior, Geological Survey. *The Oil and Gas Potential of the Arctic National Wildlife Refuge 1002 Area, Alaska.* U.S.G.S. Open File Report 98-34. (Washington, DC: 1999). Summary, and Table EA4. (Report available on 2-disk CD-ROM.) (Hereafter cited as USGS, *Oil and Gas Potential of ANWR.*)

[43] The USGS technically recoverable figures in the 1998 assessment are based upon the percentage of oil in place that was recoverable by the oil industry in the 1980s. Inasmuch as recovery rates have improved since then, the USGS figures may underestimate recovery rates in ANWR.

[44] U.S. Dept. of Energy, Energy Information Administration, *Potential Oil Production from the Coastal Plain of the Arctic National Wildlife Refuge: Updated Assessment* (Washington: May 2000). The development rates are postulated with the implicit assumptions of sufficiently high crude oil prices (current and projected) and constant technology.

development, with maximum daily production rates of roughly 0.00015 (0.015%) of the resource. Slower development rates would peak about 25 years after the start of development at a daily production rate of roughly 0.000105 (0.0105%) of the resource. (Peak production associated with a resource of 5.0 billion barrels at the faster development rate would be 750,000 bbl/d.)

Figure 4. Petroleum Discoveries and Exploratory Wells of 1002 Area and Adjacent Areas.

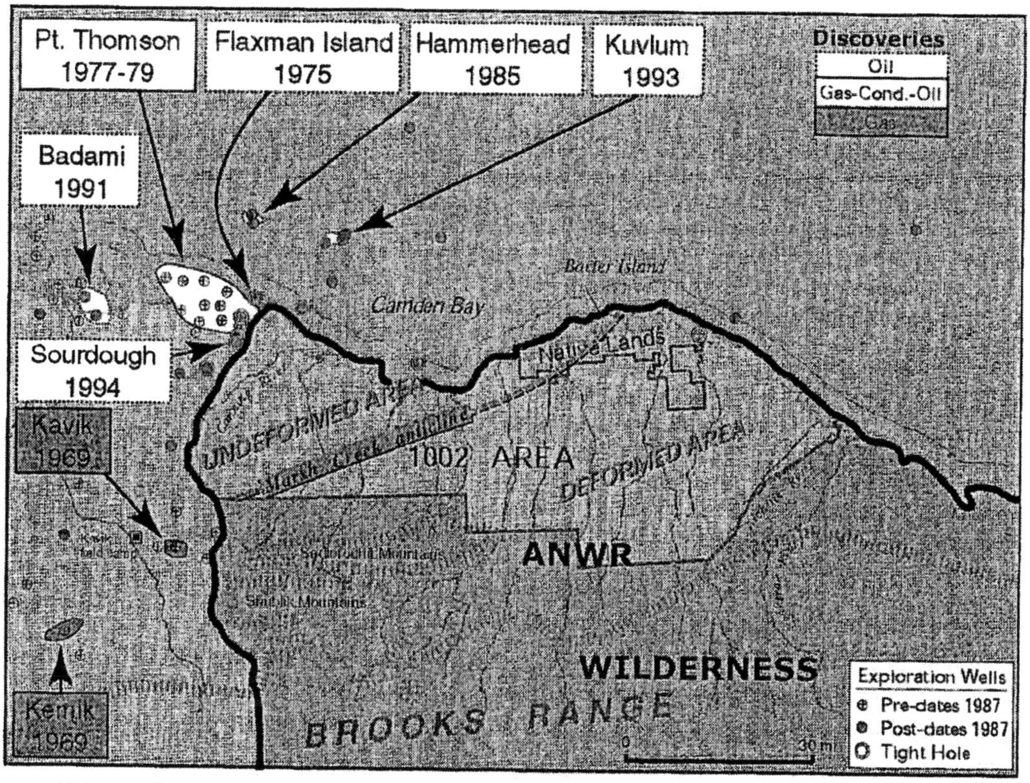

Notes: This map shows "petroleum discoveries and status of exploratory wells relative to the 1987 USGS [FLEIS] assessment. ... [D]ashed line marks approximate boundary between undeformed area, where rocks are generally horizontal, and deformed area, where rocks are folded and faulted." **Source:** Figure AO2 of USGS, *Oil and Gas Potential of ANWR*. Oil was found at Flaxman Island, Hammerhead, Kuvlum, Badammi, and Sourdough. Gas was found at Kavik and Kemik, and Point Thompson showed gas condensate and oil.

It is not known if the development rates and production schedules developed by EIA would apply to discoveries of *economically* recoverable oil in ANWR. If they did, the peak production level in a scenario with the world price of oil at $24 per barrel could range from 200,000 to 1,400,000 barrels per day depending upon the size of the discovery (Table 2). For simplicity, it is assumed that oil prices do not fluctuate during the lives of the fields being produced.

Table 2. Approximate ANWR Peak Production Levels Under Selected Discovery and Development Scenarios

Oil Price per Barrel (1995 dollars)	Hypothetical Volumes of Economically Recoverable Crude Oil[a] (billions of barrels)			Approximate Peak Production Associated with Respective Volumes and Different Rates of Development[b] (thousands of barrels per day)		
	95%	mean	5%	95%	mean	5%
$18	-0-	2.40	6.15	-0-	250 – 350	650 – 925
$24	2.03	5.24	9.37	200 – 300	550 – 775	975 – 1,400
$30	2.98	6.30	10.47	300 – 450	650 – 950	1,100 – 1,575

Note: Production levels (and implicit development rates) are based upon the assumption that crude oil prices (current and projected) would be high enough to justify continued development and production. For simplicity, it is assumed that oil prices do not fluctuate during the lives of the fields being produced.

[a] These volumes correspond to those shown in Table 1 as economically recoverable oil at market prices of $18, $24, and $30 per barrel at different degrees of uncertainty.

[b] Production volumes associated with a slower and a faster rate of development; thus at $24/bbl, the mean expectation of economically recoverable oil is 5.24 billion bbl. This would result in a production rate of 550,000 to 775,000 bbl/day in the slower and faster production rates, respectively.

Sources: Energy Information Administration. Potential Oil Production from the Coastal Plain of the Arctic National Wildlife Refuge: Updated Assessment. May 2000. Table 1 and CRS estimates.

Natural Gas Potential

Not only crude oil but also large amounts of natural gas are believed to exist in the 1002 area. This expectation together with huge amounts of proven gas reserves in the Prudhoe Bay area may increase the appeal of oil and gas development of ANWR to energy producers.[45] For economic reasons, natural gas was not emphasized in the 1980s, but has become more important in recent years as demand has grown.

Estimates of Prudhoe Bay Complex

The Alaska Department of Natural Resources estimated the original recoverable gas reserves of Prudhoe Bay at 30.5 trillion cubic feet (tcf), and estimates current overall North Slope reserves at 30.9 tcf (including amounts in oil fields subsequently discovered).[46] On an energy equivalent basis, 30 tcf of natural gas is equivalent to about 5.3 billion barrels of crude oil.[47] The Energy Information Administration originally counted all of the ANS gas volumes noted above as proved reserves. Since 1988, however, the EIA has omitted about 80% of those volumes on the basis that, without a pipeline or near-term prospects of a pipeline, the gas has no market and therefore is not commercially recoverable. EIA counts the remaining

---

[45] See CRS Report RL31165, *Natural Gas Reserves in Alaska: an Overview of Conventional and Non-conventional Development and Transport Options*, by Terry R. Twyman (Oct. 25, 2001, 23 p. (Hereafter referred to as CRS Report RL31165.)

[46] "Original estimate" figure from Alaska Dept. of Natural Resources, as reported in *Alaska Oil and Gas, Energy Wealth or Vanishing Opportunity? (Final)*. Prepared for the U.S. Dept. of Energy by EG&G Idaho, Inc. January 1991, p. 2-8. Current estimate from *2000 Annual Report*, Alaska Dept. of Natural Resources, Division of Oil and Gas, not dated, p. 12.

[47] There are approximately 1,030 btu per cubic foot of natural gas, and 5.8 million btu per barrel of crude oil. A btu, or British Thermal Unit, is the amount of heat required to raise the temperature of a pound of water one degree

portion of the gas reserves because they are used to power oil field and transport operations. EIA estimates that proved natural gas reserves in the entire state of Alaska totaled 9.7 tcf at the beginning of 2000.[48]

Most of the gas produced so far on the North Slope has been reinjected into the ground by oil field operators to maintain pressure in the reservoir zones. Currently, 80-90% of the 8 to 9 billion cubic feet of natural gas produced per day are reinjected.[49] The remainder is used for lease operations, electric power generation, and for powering oil flow through pipelines.

Estimates of 1002 Area

Natural gas is also estimated to be in the 1002 area, although seemingly not as much as so far discovered in the rest of the North Slope. The USGS 1998 assessment of ANWR gas resources estimated a 5% chance that there are 10.02 tcf or more of technically recoverable gas not associated with oil in the 1002 area, with a mean "expected" amount of 3.48 tcf. The mean 'expected" amount of technically recoverable dissolved natural gas (*i.e.,* associated with oil) was 3.56 tcf (Table 3). Non-associates gas probably would not be targeted until after oil field infrastructure was in place.

Table 3. Mean Estimates of the Amounts of Undiscovered Natural Gas and Natural Gas Liquids in the 1002 Area

Natural Gas Resource	Technically Recoverable	Economically Recoverable at a Market Price of ...		
		$18 per bbl of oil	$24 per bbl of oil	$30 per bbl of oil
In Oil Fields				
Associated dissolved gas (tcf)	3.56	n.a.	n.a.	n.a.
(Crude oil equiv. (million bbl))	(630)			
Natural gas liquids from associated dissolved gas (million bbl)	143	10	70	100
(Crude oil equiv. (million bbl))	(92)	(6)	(45)	(64)
In Gas Fields				
Non-associated gas (tcf)	3.48	n.a.	n.a.	n.a.
(Crude oil equiv. (million bbl))	(616)			
Natural gas liquids from non-associated gas (mil. of bbl)	112	n.a.	n.a.	n.a.
(Crude oil equiv. (million bbl)	(72)			

Notes: Crude oil equivalents are based upon inherent heat contents. The mean is the arithmetic average of all the estimated amounts, and is sometimes called the "expected" value, or amount.
bbl – barrel; n.a. – not applicable; tcf – trillion cubic feet.
Source: U.S. Dept. of the Interior, Geological Survey. *The Oil and Gas Potential of Arctic National Refuge: 1002 Area, Alaska.* U.S.G.S. Open File Report 98-34. (Washington, DC: 1999). Tables EA4 and RS14.

Fahrenheit. (30 tcf x. 1,030 btu/cf = 30.9 quadrillion btu. 30.9 quadrillion btu divided by 5.8 million btu/bbl = 5.3 billion bbl.)

[48] U.S. Dept. of Energy, Energy Information Administration, *U.S. Crude Oil, Natural Gas, and Natural Gas Liquids Reserves, 1999 Annual Report*, (Washington, DC) p. 28.

[49] Alaska Dept. of Natural Resources. *2000 Annual Report*, p. 8; and T.J. Glauthier, Deputy Secretary, U.S. Dept. of Energy, "Testimony to the Senate Committee on Energy and Natural Resources," September 14, 2000.

In addition, the USGS estimated natural gas liquids extractable from the technically recoverable gas in mean amounts of 143 million barrels from oil fields and 112 million barrel from gas fields. With an energy content of about 3.8 million btu per barrel, the former figure is roughly equivalent to 95 million barrels of crude oil and the latter to about 75 million barrels. The mean amounts of natural gas liquids economically recoverable at $18, $24, and $30 per barrel of oil would be 10 million, 70 million, and 100 million barrels, respectively.

Because, without a pipeline, there presently is no way of transporting natural gas to markets and generating revenue streams with which to compare costs, it is not possible to derive estimates of *economically recoverable* natural gas in the 1002 area.

Natural Gas Pipeline from North Slope

Construction of a pipeline to transport natural gas to North American markets and/or a warm-water port for shipping liquefied natural gas (LNG) could enhance Prudhoe Bay economics – oil as well as gas. The prospect of producing both oil and gas would also enhance the commercial promise of the 1002 area. Until recently, estimated costs of transporting the gas precluded serious consideration of pipeline construction. However, the steep increase in the price of natural gas in the winter of 2000-2001 and some projections of continued high prices relative to the average of he past 15 years have suggested some improvement in the relationship between market price and the cost of known gas resources in the North Slope. Economic growth, environmental regulations, and gains in gas-fired electric power generation have increased current and projected demand for natural gas. In addition, the technology of converting gas into a liquid has advanced. As a result, serious consideration of pipeline construction. However, the steep increase in the price of natural gas in the winter of 2000-2001 and some projections of continued high prices relative to the average of the past 15 years have suggested some improvement in the relationship between market prices and the cost of known gas resources in the North Slope. Economic growth, environmental regulations, and gains in gas-fired electric power generation have increased current and projected demand for natural gas. In addition, the technology of converting gas into a liquid has advanced. As a result, serious consideration is being given to building the means of transporting "proven" gas and the prospective gas of the North Slope to markets.

There appear to be several route options. (See Figure 5.) One is a pipeline that would parallel the existing TAPS from the North Slope to Fairbanks, then veer eastward along the Alaska Highway through the Yukon Territory, northern British Columbia, and into Alberta. This, the Alaska Natural Gas Transportation System (ANGTS), was presidentially and congressionally approved in the 1970s, and agreed to by the Canadian government. Two "legs" have been built – extending from Alberta to the Chicago area and from Alberta to northern California – and already transport Canadian gas to those markets. The legal framework and permits are still in force. Another proposed gas pipeline, the TransAlaska Gas System (TAGS), would move the gas via a buried route paralleling TAPS all the way to slightly west of the TAPS terminal at Valdez. The gas would be liquefied there for shipment to Asian markets. Various environmental and other approvals have been obtained.

A northern pipeline route (Northern Gas Pipeline Project) would run eastward from Prudhoe Bay buried under the Beaufort Sea and come ashore in the Mackenzie Delta. It would then link with a pipeline running through the Mackenzie Valley into northern Alberta, or with a pipeline running through the Yukon Territory, which would then link with the ANGTS.

Various factors would come into play in determining a route or routes.[50] A study prepared for the INGAA Foundation[51] estimated that an overland pipeline route would cost $100,000 per diameter-inch-mile, and an offshore pipeline route would cost $150,000 per diameter-inch-mile in up front capital.[52] According to this estimate, a 30-inch, 500-mile overland pipeline would cost $1.5 billion. The proposed northern pipeline route would be shorter, but the underwater nature may subject it to technical and environmental risks, and whalers from Alaskan Native villages object. Environmental impact statements prepared 25 years ago may not be accepted now.

Figure 5. Proposed Routes to Transport Alaskan and Canadian Natural Gas to Markets

Source: T.J. Glauthier, Deputy Secretary, U.S. Department of Energy, "Testimony to the Senate Committee on Energy and Natural Resources," September 14, 2000. Cited in "SPECIAL TOPIC – Alaskan North Slope Gas: From Stranded Asset to a Prize of the Decade: [http://www.eia.doe.gov/emeu/perfpro/chapter4.html]. Figure is slightly modified for clarity in monochrome.

Advances in the technology of converting natural gas into a liquid could provide another transportation option. A gas-to-liquids process (now being developed) chemically converts natural gas into a diesel-like liquid that can be mixed with crude oil for transportation and then refined in the lower 48 states.[53] Converting the gas into a liquid at or near the oil and/or gas fields would eliminate the need for a separate gas pipeline and potentially extend the economic life of the existing oil pipeline. Oil produced from existing North Slope fields is

---

[50] For more on transportation options for natural gas, see CRS Report RL31165, previously cited.
[51] INGAA stands for "Interstate Natural Gas Association of America," though the official name of the Foundation uses the acronym.
[52] Houston Energy Group, LLC and URS Corporation, *Future Natural Gas Supplies from the Alaskan and Canadian Frontier*, Prepared for the INGAA Foundation, Inc. (2001), p. 22.
[53] Basically, a mixture of oxygen and the methane component of natural gas is passed through a ceramic membrane containing a catalyst, producing a synthetic gas, that is then reacted with another catalyst and converted to high-quality diesel and heavier oil liquids. Low levels of sulfur, metals, and nitrogen in either the pure product or the mixture make it attractive in terms of reducing pollution.

projected to decrease and fall below the minimum economic flow of the TAPS within a decade or two.

Alaskan Position on Northern Route

Alaska has enacted legislation that bans construction of a gas pipeline in northern state waters. The Alaska state legislature strongly supports proposals for a pipeline to the south. While the royalties to the state (for those natural gas resources actually owned by the state) would be higher under the shorter, less costly northern route, thereby making the wellhead prices higher,[54] state officials see a greater gain through the income multiplier effect of construction within the state and greater access by Alaskan communities to the new gas supplies. Also at issue is the fact that a Canadian route would likely serve new Canadian gas fields, which would then compete with Alaska in U.S. markets. This, together with the factors cited above, suggests a potential conflict between maximizing energy company profits and benefits to the state.

Economic Effects of Development

The U.S. economy as a whole would be affected by development and production of oil in the Arctic National Wildlife Refuge through the direct effects of the economic activity constituted by the development and production itself. The economy would also be indirectly affected by an change in oil prices resulting from ANWR production and any effects on the amount spent on imported oil. A major unknown and driving factor is the amount of economically recoverable oil discovered and eventually produced.[55]

Development Stimulus

Oil and gas development in ANWR would generate primarily mining, construction, manufacturing, and transportation activity, but also many types of other supply and support services such as food, fuel, power, and management services. Such demand for goods and services equipment would be felt in the lower 48 states as well as in Alaska.

Major determinants of the cost of developing ANWR, and its direct stimulus, would be the size of any overall discovery of economically recoverable oil resources and the sizes of the individual fields continuing such resources. There are high degrees of uncertainty in both areas. (See Table 2.)

The USGS estimates also have very wide ranges with respect to oil field sizes. Among the larger sizes, which oil companies probably would consider first, the estimates show a 95% chance of three or more fields and a 5% chance of six or more fields with 256-512 million bbl of technically recoverable oil; a 95% chance of one or more fields and a 5% chance of four or more fields with 512-1,024 million bbl; and a 95% chance of a field of three-tenths of a field or more and a 5% chance of one and a half fields or more with 1,024-2,048 million bbl.[56] Each company would have data on j1002 area prospects from its preliminary exploration and

---

[54] The wellhead price of oil or gas obtained by Alaskan producers equals the delivered price (per barrel or thousand cubic feet) less the cost of transportation, which increases according to the length of the pipeline. State royalties and other revenues are proportionally affected.

[55] The economic effects of development are also discussed in CRS Report RS20130, *ANWR Development: Economic Impacts,* by Bernard A. Gelb, (Dec. 3, 2001). 6 p.

[56] USGS, *Oil and Gas Potential of ANWR*. These are arithmetic means of distributions of estimated fields sizes; results can have numbers with fractions. The numbers of fields used in the text are rounded.

comparisons with existing information; it would then select the most attractive prospects based upon existing information; it would then select the most attractive prospects based upon its own interpretation of geologic data, its own resource assessment, and its own financial criteria. Smaller fields probably would become attractive if and when larger fields were developed and infrastructure was in place.

Thus, if commercial oil fields were discovered, they most likely would be of different sizes and the collective overall quantity of economically recoverable oil could be in a very wide range. And, given that the size of a possible overall discovery is unknown, estimations of the overall cost of developing ANWR are hypothetical.

Advances in arctic oil and gas development technology, equipment, and facility configuration reduce both the extensiveness of facilities and the development cost per barrel of discovery.[57] These advances have made such development more capital intensive onsite and moved more labor offsite, to locations where data analysis is performed. A very crude benchmark to use as a basis for estimating the outlays that would be entailed is the roughly $1 billion cost of developing the Alpine field, which has about 430 million bbl of reserves.[58] Alpine is a recently developed field on the North Slope of Alaska that employs advanced arctic technologies. However, Alpine is appropriate as a cost benchmark only to the extent that the geological conditions, pristineness, and accessibility of the hypothetically discovered fields at ANWR were similar to those at Alpine.[59]

Two illustrative *hypothetical* cases might be as follows: (1) A discovery of 2.40 billion bbl economically recoverable oil in four 100-million bbl fields, three 200-million-bbl fields, two 400-million-bbl fields, and one 800-million-bbl field. (2) 5.24 billion bbl fields, two 800-million-bbl fields, and one 1,200-million-bbl field.[60]

In the first case if, hypothetically, the fields associated with an overall 2.40-billion-bbl discovery of economically recoverable oil are of the same nature and degree of difficulty to develop as Alpine, and if, *as is unlikely*, development costs for ANWR are proportional to field size (using Alpine as the benchmark), total development cost of an ANWR discovery of that size would approximate $6.5 billion. With identical caveats for a 5.24-billion-bbl overall discovery, total development cost of that overall discovery would approximate $14.0 billion.[61] At roughly $2.70 per barrel discovered ($14 billion divided by 5.24 billion bbl), these hypothetical estimate totals, which may well exclude exploration costs, appear low. In recent years, major oil companies have experienced onshore finding costs of about $5.25 per barrel (with exploration costs accounting for about one-third), based upon Energy Information Administration (EIA) surveys,[62] but such costs have been declining over time.

---

[57] For more detailed treatment of ANWR petroleum development technology in the arctic, see CRS Report RL31022, previously cited.
[58] Alan Petzeet, "Alaska operators start Alpine field, take more leases," *The Oil and Gas Journal*, (December 4, 2000); Phillips Alaska, Inc., *Fact Sheet* (January 1, 2001).
[59] Additional outlays for infrastructure, including the cost of connecting to the TransAlaska Pipeline System, would be required if fields are distant from existing staging areas.
[60] The hypothetical distributions of field sizes are based upon Field EA2 in: USGS, *Oil and Gas Potential of ANWR*, Chapter EA.
[61] Using a ratio of $1 billion per 400-million-bbl field, the arithmetic is as follows. For the smaller discovery: (4 x $250 million) + (3 x $500 million) + (2 x $,000 million) + (1 x $2,000) = $6.5 billion. For the larger discovery: (6 x $500 million) + (4 x $1,000 million) + (2 x $2,000 million) + (1 x $3,000 million) = $14.0 billion.
[62] U.S. Dept. of Energy, Energy Information Administration, *Performance Profiles of Major Energy Producers, 1999.* (Washington, DC) Table 20, Table B14.

Oil Market Response

Other things being equal, an increase in production, or supply, would be expected to result in a price decline (or a lower price than would occur otherwise). The size of the decline would depend to some extent on how close world oil output would be in relation to world oil production capacity and upon the reaction of other suppliers to the market.

As noted above, peak production from any economically recoverable volumes of 2.03 billion and 9.37 billion bbl at $24 per barrel[63] probably would be reached in about 2020, and would range from roughly 300,000 to 1,400,000 bbl per day. EIA projects world oil production to total 106.6 million bbl per day in 2015.[64] Thus, ANWR production (from the respective discovery volumes) at their peaks around the years 2013-2015 would range from about 0.3% to 0.9% of world output.

Opponents of ANWR have suggested that potential ANWR resources are equivalent to U.S. daily demand for oil for a matter of just months.[65] This does not consider the role, which any incremental source of petroleum plays in markets, which are dynamic. Consequently, the impact of ANWR production on world oil prices is likely to be variable depending upon market and political factors prevailing in the moment. For proponents of development, the oil shocks to the market in 1973-74, 1979-80, 1991, and 2000-2001 tend to loom large.

However, a review of the nearly thirty years since the time of the Arab oil embargo and first oil price shock in 1973 suggests that it is more accurate to see this nearly thirty-year period as one of general price and supply stability that is periodically broken with shorter episodes when price became volatile and supplies of fuel less certain. During any of these episodes, even an additional 100,000 bbl/day of refined product in certain regional markets might have eased prices.[66] In times of uncertainty – and even at the low range of estimates of potential ANWR production – these volumes might help contain a short-term spike the prices. In these moments, it matters little whether the incremental supply comes from a field holding six months' national demand, or sixty years' potential supply, because the price of product at the pump will not discriminate between the two.

Some argue that ANWR production could result in lower world oil prices if supply in the world market were relatively tight in 2015 and the market was reasonably competitive. In a period of general stability and balance in supply and demand, production from ANWR at the lower range of the estimates would probably have a small effect on prices. There is also the prospect that, depending upon market factors and their internal economies, OPEC and other producers could cut their output to offset the supply effect of ANWR, as has occurred before. This would depend upon the commitment of OPEC nations to try to support or deal a price band for crude oil by cutting production, as they did three times in 2001. At the same time, internal revenue needs have sometimes prompted producing nations to sell output above their

---

[63] EIA projects the average price of landed oil imports at $21.37 per barrel in 2010 and $21.89 in 2015 (1999 dollars). *International Energy Outlook 2001.* (Washington, DC: March 2001), p. 41. EIA's oil price, oil production, and economic growth projections used here are its best-guess ", reference case."

[64] *International Energy Outlook 2001,* p. 42.

[65] Actual extraction of the oil would require decades.

[66] Mention should be made that a shortage of refining capacity or configuration, and transportation infrastructure were contributing factors to some of the observed increase in price, and under these circumstances, the effect upon price of incremental crude production will be perhaps more selective and regional.

quotas. Additional oil supply from non-OPEC producers also makes it more difficult for OPEC to affect prices.[67]

Macroeconomic Effects

In general, if energy prices fall, the drop would tend to increase the amount of inputs afforded by businesses, boosting the overall supply of goods and services. Higher aggregate income and lower prices would enable households to buy more goods and services. Economic growth would speed up; and, if the economy is not a full employment, more labor and capital would be employed. Once the adjustment to lower prices is completed, growth would return to its prior rate, but at a higher output level.

However, in analyzing the impact of changes in energy costs on the economy as a whole or on individual sectors, one needs to be aware that the relative price of oil has decreased since the oil price spikes of the 1970s and early 1980s, and energy use per unit of output has fallen as well. The proportions of production costs account for by energy have dropped across the economy; and energy costs as a share of Gross Domestic Product (GDP) have declined. Consequently, the relative impacts of energy price changes on the economy in general and on particular sectors can be expected to be smaller than they were 20-25 years.

It appears also that any price effect would have to be considerable and sustained for the macroeconomic effects to be reasonably noticeable. For example, the Organization for Economic Cooperation and Development estimated that an increase in oil prices of $10 per barrel above its baseline scenario would result in U.S. GDP being 0.2% lower one year and two years after the shock.[68] In contrast, as noted above, the price effect of a 0.3% - 0.9% addition to world oil supply resulting from ANWR production probably would be small, although econometric research findings suggest that the beneficial macroeconomic result of a price drop would not necessarily be proportional.

Oil and gas producers that do not participate in ANWR development, their suppliers, and their local economies in the contiguous 48 States would be *harmed* should oil prices decline. Producers' revenues would decline indirectly as well as directly through reductions in output – both effects leading to cutbacks in employment and in purchases of other goods and services.

With respect to ANWR development, hypothetical outlays of $6.5 billion and $14.0 billion with an income multiplier of two[69] applying to both would come to roughly 0.12% and 0.26% of projected GDP for they year 2002 (on the unlikely assumption that all the outlays occur in one year).[70] If the outlays are spread over more than one year, the impact in each year would be less, but the total effect would be about the same. The percentages would be much lower in 2020, when the economy is projected to be about 45% larger.[71] If there is some

---

[67] For more on U.S. energy policies, see CRS Issue Brief IB10080, *Energy Policy: Setting the Stage for the Current Debate.* 16.p

[68] Organization for Economic Cooperation and Development, *Economic Outlook.* (December 1999), p. 9. Macroeconomic simulations by other organizations have had similar results.

[69] Changes in investment spending have a magnified impact on the economy as a result of the ripple effects on the income and spending of other businesses and of households. Income multiplier is the term used to denote the total impact of the initial spending. Such multipliers differ depending upon the sector of the economy in which the investment takes place. A multiplier of two is generally considered reasonable for the type of spending discussed here.

[70] DRI-WEFA, *U.S. Economic Outlook*, (August 2001) p. 9. The projection is in current dollars.

[71] EIA, *Annual Energy Outlook 2001*, p. 152.

spare capacity in the oil and gas industry, producers and their suppliers would benefit. However, if the economy is at full employment, the multiplier effect would be transitory.

Employment Effects

Oil and gas development in ANWR would generate *additional* jobs in the national economy to the extent that development resulted directly and indirectly in a *net* economic stimulus. A key factor would be whether the economy is at full employment or less than full employment. The direct effects are clearer than the indirect, given the uncertainty of the effects of ANWR oil on world oil prices and any consequent beneficial effects of lower energy prices on the economy as a whole.

Rough estimates can be made for jobs generated by the hypothetical development outlays by using the national averages of 3.89 jobs directly and indirectly generated per $1 million of sales by oil and gas producers and 16.53 jobs per $1 million of sales by oil and gas field services companies, as estimated by the Bureau of Labor Statistics (BLS).[72] Adjusting for price increases since 1992 and assuming that half of the outlays are attributable to each group, $6.5 billion in outlays would lead to about 60,000 jobs, and $14.0 billion would lead to about 130,000 jobs.[73]

If the economy were at full employment, however, investment in ANWR may crowd out other spending in the economy; moreover, ANWR development may draw oil industry resources (capital and labor) from oil prospects elsewhere in the country. In the long run, the unemployment rate is determined by the structure of the labor market, and, at full employment, any jobs generated by ANWR development would come at the expense of an equal number of jobs lost in the rest of the economy.

Because the impact of ANWR oil prices would be uncertain, and any decrease would have to be considerable and sustained for the macroeconomic effects to be reasonably noticeable, the effects on employment would be highly uncertain. Any gain in employment from beneficial macroeconomic effects of a drop in oil prices, however, may be offset by the harm to oil producers elsewhere in the United States, who may reduce their operations and workforce.

Other Job Impact Estimates

Some proponents of ANWR development assert that such development would result in a gain of more than 700,000 jobs in the economy. This is based upon a 1990 report by The WEFA Group[74] that estimated that the economic impact of oil development in ANWR would result, through direct and indirect effects, in a net gain in employment of 735,000 in the peak year of job creation. The major portion of WEFA's employment gain results from large estimated beneficial macroeconomic effects of lower world oil prices caused by an increase in

---

[72] U.S. Bureau of Labor Statistics, Web site [http://www.bls.gov/emp/empiknd4.htm]. While in terms of sales in 1992 dollars, the ratios (which BLS calls "employment requirements") are based upon 1998 productivity relationships.

[73] Hypothetical $6.5 million scenario: ($3.25 billion by oil producing companies divided by 1.097 (deflator)) x 3.89 (jobs per million $) = 11,525 jobs; ($3.25 billion by oil field service companies divided by 1.097 (deflator)) x 16.53 (jobs per million $) = 48,9075 jobs. Together, the result would be 60,500 jobs. Hypothetical $14.0 scenario: ($7.0 billion by oil producing companies divided by 1.097 (deflator)) x 3.89 (jobs per million $) = 24,825 jobs; ($7.0 billion by oil field service companies divided by 1.097 (deflator)) x 16.53 (jobs per million $) = 105,475. Together, the result would be 130,300 jobs.

[74] The WEFA Group merged with DRI, forming DRI-WEFA. DRI had been a subsidiary of Standards & Poor's.

world oil supply attributable to ANWR oil. WEFA based that increase upon an oil discovery near the high end of the 1987 FLEIS estimates.

The study's estimates of effects on GNP[75] and employment appear large in the context of WEFA's essentially full employment base case. They are large also compared with actual economic consequences of oil price changes, and in view of decreased importance of energy input in the economy compared with the 1970s (noted above). It may have been reasonable for WEFA to posit that the world oil supply situation in 2005 would be much tighter than in 1990, and that an injection of an additional 1.7 million barrels per day would tend to lower prices somewhat; and the model used by WEFA allowed for some response by OPEC. The estimated price effect is large nevertheless. In general, the report tended to select the more or most optimistic of underlying scenarios when there was a choice to be made in the sequential analysis required in estimating efforts of this type.[76]

A recent report by Dean Baker of the Center for Economic and Policy Research (CEPR) examined The WEFA Group study and re-estimated the employment effects. It followed WEFA's paradigm but applied different assumptions about some basic data, the degree of response by the market and by OPEC to ANWR oil, and the degree to which the economy responds to an oil price decline. CEPR estimated that oil production in ANWR would result in the creation of 46,300 jobs.[77] The CEPR report, however, does not purport to be a full-fledged estimate of job effects under current oil market, oil industry, and economic conditions.

Import Reduction

As any ANWR oil would be the marginal source of petroleum for the United States, net imports (total imports minus exports) probably would be reduced by virtually one barrel of ANWR output. This is true regardless of the amount of exports of North Slope oil (now nil), which would affect *gross* imports. The economy would benefit temporarily through a reduction in the income transferred overseas to pay for the oil. Using the EIA's projection of refiners' acquisition cost of foreign crude oil of about $21.50 per barrel in 2015,[78] the oil import bill would be cut by $2.4 billion to $11.0 billion in that year, improving the U.S. merchandise trade balance in the short run.

The relative reduction in dollars flowing abroad, however, could cause the dollar to appreciate. This would tend to reduce other exports and expand other imports to some extent, reversing the initial improvement. A possibly greater increase in demand for imports of other goods and services could result from the higher level of economic activity caused by lower oil prices. Basically, the trade deficit reflects the desire of Americans to borrow abroad versus the desire of foreigners to invest or borrow in the United States. Assuming that oil development of ANWR did not influence this dynamic, it would likely have no permanent effect on the trade balance.

---

[75] Before 1991, the main indicator of total economic output used by the U.S. Department of Commerce was Gross National Product, rather than the Gross Domestic Product now used.

[76] A 1992 CRS report, which examines the economic impact question, judged that, overall, the WEFA estimates were generous. See *ANWR Development: Analyzing Its Economic Impact*, Report 92-169 E, by Bernard Gelb (Feb. 12, 1992), 6 p.

[77] Baker, Dean. *Hot Air Over the Arctic? An Assessment of the WEFA Study of the Economic Impact of Oil Drilling in the Arctic National Wildlife Refuge*. Center for Economic and Policy Research. September 4, 2001. 11 p.

[78] EIA, *Annual Energy Outlook 2000*, p. 133.

Effects on the Alaskan Economy

The Alaskan economy could be affected substantially by development and production of oil in ANWR through the direct effects of the exploration, development, and production, and indirectly through the ripple effects of the money spent in Alaska by the producing companies and their workers. A major unknown is the amount of oil that might eventually be produced.

Oil and gas production already is a major industry in Alaska, directly accounting for about 4,500 jobs and $425 million in annual payroll,[79] and about 20% of state gross product on average.[80] ANWR development would affect primarily the oil and gas industry, but also construction, telecommunications, manufacturing, transportation, and other mining, as well as employment in these industries. Many types of other supply and support services such as food, fuel, power, and management services would also benefit. A study of the current economic impact of the oil and gas industry on Alaska indicates substantial effects of the industry on individual regions in the state. And it found indirect and "induced" employment impacts equal to six times employment in the industry itself.[81]

The direct stimulus of the outlays for exploration, development, and production would be felt more in Alaska than elsewhere in the United States – the amount of economically recoverable oil discovered and eventually produced being a key factor. However, much of the equipment and other goods required would be manufactured in the lower 48 states as well as in Alaska. Working with the hypothetical outlays of $6.5 billion and $14.0 billion for wells, pipeline extension, and other facilities, and making the simplifying assumption that half of these outlays would be spent for goods and services (including labor) in Alaska, they would come to $3.25 billion and $7.0 billion. Again adjusting for price increases since 1992 and assuming that oil producing companies and oil field service companies each accounted for half of he outlays, it would lead to about half of the hypothetical jobs estimated for the United States as a whole – 30,000 and 65,000, respectively.

The ratios used, however, are national averages, and oil and gas industry wages in Alaska are higher than average. While the later is beneficial in one respect, I may translate into a smaller number of jobs per billion dollars of outlays. Also, advances in oil and gas development technology and facilities since 1990, reducing the size of facilities, may also reduce the number of jobs generated by such development.

Furthermore, if there were some slack in the Alaskan economy if or when ANWR energy development occurs, jobs created by ANWR could result in a reduction in Alaskan unemployment. If the Alaskan economy were at full employment, the job gain could be transitory. Moreover, as noted earlier, any jobs generated by ANWR development could come at the expense of an equal number of jobs lost in the rest of the economy. This could include drawing oil industry resources (capital and labor) from oil prospects elsewhere in the country to some extent.

---

[79] Employment and payroll figures are calculated from data in U.S. Dept. of Commerce, Bureau of the Census, *1999 County Business Patters, Alaska* and information Insights, Inc. and McDowell Group, *Economic Impact of the Oil and Gas Industry on Alaska*, (Fairbanks, AK: January 15, 2001).

[80] U.S. Dept. of Commerce, Bureau of Economic Analysis at [http://www.bea.doc.gov]. State gross product is the total market value of the goods and services produced in the state. Gross product originating in oil and gas extraction varies widely with crude oil prices and the consequent effects on oil company profits, which are a component of gross product.

[81] *Economic Impact of the Oil and Gas Industry in Alaska. op. ct.* The study is based upon a survey of state oil and gas producers and businesses in the state that sell them goods and services. CRS observes that while there are indirect effects, frequently studies of this type use estimating approaches that tend to overstate indirect impacts.

The Alaska state government, and ultimately Alaskan citizens, could benefit substantially form ANWR development via its share of potentially billions of dollars of revenues from bonuses, rents, and royalties. Alaskan citizens receive annual distributions from the state's Permanent Funds, which is endowed by revenues from mineral lease rentals, royalties, and bonuses, and the state's share of federal mineral-derived revenues. The distribution in 2000 was $1,963.86 per resident.

Regarding only royalties, a discovery sufficient to produce the modest amount of $750,000 barrels per day with a wellhead price of $20 per barrel and a royalty rate of 12.5% could yield about $700 million per year for Alaska's 627,000 residents. As discussed subsequently in this report, however, it is uncertain at this point what Alaska's share of the various revenue streams might be.

Relationship to Recent U.S. Energy Difficulties

The current interest in oil exploration and development in ANWR was at least partly prompted by the increase in the retail prices for refined petroleum products that began with gasoline in early 1999, and California's electric power problems. Any energy and/o economic benefits that would accrue from oil and gas development of ANWR essentially would not address the power difficulties experienced in California – which were related to insufficient generation capacity, natural gas price spikes, and the electric power market deregulation plan adopted by the states.

Similarly, some of the increase in the prices for gasoline, diesel and home heating oil were a function of insufficiently available refining capacity, and a brittle petroleum supply infrastructure. Much of this effect has now been mitigated. Under these circumstances, the effect upon price of incremental crude production from ANWR might have been party muted, or at least more selective and regional.

Biological Resources: Status and Effects

At a House hearing on July 1, 1959, testimony was provided by Ross L. Leffler, Assistant Secretary of the Interior for Fish and Wildlife, on H.R. 7045 to authorize the establishment of the Arctic National Wildlife Range. Speaking of the entire area of the proposed refuge, he said:

> The great diversity of vegetation and topography ... in this compact area, together with its relatively undisturbed condition, led to its selection as the most suitable opportunity for protecting a portion of the remaining wildlife and its frontiers. The area included within the proposed range is a major habitat, particularly in summer, for the great herds of Arctic caribou, and the countless lakes, ponds, and marshes found in this area are nesting grounds for large numbers of migratory waterfowl that spend about half of each year in the rest of United States; thus, the production here is of importance to a great many sportsmen .... The proposed range is restricted to the area, which contains all of the requisites for year-round use. The coastal area is the only place in the United States where polar bear dens are found.[82]

Twenty-eight years later, the FLEIS echoed these remarks with the following: "The Arctic Refuge is the only conservation system unit that protects, in an undisturbed condition, a complete spectrum of the arctic ecosystems in North America" (p.46). It also said "The 1002 area is the most biologically productive part of the Arctic Refuge for wildlife and is the center of wildlife activity" (p. 46). The biological value of the 1002 area rests on the very intense productivity in the short arctic summer; many species arrive or awake from dormancy to take advantage of this richness, and leave or become dormant during the remainder of the year. Caribou have long been the center of the debate over the biological impacts of Refuge development, but other species have also been at issue. Among the other species most frequently mentioned are polar bears, musk oxen, and the 135 species of migratory birds that breed or feed there. To some extent, the effects of development on animals in the Refuge can be estimated by examining past effects on the same species as they exist in developed areas on the coast plain.[83] However, these comparisons must be made with some caution for several reasons:

- The coastal plain in the 1002 area is much narrower (as little as 15 miles) than around Prudhoe (roughly 100 miles) or the NPR-A (as much as 130 miles).
- The form development takes in the 1002 area would likely be quite different from earlier development, with fewer roads and more overflight, for example.
- Conditions have changed since Prudhoe Bay development began nearly 30 years ago: winters tend to be milder; tundra thaws earlier and freezes later; and vegetation patterns have already begun to change in response to these changes.[84] Animal life would be expected to respond to these changes, sooner or later.

This section presents background information on various species as it might relate to energy development in the Refuge and the potential effects of development on these species.

Caribou

In 1987, the Porcupine caribou herd (PCH) was estimated at 180,000 animals, and is now estimated at 129,000 animals.[85] The herd winters south of the Brooks Range in central Alaska and northwestern Canada. Its winter range is centered on the Porcupine River in Canada and Alaska. In the spring, the males and yearlings migrate north first, followed by the cows, who move north with the retreating snow line; the entire herd calves in only a few days. In most years, the cows reach the 1002 area and give birth there, concentrating their activity in areas that are greening most rapidly and that offer the high protein content required by growing

---

[82] U.S. House of Representatives, Committees on Merchant Marine and Fisheries, *Miscellaneous Fish and Wildlife Legislation*, 86th Congress, First Session, July 1, 1959, Washington, DC: 1959), p. 140.

[83] Development of Native lands may operate under different legal authorities or management goals, depending on existing laws and such changes as Congress might make in legislation to open the 1002 area to development. Such differences could affect not only these lands themselves but also surrounding federal lands.

[84] Margie Mason, "Increased Shrubbery Found in Arctic," *Reuters* (May 30, 2001); Zaz Hollander, "Global climate changes rule Senate hearing," Anchorage *Daily News* (May 30, 2001).

[85] Like many arctic species, caribou *(Rangifer tarandus)* population numbers are highly variable, and the causes of these "boom and crash" cycles are not well-understood. The Central Arctic Herd calves closer to the existing oil fields, and is about 20-25% the size of the PCH.

calves and lactating cows.[86] If snowfall has been heavy, or if a cool spring delays snowmelt, the cows are delayed, and dropt heir calves short of the 1002 area. (Maps of the distribution of radio-collared caribou throughout their annual cycle can be found at [http://www.taiga.net /caribou/pch/pc_cycle.html] and annual calving maps at [http://www.r7.fws.gov/nwr/arctic /pchmaps.html].)

Much has been made of the failure of caribou cows to calve in the 1002 area in some years, notably 1986, 1987, and 2000. In these years, heavy snowfall or cool spring temperatures slowed the northern migration, so that when calving occurred, most cows had not yet crossed large flooding rivers or passed the Brooks Range. Many newborn calves died in river crossings or fell prey to the golden eagle, wolf, and grizzly populations in the Brooks Range. For radio collared cows in 2000, the June calf survival rate and the July calf to cow ratio were the lowest ever recorded.[87]

Even if migration is delayed, the cows continue on to the 1002 area, where they continue to forage. As June days lengthen and become warmer, mosquitoes, bot flies, and warble flies can reach tremendous numbers on the coastal plain. While the blood-sucking habits of mosquitoes are well-known, the flies present major health problems as well. These flies deposit their eggs in the nasal passages of the caribou or in wounds; larvae feed and migrate through the skin, making holes in the skin when ready to emerge. Severely infested animals, or those in weakened condition (*e.g.*, injured or older animals, young calves, lactating cows) have restricted breathing or are otherwise weakened. They may die or fall to predators. When these flies are numerous, herds may appear panicked, seeking relief in areas where flies are less numerous.

Mosquitoes become active earlier in the summer and are deterred by cool, windy, humid conditions. When they are numerous, caribou congregate near the coast, where breezes are typically stronger, temperatures lower, and mosquitoes consequently rarer. The larger bot and warble flies tolerate somewhat higher winds, but not shade; they too prefer warmer temperatures, and become active later in the summer.[88] Consequently, after calving is over and the herd has reached the 1002 area, the herd generally moves to the coast to escape mosquitoes; as mosquito populations decline and fly populations increase, the herd may return to inland areas where patches of snow, gravel bars, or hills offer less favorable conditions for the increasing numbers of bot and warble flies. At this time of year, cows are at their lowest energy levels, and according to the FLEIS, "[a]ccess to insect-relief habitat and forage during this period may be critical to herd productivity" (p. 25).

The effects of exploration, production, and development in the 1002 area on caribou cannot be known with certainty unless such events actually occur, and even then will undoubtedly be debated. When the 1987 FLEIS was released, debate centered on the potential for displacement of the herd from (a) its preferred calving area and (b) the coastal areas needed for relief from clouds of biting insects. These remain the primary concerns. A major point of debate has been the comparison of effects of development on the Central Arctic Herd (CAH), whose range is partly in the developed areas west of the Refuge, and the potential

---

[86] Gibbs, "The Arctic Oil and Wildlife Refuge," pp. 62-69.
[87] Stephen M. Arthur, "Porcupine Caribou Herd Calving Survey, June 2000," unpublished memorandum, (July 12, 2000), 7 p.
[88] Warren B. Ballard, Matthew A. Cronin, and Heather A. Whitlaw, "Caribou and Oil Fields" in *The Nature History of an Arctic Oil Field*. (New York, NY: Academic Press, 2000), p. 91. (Hereafter cited as *The Natural History of an Arctic Oil Field).

effects of development on the PCH, whose summer range is primarily in the 1002 area. Comparisons of the two herds must be made cautiously, since the PCH is about 5 times larger than the CAH, calves in about 1/5 the area of the CAH, and annually migrates to overwinter south of the Brooks Range, while the CAH generally remains year-round in the much broader coastal plain in and south of the existing oil fields.

Would Caribou Be Displaced from Calving in the 1002 Area?
This question can be divided into two parts: *would the PCH likely be displaced from calving in the 1002 area?* And more importantly, if it were displaced, *would displacement have harmful effects on calving success*? For the first question, the answer for the herd as a whole, based on the Prudhoe Bay experience, appears initially to be a qualified "no." Individual animals, especially adult males, habituate to the disturbance, and sometimes seek out gravel pads and roads, where insect attacks may be less severe. The CAH has grown since development began, from 5,000 to about 27,000. However, warning signs exist. For instance, Brad Griffiths and Ray Cameron and their students at the University of Alaska (Fairbanks) have shown that for the western portion of the CAH, cows have shifted their calving southward, out of the development area, and return to this rich foraging area only after their calves are older. These studies also show that "the greatest incremental impacts are attributable to initial construction of roads and related facilities" and that "the extent of avoidance greatly exceeds the physical 'footprint' of an oilfield complex."[89] Thus, it is possible that habituation could occur, especially with males and yearlings, but some displacement of cows with young calves also seems likely.

The second question is the most crucial, since displacement to another area is inconsequential only if calving success is equally good in the alternative area(s). More precisely, if the herd is significantly less productive in he alternative area(s), the difference serves not to show the availability of alternatives but rather to highlight the importance of the preferred area. For clues, scientists have examined the reproductive success both of displaced cows in the CAH, and of the PCH in years when natural events prevented it from calving in the 1002 area. Griffiths and Cameron have shown a correlation of calf survival in the CAH with the amount of high-protein food in the calving area. In the much narrower coastal plain of the 1002 area, any cows displaced southward would calve in or nearer the rooks Range, where grizzly bears, golden eagles, and wolves (all calf predators) are more abundant than on the plain. As noted above, in 2000, when snows delayed migrating cows, effects on calf survival were severe.[90]

In sum, calving can – and in some years does – occur in areas other than the preferred 1002 area. However, evidence exists to suggest that calving success will be reduced when this occurs. At present, displacement from areas of the most nutritious forage is a rare event; if it were to become common, reduced fecundity could be expected. Smaller drill pads and fewer roads could combine to reduce displacement, and with directional drilling, pads might be sited to avoid areas of high quality forage. However, full effects would be uncertain unless development were actually carried out. Even then, the naturally cyclic nature of caribou populations might conceal all but large effects for a considerable time.

---

[89] C. Nellemann and R.D. Cameron, "Cumulative impacts of an evolving oil-field complex on the distribution of calving caribou," *Canadian Journal of Zoology*, Vol. 76 (1998): p. 1435.
[90] Stephen M. Arthur, "Porcupine Caribou Herd Calving Survey, June 2000," unpublished memorandum (July 12, 2000). 7 p.

Would Caribou Be Displaced from Insect Relief Areas?

Relief from massive mosquito populations and then fly populations can be critical to the herd. Given the particular aversion of cows with young calves to developed areas, the potential for conflict with development seems likely to be more important early in the calving season. Immediately along the coast, breezes deter mosquitoes. Any shore facilities or activities that block access to the coast could be most significant in this potential conflict. Later, when bot and warble fly populations are peaking and calves are older, cows with calves are likely to leave the coast and move inland. In the CAH, they may join the rest of the herd when it rests on drill pads or under pipelines or other structures, where shad discourages fly populations. Studies by Pollard *et al.* have shown that temperatures were lower and wind speeds higher on gravel pads, and mosquitoes and flies were less common on gravel pads than on tundra.[91] Thus, gravel drill pads could join other features in providing fly relief to the PCH, once caribou become accustomed to the facilities. The aversion of cows with younger calves to such features would suggest that cow/calf pairs would benefit primarily after calves had passed a certain age.

Polar Bears

Polar bears (*Ursus maritimus*) probably rank right after caribou in generating attention in the ANWR debate. The Beaufort Sea population is estimated at about 2000 bears and ranges along the Alaskan and northwestern Canadian coasts. Bears spend most of their adult lives at sea on the ice, feeding primarily on seals. Female bears give birth about once every three years (or less, if previous cubs died young) as they hibernate. While some females den on the ice pack, other adult females come ashore. In either case, they give birth to one to three cubs. In the spring, the females and cubs leave the dens; those with onshore dens return to join the rest of the populations on the ice pack. As a result of this pattern, only a small part of the population is on shore at any one time. The Refuge has the highest density of onshore dens of any area along the Alaskan coast. Researchers have shown that female polar bears are very sensitive to disturbance and will abandon their dens and young cubs if sufficiently disturbed (FLEIS, p. 129-130).

The shift to winter for virtually all exploration and certain other activities during development and production benefits many species. However, for polar bears this activity would occur at the times when female bears would be denning. To the west, industry has worked to avoid known den sites, but fewer dens are present in that area that in the 1002 area. Paradoxically, one new technology may present more difficulties. Use of 2-D seismic exploration can be accomplished with crews working at considerable intervals between survey lines. But for finer analysis of geological data, industry may find 3-D seismic exploration to be a cost-effective and preferable supplement. However, 3-D crews must work at much closer space than 2-D, thereby increasing the potential for conflict with denning bears.

Other possible conflicts include inhibition of bears coming ashore for denning, and the habituation of polar bears to human presence, and the subsequent risk to human life. Protected under the Marine Mammal Protection Act, and an international agreement (though not under the Endangered species Act), polar bears are hunted relatively infrequently in Alaska (for

---

[91] Cited in *The Natural History of an Arctic Oil Field*, p. 91.

subsistence), and some may lose their fear of humans. If human presence increases in the 1002 area as a result of development, conflicts with scavenging bears might become more common in the 1002 area. Polar bears are attracted now to the Kaktovik area (especially on occasions when whale carcasses have been landed). Generally, when such conflicts have occurred on the North Slope, habituated nuisance bears are relocated or destroyed.

The FLEIS suggested buffer zones of at least 0.5 miles around known dens in order to prevent abandonment. It also recommended orienting facilities to permit inland access for pregnant polar bears, relocating problem bears, and as a last resort, humane killing to protect human welfare. These actions continue to be the primary forms of mitigation.

Musk Oxen

Musk oxen were hunted to extinction in the area in the late 1800s, but 64 animals were re-introduced into the 1002 area in 1969-1970, and a growing population of about 250 is found there year-round; about twice that many area present during spring calving. They survive brutal winters protected by their thick fur, and conserve energy by moving little form their preferred riparian habitats. River corridors are used both for feeding and for travel all through the year, particularly in western portions of the 1002 area. Limited hunting of bulls is permitted by the Alaska Department of Fish and Game.

The high demand for water could create conflicts with the needs of musk oxen. The preferred habitat for musk oxen is riparian areas; if riparian areas are heavily mined for gravel, or altered for capture of spring runoff, this species could be affected. In addition, the extreme metabolic slowdown that this species undergoes to survive the harsh winter could be threatened if herds are forced to flee frequent disturbances. The latter seems more easily mitigated than habitat alteration, since knowledge of the specific whereabouts of herds through radio collars could permit workers to avoid them.

Migratory Birds

A variety of bird species nest or forage in the 1002 area, taking advantage of the explosion of insect life and rapid plant growth that occurs in the short summer. Compared to birds breeding in temperate areas, these species cycle from spring arrival, to nesting, to southern migration at a furious page. A large variety of birds, both familiar and rare in the lower 48 states, breed or fatten for migration in the Refuge. (See FWS web site: [http://www.r7.fws.gov/nwr/arctic/wildlife.html].) Among these are many popular game species: snow geese, Canada geese, white-fronted geese, brant, pintails, widgeons, and others. A wealth of shorebirds (plovers, dunlin, sandpipers, turnstones, phalaropes, and others) also frequent the area. Population data on most ANS bird species come from studies done in or near developed areas around Prudhoe Bay. The populations of many species oscillate, as is common in the arctic. Among shorebirds, only dunlin have shown long term declines, though this trend is shown in other arctic areas, and may be due to losses in their wintering habitat in east Asia.[92] Only 6 bird species are regularly found in the 1002 area in winter: snowy owls, gyrfalcons, rock and willow ptarmigans, common ravens, and American dippers.

---

[92] Declan M. Troy, "Shorebirds" in *The Natural History of an Arctic Oil Field*, p. 283.

The spectacled eider, a large sea duck, is a rare to uncommon breeder along the coast of ANWR. It is listed as threatened under the Endangered Species Act (ESA). (See FWS fact sheet, including distribution map, at http://alaska.fws.gov/es/spei.pdf.) Reasons for the decline are unclear and may vary in different parts of the bird's range, but increased lead poisoning from ingested lead shot, hunting, and increased predation due to augmented predator populations near human development and garbage dumps are thought to play a role.

Steller's eider is a casual visitor along the coast of the Refuge. It too is listed as threatened under ESA. (See FWS fact sheet, including distribution map, at http://www.r7.fws.gov/es/steller/stei.pdf.) Reasons for the decline of this species are also unclear, but may be similar to those for the spectacled eider.

In comparing likely environmental effects of potential energy development on the birds of the 1002 area under a modern scenario and under that envisioned in 1987, only one feature seems to have changed markedly: much greater reliance on aircraft. Many more airstrips are now likely to be built, and many more flights made, especially in summer when more birds are present, than seemed likely in 1987. The species most likely to be affected by these flights is the snow goose, since their huge feeding flocks are highly sensitive to overflights, and are easily startled away from foraging sites. Mitigation measures suggested in the FLEIS were "careful facilities siting and controls on surface activities, air transportation, and hunting" (p. 133). These remain important, and it seems likely that a reduced number of facilities could make siting easier, but controls on air traffic seem more likely to be difficult than was assumed the. Protection of eiders, which were not listed under ESA at that time, could also be an issue in the western part of the Refuge where these rare birds are more likely to occur. Measures to protect both species of eiders could include restrictions on certain activities such as vehicular traffic, noise, construction within about 200 meters (660 feet) of active nests, and habitat alteration.

Other Species

Arctic fox populations and brown (grizzly) bear populations on the coastal plain have increased from development due to increased scavenging. The FLEIS noted that the increased population of foxes had damaging effects on their normal prey species, such as young birds, on which they continue to feed. Scavenging arctic grizzlies can become habituated to humans, as they do elsewhere, and become dangerous to human life. As noted in the FLEIS, careful control of trash can mitigate both problems.

Special Areas

If Congress-opened ANWR, it could choose to afford special protections to special areas. Four areas within the coastal plain are commonly considered to have exceptional ecological value and were identified as such in the FLEIS.

- By far the most frequently mentioned is *Sadlerochit Spring* in the southernmost part of the 1002 area. The spring maintains a flow of water at 50°-58°F year-round, and keeps the river open for nearly 5 miles, even in winter. It represents the extreme northern range of some plants and birds, and provides wintering habitat for fish; muskoxen frequent the area. During the research leading up to the Section 1002 study, 4,000 acres around the spring were closed to exploration. There are individual Native allotments in the Sadlerochit area, which could complicate attempts to set it aside.

- The *Kongakut River* lies between the 1002 area and the Canadian border, and flows into the Beaufort Lagoon. Because of the unusual and diverse offshore ecosystem, and the presence of some of the North Slope's very rare trees in the upper part of the watershed, the area is considered ecologically valuable. About 25,000 acres of this system are included in the extreme northeastern part of the 1002 area.

- The *Angun Plains* are in the eastern part of the 1002 area, where evidence of Pleistocene glaciation is considered special. It comprises 36 square miles (23,040 acres).

- Parts of the *Jago River* drainage were identified in the FLEIS as nominees for "a system of 'Ecological Reserves.'" The river flows from the Brooks Range, into the 1002 area, and to the sea east of Kaktovik. The report notes that the drainage "contains a complete array of tundra and flood-plain vegetation types and provides habitat for a cross-section of all Arctic Slope wildlife species" (p. 20). The particular areas suitable for such ecological reserves were not named by proponents of the idea, and the FLEIS gave no acreage figure for it.

Physical Environment: Status and Effects

Much of the attention and controversy over exploration and development of the 1002 area have focused on potential impacts on biological resources in the area. However, if development occurs, there also will be impacts on the physical environment and resources of the area – land, air, and water – as a result of construction, operations, and human habitation. Currently, because the area is largely uninhabited, the condition of the physical environment is almost pristine (although rugged and challenging for man's use) and essentially unaffected by human activity. Especially in terms of land and water, the dominant physical characteristic is permafrost, the permanently frozen, layer which starts between 1 and 2 feet below the surface and has been found at a depth of 2,000 feet, that impedes drainage and creates saturated soil conditions in most areas of the entire North Slope. Permafrost and the surface layer on top of it are fragile, and special construction techniques (such as ice roads and structures built on pilings) have been devised to protect them.

It is undisputed that exploration and development activities will alter the existing physical environment. Oil field operations will result in air pollution emissions. There will be a need for large amounts of water for drilling and ancillary activities, including construction of roads, drill pads, and airstrips. Some amount of gravel will e mined as part of some of these activities, and there likely will e impacts from both the mining and use of gravel. Exploration and development activities will result in the generation of several types of waste streams, both wastes from industrial operations and domestic wastes, requiring disposal technologies. At issue are the individual and cumulative effects of such alternations and the ability of the natural environmental to recover and be reclaimed when oil-related activities have ceased.

The industry strongly believes that the 1002 area can be explored and developed in an environmentally sensitive manner. Industry points out that companies use improved technology (compared with that used in the past for development of existing sites in the arctic region) which greatly reduces the "footprint" of operations and relies on practices that minimize and provide for better disposal of waste. The result is less direct and indirect impact in terms of habitat loss and environmental contamination. Moreover, there are numerous environmental protection requirements administered by federal and state authorities that are intended to govern and regulate activities that might take place. Critics, however, are concerned about effects of routine operations in the fragile 1002 environment, as well as the possibility of leaks and spills of various contaminating substances, and whether adequate safeguards will be included in legislative proposals, and adopted and enforced by regulators.

Air Quality

Air quality on the North Slope of Alaska, including that in ANWR, currently meets all National Ambient Air Quality Standards (NAAQS) and would likely continue to do so even with ANWR development. Areas such as ANWR (i.e., those that meet the NAAQS) are regulated under the Prevention of Significant Deterioration (PSD) requirements of the Clean Air Act. The PSD program requires pre-construction review and permitting of major new sources of pollution to determine the impact of projected emissions, and the imposition of Best Available Control Technology on emission sources.

Emissions and Expected Air Quality

Oil field operations – and the natural-gas-fired turbines and heaters associated with them in Alaska – generate significant amounts of air pollution. The power facilities needed to support operations on the North Slope are quite large: according to BPAlaska, the Central Compression Plant at Prudhoe Bay has turbines capable of generating the equivalent of 429 megawatts of electric power – enough power for a city of 150,000 people.[93] Even though it burns relatively clean fuel (natural gas), the North Slope complex emits an estimated 63,786 tons of air pollution per year.[94] Nitrogen oxide emissions, which account for more than two-thirds of the total, are "2-3 times the amount emitted by Washington, DC."[95]

Despite these emissions, as noted, air quality on the North Slope of Alaska, including that in ANWR, currently meets all National Ambient Air Quality Standards. Annual concentrations of nitrogen dioxide, measured at three monitoring stations in the Prudhoe Bay field, were, in fact, 70% to 90% below the NAAQS in each of the years 1996-2000. Emissions of other criteria pollutants were also within limits.[96]

Potential emissions from ANWR sources were discussed in the Final Legislative Environmental Impact Statement (completed in 1987, and not subsequently updated). The FLEIS concluded that the likely effect on air quality of the full leasing and development alternative would be minor.[97] It is also noted that while "it is difficult to predict the impacts on air quality in the 1002 area without knowing the scope, timing, and location of oil

---

[93] *BP Environmental Performance Report, 2001*, Part 3, Status of Environmental Protection, p. 3-19, available at [http://www.bp.com/Alaska/index_envperf.htm].

[94] Personal communication, Don Bodron, Alaska Department of Environmental Conservation, January 9, 2002.

[95] Steven Brooks, atmospheric scientist, National Oceanic and Atmospheric Administration, Oak Ridge, TN, as cited in Janet Pelley, "Will Drilling for Oil Disrupt the Arctic National Wildlife Refuge?" *Environmental Science & Technology*, June 1, 2001, p. 244A.

[96] *BP Environmental Performance Report, 2001*, previously cited.

[97] U.S. Department of the interior, *ANWR FLEIS*, previously cited, p. 166.

development," which is impossible to predict without further exploratory activity, "The maximum annual emissions from the 1002 area would probably be analogous with present North Slope operations."[98]

PSD Regulatory Structure

Facilities in the 0102 area would be subject to the Clean Air Act's Prevention of Significant Deterioration rules. The PSD program is designed to protect air quality where ambient concentrations of pollutants are better than required by National Ambient Air Quality Standards. Pollutants subject to PSD requirements are particulate matter, sulfur oxides, and nitrogen oxides. Of these, only the nitrogen oxide increment[99] is expected to pose any challenge to the development of the 1002 area.

Under the PSD program, the type of area affected by a proposed facility's emissions determines the amount of air quality degradation to be allowed. All international parks, national parks larger than 6,000 acres, and most wilderness areas larger than 5,000 acres are mandatory Class I areas – those for which the least increment of pollution is allowed. Facilities affecting Class I areas may increase annual ambient concentrations of NOx by only 2.5 $\mu g/m^3$ - 2.5% of the NAAQS.

ANWR, and specifically the 1002 area, are not Class I areas, however: the 1002 area has not been designated wilderness, and the remainder of ANWR, while it is officially wilderness, was not designated so until after the statute establishing the PSD program was enacted. Thus, like most other areas of the United States, ANWR is a Class II area. In such areas, new facilities may increase concentrations of NOx by 25 $\mu g/m^3$, 25% of the NAAQS – 10 times the amount allowed if the area were designated Class I.

Even this allowed increment could pose constraints for full ANWR development. In establishing the PSD increments for nitrogen oxides in 1988, the Environmental Protection Agency (EPA) made specific note of their potential impact on the North Slope, stating that "certain Class II areas such as Prudhoe Bay, Alaska, have ambient concentrations as much as 40 $\mu g/m^3$ higher than in 1980,"[100] which exceeds the 25 $\mu g/m^3$ increment adopted. If the FLEIS is accurate in projecting NOx emissions from full development of ANWR as analogues to levels observed at Prudhoe Bay, emissions might exceed allowed levels unless additional pollution control measures are adopted.

Major new sources of air pollution in PSD areas must undergo preconstruction review and must install Best Available Control Technology (BACT). State permitting agencies (in this case, the Alaska Department of Environmental Conservation) determine BACT on a case-by-case basis, taking into account energy, environmental, and economic impacts. More stringent controls can be required if modeling indicates that BACT is insufficient to avoid violating an allowable PSD increment or the NAAQS itself. Thus, the permitting process should ensure that ambient concentrations of NOx increase no more than 25% of the NAAQS level.

---

[98] Ibid., pp. 198, 112.
[99] Allowed levels of pollution in the PSD program are terms "increments" because the standards specify maximum incremental concentrations of pollution to be allowed. The specific increments for NOx are discussed later in this section.
[100] Prevention of Significant Deterioration for Nitrogen Oxides, Proposed Rule, 53 Federal Register 3706, February 8, 1988.

Arctic Haze

Another air quality concern that was much discussed when ANWR development was first considered in the 1980s in a phenomenon known as arctic haze. Beginning in the 1950s, arctic observers have noted the presents in late winter and early spring of persistent bands of haze that reduce visibility and change the color of clear skies from deep blue to a pale blue or hazy gray. The haze consists of suspended particles, primarily sulfates, that originate in Europe and the former Soviet Union.[101] The Arctic's cold, dry air, with little precipitation and weak sunlight, produces remarkably stable air masses in winter and early spring, allowing the particles to remain airborne for weeks at a time and to spread thousands of miles form their point of origin.

Arctic haze appears to be less of a concern at present than it was in the 1980s. With the breakup of the former Soviet Union and the closure of many of the most heavily emitting industrial facilities in Eastern Europe and Russia, the haze has declined by as much as 50% since the mid-1980s.[102] Emissions from Alaska's North Slope appear to contribute relatively little to the problem.

Water Resources and Wetlands

Issues of concern for potential oil exploration and development in the 1002 area are the availability of water supplies and the impacts of production activities on the water and wetland resources of the area. Large amounts of water are needed for drilling and ancillary activities, such as ice roads and airstrip construction, as well as domestic use.

Description of the Resource

According to the 1987 FLEIS, free water is limited in the 1002 area and is confined to the surface and the shallow zone of soil located above the impermeable permafrost layer. The refuge receives an average of 6 inches of precipitation annually. A study done in 1989 found 255 lakes, ponds, and puddles within the 1002 area. Most lakes are shallow and freeze solid in winter. Less than 25% were deeper than 7 feet, and only 8 contained enough unfrozen water to build a mile or more of ice road.[103] A number of rivers and streams exist in the 1002 area, most draining to the coast and the Beaufort Sea; these too are also usually shallow.

According to the FLEIS, 99% of the 1002 area is classified as wetlands, which are transitional lands found between terrestrial and aquatic systems where the water table usually is at or near the surface, or the land is covered by shallow water. Arctic wetlands are different from those in the Lower 48 states, however. In warmer areas outside of Alaska, wetlands play a significant role in floodwater storage, lateral water movement, groundwater recharge, and sediment and erosion control. But in the arctic area, the permafrost layer impedes drainage and prevents many of the processes normally attributed to wetlands from occurring, because most arctic wetlands are not hydrologically linked to underground aquifers. However, this thin surface layer of soil and rock, located above the permanently frozen layer, is the area

---

[101] Leonard A. Barrie and Jan W. Bottenheim, "Sulphur and Nitrogen Pollution in the Arctic Atmosphere," in W.T. Sturges (ed.). *Pollution of the Arctic Atmosphere* (New York: Elsevier Science Publishers, 1991), p. 173, 177.
[102] John Ogren, NOAA Climate Monitoring and Diagnostics Laboratory, Boulder, CO, "Measurements of the Climate-forcing Properties of Atmospheric Aerosols," Slide 18, at
[http://www.cmdl.noaa.gov/aero/pubs/sem/ogren/Mexico_980123/sld018.htm].
[103] Gibbs, "The Arctic Oil and Wildlife Refuge," p. 68.

where the processes that sustain life in the arctic occur, including the cycle of freezing in winter and thawing in the brief summer and where biological activity of micro-organisms and growth of plant roots take place.[104] Plants that grow in the perpetually saturated soils of the area include sedges, grasses in flat areas, and tiny shrubs and dwarf trees in the foothills and uplands.

Water availability is cyclical during the year. In the spring, rapid snowmelt occurs throughout the area, and melting snow flows to rivers because it does not penetrate the permafrost. Rivers run full, riverbanks are severely eroded by ice and snow, and there is extensive spring flooding. Turbidity from suspended sediments is high, which impairs water quality. IN summer and fall, rain follows, which can also lead to flooding. But at the time of freezeup in the fall, low water supply conditions prevail. Most rivers go dry or freeze to the bottom, and streamflow ceases during winter except below a few warm springs.

Currently, water quality conditions in the 1002 area are not affected by human activity. While the state does not have extensive information about water quality in the vast majority of Alaska's watersheds, because they are not actively monitored, most are presumed to be in relatively pristine condition – including the 1002 area – due to the state's size, sparse population, and general remoteness. As of 1987, no data were available on water quality below the permafrost in the 1002 area, but the water beneath it is probably brackish, according to the FLEIS.

Effects of Oil Exploration and Development

The 1987 FLEIS identified the use of limited fresh water sources for industrial purposes as having the potential for major adverse effects, if exploration and development of 1002 area occur. It estimated that one exploratory well could require 15 million gallons of water: 7 to 8 million gallons for construction and maintenance; and 1.7 to 2 million gallons for drilling operations and domestic use. Despite technological improvements and a smaller "footprint" for oil and gas operations in the arctic today (discussed below), estimates of water requirements are generally the same as presented in the FLEIS.

These water supply needs result from the fact that ice is the construction material of choice for the winter exploration season to make temporary roads, winter airstrips, and drill pads, in preference to mining of gravel (discussed below). This is done by spreading 6 inches of chipped ice from rivers and lakes, then spraying the area with fresh water to make temporary roads and pads that melt in the spring. When they melt, they leave no significant damage to the tundra. Road construction techniques have evolved since early days of oil activity in the arctic. Temporary ice roads now allow construction of oil field pipelines during the winter months, thus largely eliminating the need for permanent gravel roads adjacent to pipelines.[105]

A source of water for ice roads, airstrips, and drill pads would need to be located, but there is little evidence on whether North Slope rivers and lakes can support the amount of water used by oil fields. One FWS hydrologist suggests that drawing too heavily from deep lakes would diminish the aquatic species that are food for migratory waterfowl; heavy withdrawals from the Canning River, which flows freely in winter for many miles below

---

[104] British Petroleum Corp. "Exploring Alaska: Alaska's Terrestrial Environment. [http://www.bp.com/Alaska/environment/env.htm]
[105] British Petroleum Corp. 'Exploring Alaska: Ice Roads and Pads." [http://www.bp.com/Alaska/bpamoco/env_record/10.htm].

warm springs, could harm over-wintering fish.[106] The deepest river basins are near the mouths of the Canning and Jago Rivers; if the brackish water from these basins were used for ice roads, the result could be harm to tundra vegetation when the ice melts in the spring.

Because the Refuge has few deep lakes or lakes that do not freeze solid in winter, it is believed that there is only enough water in the 1002 area for less than 50 miles of ice roads.[107] To meet water needs, alternatives that might be considered include crating water reservoirs by excavating deep pools in conjunction with gravel removal. Overflow during spring runoff would fill the basins, and the accumulated water could be used for construction. With sufficiently deep basins, habitat could be created for over-wintering fish. If economic quantities of oil were not found, basins might be left in place, or it would be necessary to find clean gravel to fill in the basins. Riparian habitat is heavily used by musk oxen in winter, and siting of facilities in riparian areas (with or without oil discovery) would likely to be an issue.

Companies might also melt lake and river ice and snow, or desalinate marine water. Oil companies also might consider transporting water by truck from existing developed areas, such as Prudhoe Bay, although the economics of doing so for long distances could be impractical. Another possibility is that oil companies might revert to building gravel roads for exploration and production, as in the past elsewhere on the North Slope.

On the North Slope today, most wastes associated with drilling, as well as sewage and garbage, are injected in dedicated disposal wells, rather than in waste pits, which greatly reduces surface impacts and water pollution incidents. The oil industry has improved both technology and practices to prevent and clean up accidental releases that could harm the surface layer and water. However, critics are concerned about the possibility of spills of various substances, including waste oil, acid, ethylene glycol, and drilling fluids, especially given the relatively few lakes and streams in the 1002 area. Even small spills, if not cleaned up, can affect lakes and streams, for example if a spill on an ice pad melts in the spring. The primary impact of contaminated water is its potential to reduce oxygen availability in receiving waters, plus possible toxicity of the waste.[108] Critics also are concerned that leaks and spills of oil, fuel, chemicals, or brine could contaminate soils, thus killing vegetation and resulting in scattered small habitat loss. In addition, they are concerned about the environmental standards that would have to be met for development on these federal lands.

Regulatory Setting

If oil exploration and development were to occur in the 1002 area under current law, a regulatory regime that is carried out both by federal and state agencies would apply to water quality protection. Federal laws applicable to activities taking place in the 1002 area include the Clean Water Act, Safe Drinking Water Act, Rivers and Harbors Act, Coastal Zone Management Act, and the Ocean Dumping Act. In Alaska, permits required by federal laws are issued by federal agencies, especially the Environmental Protection Agency (EPA) and the U.S. Army Corps of Engineers (Corps).

The state of Alaska has limited separates regulatory authorities and regulatory authorities and requirements. One important role that the state plays in establishing water quality

---

[106] ANWR chief hydrologist Steve Lyons, cited in Gibbs, "The Arctic Oil and Wildlife Refuge," p. 68.
[107] Pelley, Janet. "Will Drilling for Oil Disrupt the Arctic National Wildlife Refuge?" *Environmental Science & Technology*, June 1, 2001: 244A. (Hereafter referred to as Pelley, "Will Drilling for Oil Disrupt ANWR?")

[108] British Petroleum Corp. "Water." [http://www.bp.com/corp_reporting/hse_perform/env/water/index.asp]

standards to protect waters within its jurisdiction, as required by the federal Clean Water Act (CWA). Alaska's statewide standards apply to surface waters and to groundwater, at the state's discretion, and include specification of designated uses (such as use for water supply or recreational purposes), numeric and narrative criteria, and general policies to ensure protection of the designated uses. State standards do currently apply to waters through the state, including the 1002 area. Any permits written by federal or state agencies must provide that state water quality standards will not be violated. In addition, the state requires development of oil discharge prevention and contingency plans for exploration or production facilities and proof of financial responsibility to ensure that owners and operators maintain adequate financial resources to respond to any spill and mitigate environmental damages. The state's Department of Fish and Game also would conduct a review of any proposed project for possible impacts on anadromous fish.

There is little public information available concerning oil industry compliance with state water quality standards, permits, and other environmental requirements. The industry believes that as a result of improved technology and operating practices – especially in recent years – its environmental performance in the arctic is good. Critics, however, point out that data compiled by the Alaska Department of Environmental Conservation demonstrate that on average several hundred spills of hazardous substances, refined oil products, and crude oil occur each year at existing North Slope operations, and some argue that the oil industry should not be allowed into the 1002 area until it fixes chronic problems with leaky and poorly maintained physical structures.[109]

The Clean Water Act requires that facilities must obtain permits which authorize discharge of processed wastewater. These permits, issued in Alaska by EPA, establish specific limitations on pollutants in industrial waste or sewage that may be discharged from any facility to waters of the United States, as well as general requirements such as monitoring and reporting. CWA permits for oil and gas operations in the arctic typically require Best Management Practices (BMP) plans which focus on pollution prevention rather than end-of-pip discharge limits through specification of structural and operational controls, maintenance, and inspections. Outside of the 1002 area, EPA has issued a general permit for onshore and offshore oil and gas extraction in Alaska that covers rest of the North Slope Borough. It provides general authorization to different facilities having similar discharges for such activities as discharges from ice roads constructed of gravel pit water, discharges of sanitary and/or domestic wastewater from covered facilities, and construction de-watering. The general permit application process is streamlined, because individual sources covered by a general permit do not need to apply to EPA for a source-specific permit; if they file a Notice of Intent and meet certain other qualifications, they can be covered by the general permit. The current general permit was issued in 1997 and extends to April 10, 2002. It is possible that EPA would also choose to issue a general permit for any activities in the 1002 area.

EPA also issues CWA permits for stormwater discharges of uncontaminated rainwater and snowmelt. Arctic drilling and production pads do not have conventional storm drains, as in other parts of the country, so stormwater discharges are in the form of surface runoff during the spring thaw season. Stormwater permits focus on plans to prevent releases of contaminated runoff to waters of the United States.

---

[109] Pelley, "Will Drilling for Oil Disrupt ANWR?" p. 43A. Reports and data on spills can be found at: [http://www.state.ak.us/local/akpages/ENV.CONSERV/dspar/perp/datanews.html]

The Safe Drinking Water Act (SDWA) authorizes a program to protect underground sources of drinking water (USDWs) from contamination by injection through wells. In Alaska, primary responsibility for regulation of injection wells through this program is split between EPA and the Alaska Oil and Gas Conservation Commission (AOGCC). EPA issues permits authorizing subsurface injection of nonhazardous industrial wastes associated with oil exploration and development, while the AOGCC issues permits for wells used for injection of fluids brought to the surface from oil and gas production operations or liquid hydrocarbons which are stored underground. Injection of fluid wastes which cannot be recycled is preferred to the discharge to surface disposal pits or ponds. Underground injection is to be conducted so as to protect USDWs. However, in existing oil production areas on the North Slope, EPA has determined that there are most likely not any aquifers beneath the permafrost which are fresh enough to qualify for protection as USDWs. Thus, the agency has granted several waiver requests from oil companies authorizing underground injection with less stringent requirements than normal. This could be a precedent for ANWR, as well.

Separate from the CWA discharge permit program administered by EPA, §404 of the CWA also contains a permit program administered by the U.S. Army Corps of Engineers under which advance approval must be obtained for discharges from any project that involves dredging or filling of the nation's waters, including adjacent wetlands. Because of the extent of wetlands in the 1002 area, these requirements are likely to apply to nearly all oil exploration and development activities that might occur onshore. In addition, the Rivers and Harbors Act of 1899 requires permits from the Corps for construction of any dam or dike in a navigable waterway or any structure in or over any navigable waterway, if the structure affects the course, location, or condition of the waterbody.[110] If docks or offshore navigational components of facilities to transport people and materials to and from the 1002 area were constructed, permits under this authority as well as the CWA would likely be required.

Another permit provision that cold arise is contained in the Marine Protection Research and Sanctuaries Act (Title I known as the Ocean Dumping Act), which requires a permit from the Corps for the disposal of dredged material in the territorial seas, for example, for disposal of material dredged in the construction of channels in open seas needed to get to shore facilities. In carrying out its regulatory responsibilities, the Corps evaluates projects through a public interest balancing process, considering the public benefits and detriments of all relevant factors including conservation, economics, aesthetics, wetlands, cultural values, fish and wildlife values, and navigation. Further, the Corps shares jurisdiction with other agencies. For example, the Corps uses environmental guidelines issued by EPA to evaluate impacts of a proposed discharge and consults with other federal and state agencies before issuing permits.

The Coastal Zone Management Act (CZMA) requires certification by states that projects to be located in a state's coastal zone are consistent with the state's coastal zone management program. The CWA requires a similar state certification concerning compliance with state water quality standards. Both would presumably apply to oil exploration and development activities. Accordingly to EPA officials, however, in part because of resource limitations, the state of Alaska frequently waives CZMA and CWA certification, rather than using that authority to impose environmental conditions on projects.[111]

---

[110] Given the rapid snowmelt and high streamflow in rivers that occurs in the spring, constructing bridges could present significant challenges.
[111] Personal communication with Ted Rockwell, U.S. EPA, Anchorage, Alaska, Dec. 19, 2001.

Waste Disposal

Oil exploration and drilling result in the generation of several waste streams. There are also small quantities of solid and hazardous wastes associated with daily living activities and with running an industrial complex. The Resource Conservation and Recovery Act (RCRA) governs the generation, storage, transportation and disposal of hazardous wastes, and in Alaska the program is carried out by the U.S. EPA. Nonhazardous and RCRA-exempt solid wastes are regulated by the Alaska Department of Environmental Conservation (ADEC).

The hazardous wastes come from maintenance shops, laboratories, and other support activities. The largest categories are paint wastes, solvents, miscellaneous chemicals (particularly from laboratories), crushed light bulbs and bases, and rags, sorbents, and filters. There are no commercial facilities in the state for disposal of hazardous wastes, and they must be stored in secure areas before shipment to RCRA-permitted facilities in the lower 48 states.

RCRA-Exempt Wastes

EPA has determined that oil and gas exploration and production wastes constitute a high-volume, low-toxicity waste stream that would be better managed outside the RCRA hazardous waste regime. The ADEC regulates these drilling fluids, produced waters, and other wastes.

In the past, drilling wastes were placed in surface impoundments called "reserve pits," but they have several disadvantages: they take up a great deal of space, making the well pad's footprint larger; they require continuous fluid management, maintenance, and monitoring to prevent releases of metals, slats, and other contaminants into the environment; and, when closed down, may require years of environmental monitoring. Today these wastes are ground up and injected into dedicated disposal wells 5,000-8,000 feet deep.[112] The ADEC regulates underground injection wells, as discussed above in *Water Resources and Wetlands*. The wells are only allowed in areas where there is no underground source of drinking water, or where aquifers are too deep or briny for development. Grind and inject technology has ended the use of reserve pits for permanent disposal.

Minimization and Recycling

The companies on the North Slope employ waste minimization and recycling programs to reduce the volume of solid waste.[113] One of the waste streams is drilling muds – mixtures of natural clays and weighting materials with small amounts of specialized additives that serve to lubricate the drill bit, remove cuttings from the well bore, and control the pressure in the well. As the mud circulates back to the surface, cuttings and other solids are removed, and the muds are reused; this recycling can reduce mud requirements by 50% or more. During drilling operations, each well can generate up to 8,000 barrels of muds and cuttings. Cuttings from the upper strata are washed and used as gravel for construction of roads and pads. The remaining cuttings are ground fine and injected in a slurry in a permitted disposal well along with other production wastes.

Surface discharges of sanitary and domestic wastewater (black and gray water) have been eliminated at some facilities by injecting them in disposal wells or using them for enhanced oil recovery (EOR). Other nonhazardous and RCRA-exempt liquids that might otherwise be

---

[112] Pelley, "Will Drilling for Oil Disrupt ANWR?" p. 243A.
[113] British Petroleum Corp. "BP and the Environment in Alaska's North Slope." [http://www.bp.com/Alaska].

discarded may also be used for EOR. Used oil from vehicles and equipment is colleted at several North Slope facilities. It is blended into the crude oil and sent to refineries.

In conjunction with the Federal Trade Commission's approval of the sale of ARCO Alaska to the Phillips Petroleum Company in 2000, an agreement between the State of Alaska and the companies operating on the North Slope was reached. Called the "Charter for the Development of the Alaskan North Slope," it contained, among other things, several environmental provisions committing British Petroleum and Phillips Petroleum to clean up selected existing and abandoned sites, retrieve and dispose of abandoned empty barrels, and close inactive reserve pits.[114]

These cleanup activities are testament to the uneven environmental record of the past. And as recently as the year 2000 British Petroleum (BP) paid $7 million in civil and criminal penalties and agreed to spend $15 million to carry out a nationwide environmental management system as a result of a contractor's illegally disposing hazardous waste for at least 3 years, and of BP's failing to report it immediately on discovery.[115] Technical advances and heightened sensitivity on the part of operators to the need for careful operation in the arctic environment offer an optimistic outlook, but the possibility of an accident or deliberate violation of a waste disposal permit or regulation always exists.

Land and Gravel Use

Gravel is a necessary component of exploration and development activities on the North Slope, and gravel suitable for these activities is a relatively valuable resource there.[116] However, with the higher velocities of rivers in the narrow coastal plain of the 1002 area, gravel is more abundant than in the broader, developed portion of the coast plain to the west. Gravel roads and pads are constructed by piling gravel on top of tundra to provide a base for aboveground structures and to insulate the permafrost that lies just below the surface. The mining of gravel from streambeds and floodplains for such purposes can alter natural river drainage and cause increased erosion and sedimentation. Vegetation covered with layers of gravel dies, subtracting its resources from the food web of the ecosystem. In addition, dust blown from the gravel structure may affect freezing and thawing of nearby vegetation, as may any material washed from the gravel surface. The blown dust might convey some unexpected benefits: dust kicked up from gravel structures may cause earlier snowmelt. Early melting stimulates plant growth, and could provide earlier foraging areas for waterfowl. Possible contamination of he dust with wastes might counter benefits, however.

The need for gravel for activities in the 1002 area, if development occurs, is likely to be much less than that for earlier years of oil development in existing areas for several reasons. First gravel previously was used as the base for nearly all road and pad construction, but today it is likely to be used only for *permanent* roads and pads because ice is the preferred

---

[114] "Alaska at Peace with BP Amoco Concessions," *Gas Daily*, December 3, 1999; Mary Pemberton, "DEC: BP and Phillips Keeping Environmental Promises on North Slope," Associated Press State & Local Wire, March 28, 2001; and Alaska. DEC. *Alaska Department of Environmental Conservation's Report on the Charter for Development of the Alaskan North Slope.* March 2001. 8 p. Available at:
http://www.state.ak.us/local/akpages/ENV.CONSREV/pubs/charter7web.pdf

[115] U.S. Environmental Protection Agency. "British Petroleum (BP) Exploration Alaska Sentenced in Hazardous Waste Case." February 10, 2000. See: http://yosemite.epa.gov/R10/OWCM.NSF/28100b370fl149936882565 00005dcdf2/1eff2f7433b0da66882568b000745a01?Open Document.

[116] *BP Environmental Performance Report, 2001*, previously cited: 3-39.

construction material for *temporary* roads and pads (although the availability of adequate supplies of water is an issue for development of the 1002 area; see *Water Resources and Wetlands*, above). Second, gravel previously was mined to create reserve pits that held drilling muds and other produced wastes. Today, however, nearly all wastes are recycled, reused for disposed by underground injection, thus greatly reducing the need for reserve pits. Third, even where used for drilling pads, the amount of gravel needed will be less because of the smaller overall footprint of sites.

If development in the 1002 area followed the pattern at Alpine, it would be, if not entirely roadless, then road-reduced, compared to older developments. Alpine is not connected by road to older facilities, but the development includes a 3-mile road (14.6 acres) and a 36.3 – acre airstrip. (See Figure 3.) The latter forms part of the road connecting the two pads.[117] The road and airstrip constitute about 52% of the total permitted acreage. If anything like this pattern holds a modern scenario, it would represent a very substantial reduction in the miles of roads relative to either development.

Caribou cows in existing oil fields with calves younger than a few weeks old (roughly, during June inmost years) are known to avoid roads, pads, and other areas around human activity; avoidance during this early period extends well beyond the footprint of facilities, especially in early years of oil development.[118] (See also *Caribou*, above.) If road mileage were reduced, impacts on calves at this sensitive time could be lowered. In ANWR, as calving ends in early June, and as the Porcupine Caribou Herd (PCH) tends to move to the coast and the western portion of the 1002 area for insect relief, roads or runways oriented across the path of travel could be expected to disrupt the cows' movement more than those oriented roughly parallel to it. If calving were displaced to the foothills, greater predation would apparently result; if foraging is displaced from prime areas, weight loss in cows could result in reduced survival rates in calves.[119] On the other hand evening June, some animals (primarily males and yearlings) use pads, roads, and runways for insect relief, and so may congregate in these areas. Later in the summer, when calves are older, some cow-calf pairs may join them.

Consequently, interpretations of impacts based on the CAH must be made cautiously, due to the differing concentrations of the herds and the differing availability of similar calving areas.[120] If road mileage were limited, impacts would probably be lowered. Conversely, if roads were not limited, or if economic necessity later resulted in a change in this restriction, impacts on the PCH or other species, such as tundra swans (which tend to avoid nesting within 200 meters (about 650 feet) of roads), could be greater. (See also *Biological Resources: Status and Effects,* below.)

Changing Footprint Estimate: 1987 vs. 2001

There has been considerable focus in recent years on the reduced footprint that seems likely in any 1002 development, given advances in exploration, development, and production technologies, as well as the possibility of added congressional restrictions on environmental

---

[117] U.S. Army Corps of Engineer, Alaska District, Permit Evaluation and Decision Document, Alpine Project, Colville River 18 (2-960874) p. 2 (February 13, 1998).
[118] C. Nelleman and R.D. Cameron, "Cumulative impacts of an evolving oil-field complex on the distribution of calving caribou," *Canadian Journal of Zoology,* Vol. 76 (1998): p. 1425-1430.
[119] Gibb, "The Arctic Oil and Wildlife Refuge", p. 69.
[120] Gibbs, "The Arctic Oil and Wildlife Refuge", p. 69.

impacts. It may be useful to compare those features considered in the footprint as described in the 1987 FLEIS, and how that might differ from a scenario predicated on modern technologies. In 1987, the FLEIS described the assumptions built into its full development scenario:

> For the sake of maintaining data confidentiality, [the full development scenario] shows a highly generalized placement of production and transportation facilities based on typical North Slope prospect characteristics for three localities within the 1002 area. This assumes successful exploration in all three localities. Actual placement of oil production facilities and marine facilities on the 1002 area, or location of the trunk pipeline from producing fields to TAPS Pump Station 1, depends upon site-specific geotechnical, engineering, environmental, and economic data that can be determined only after a specific prospect ha been drilled, and a discovery made and confirmed.[121]

The features considered in the FLEIS (on p. 99) are shown in Table 4, along with the estimate given at that time for the space or miles that would be occupied by the feature in a full development as hypothesized by the FLEIS. The third column shows, in qualitative terms, how modern technology would probably change the estimate provided in 1987, assuming the same full development scenario. The highlights of the comparison are as follows.

Some features would very likely or probably be reduced in total acreage or mileage; a few might even be eliminated. These are:

- spur roads with collecting lines, connecting (fewer) pads in a given oil field,
- large permanent airfields (supporting an entire area, as at Deadhorse or Kuparuk),
- permanent drill pads,
- pits for gravel mines (borrow pits),
- major river or stream crossings (given fewer roads),
- main road paralleling main pipeline (possibly *no* such road, and
- large central processing facility, as at Deadhorse or Kuparuk (possibly no such facility).

In other instances, new technology might actually increase the demand for acreage devoted to some features:

- marine and saltwater treatment facilities, due to greater modern demand for water (but possibly substituted with smaller plants for fields near coast), and
- small permanent airfields, enough for each cluster of pads not supplied by a permanent road.

Assuming the same full development scenario as the FLESI, some features would probably remain the same:

- main oil pipeline within the 1002 area, and
- collecting lines from drill pads to main oil pipeline.

Finally, in some instances, it is simply unclear whether some features would be built:

- marine port facilities, to off-load barges and other heavy equipment,
- main road from marine facility.

In 1987, the FLEIS, in is hypothetical full development scenario, estimates that the total acreage covered would be 5,330 to 5,980 acres. A comparison with a scenario using modern technology suggests that the footprint (as defined by the FLEIS in its table) would be smaller, but perhaps not markedly so. If, as suggested by Arctic Power (a pro-development group cited earlier), full development of the 1002 area could be accomplished by building no more than 2,000 acres of facilities (scattered appropriately around development oil fields, and assuming the same oil fields as the FLEIS), then either its definition of "footprint" is different from that used in the FLEIS, or additional technological improvements may be required. It is the pads, airstrips, pad supports, and connector roads that are typically considered when development proponents have recently referred to limiting surface impacts to 2,000 acres; other features, such as pipelines, gravel mines and the like typically are not.[122]

While the technologies used would be affected by economics, direction by Congress could specify higher or lower standards than those assumed in the table. Moreover, development on Native lands is not considered in the table, since different standards could apply. (For legal issues related to Native lands, see *Alaska Native Lands and Rights*, below.)

Table 4. Comparison of the Estimated Number and Area of In-place Oil-related Facilities: 1987 FLEIS and Modern Technologies

Facility	FLEIS Full Leasing Scenario (p. 99)	Same finds, assuming Alpine-like technologies
Main oil pipeline within 1002 area	100 mi (610 acres)	probably similar for similar locations of oil
Main road paralleling main pipeline (see note below)	120 mi (730 acres)	possibly 0 miles (0 acres)[a]
Main road from marine facilities	(Included in above row, no separate figure given)	Unclear if marine facilities would be built[a]
Spur roads with collecting lines within production fields	160 mi (980 acres)	Uncertain – fewer pads in a production field, therefore probably fewer in-field spur roads for similar locations of oil[a]; collecting lines probably similar
Marine and salt-water treatment facilities	2 facilities (200 acres)	Unclear how many would be built, but demands on fresh water sources possibly greater than assumed in 1987

---

[121] FLEIS, p. 98. The full set of assumptions is given on pp. 97-98.
[122] Some development advocates do not include road connecting the pads. For example, Rep. Sununu, in an editorial discussing his amendment to H.R. 4 (adopted Aug. 1, 2001), to limit total surface occupancy in future development of the 1002 area to 2,000 acres, said his language did not include roads, saying that most roads in the 1002 area would be made of ice (*Manchester Union Leader*, August 20, 2001).

Facility	FLEIS Full Leasing Scenario (p. 99)	Same finds, assuming Alpine-like technologies
Large central production facilities	7 facilities (630 acres)	0? (facilities incorporated into one pad in each production field)[b]
Small central production facilities	4 facilities (160 acres)	0? (facilities incorporated into one pad in each production field)[b]
Large permanent airfields	2 airfields (260 acres)	0?[b]
Small permanent airfields	2 airfields (60 acres)	Many more – probably one for each production field[b]
Permanent drilling pads	560-60 pads (1,200-1,600 acres) [average size: 20-32 acres]	Probably fewer per production area, given greater reach of modern wells[b]; most recent 2 pads (at Alpine) wee 10 acres and 36 acres each.
Borrow sites (i.e., gravel mine pits)	10-15 pits (500-750 acres)	Uncertain, but probably fewer, given fewer roads and fewer pads[c]
Gravel for construction, operation, and maintenance	40 – 50 million cu yds	Uncertain, but probably less
Major river or stream crossings	Maximum 25	Uncertain, but likely fewer, due to fewer roads
Total acres of surface occupancy	**5,330 – 5,980 acres**	**Probably less**

Notes: Columns 1 and 2 are reproduced from the FLEIS with the modifications noted. Column 3 assumes the same hypothetical oil fields as the FLEIS, and the use of modern, Alpine-like technologies or better. The FLEIS table gave one figure for all main roads; this number is broken into two parts here, since an Alpine-like scenario is assumed not to have a main road for a pipeline, but such technology may not necessarily preclude a marine facility or roads associated with it.

[a]Facilities which at least some observers would likely count in current proposals to restrict development to 2,000 acres (see text); unclear in some of the marked cases whether any such structure would actually be built. Some argue that economics (cost of long-distance transportation of heavy equipment or cost of repeated construction of ice roads) could force eventual construction of a main road, especially if world oil prices do not increase.

[b]Facilities which most observers would likely count in proposals to restrict development to 2,000 acres (see text); unclear in some of the marked cases whether any such structure would actually be built.

[c]In association with the Alpine development, the Corps of Engineers issued a permit to Nuiqsut Contractors for a 150-acre gravel it, though some portion of the gravel met needs in the village of Nuiqsut, and the size of the permitted pit may have been designed to allow expansion of the Alpine development to 2 additional satellite pads and associated connector roads. It is unclear precisely what size of gravel mine would have been required to construct only the current facilities at Alpine. Consolidation of gravel pits might occur, by digging fewer, deeper pits, but no information was found on this possibility.

Sources: U.S. Dept. o the interior, Fish and Wildlife Service, Geological Survey, and Bureau of Land Management. *Arctic National Wildlife Refuge, Alaska, Coastal Plain Resource Assessment*. Report and Recommendation to the Congress of the United States and Final Legislative Environmental Impact Statement. Washington, DC, 1987. p. 99. U.S. Army Corps of Engineers, Alaska District, Permit Evaluation and Decision Document, Alpine Development Project, Colville River 18 (2-960874). February 13, 1998. p. 2. U.S. Army Corps of Engineers, Alaska District, Colville River 17 (2-960869). Alpine Gravel Pit, Nuiqsut Contractors. June 23, 1997.

Effects on Tundra Surfaces

The 1002 area has a higher proportion of rolling terrain than the flat, pond-rich Prudhoe Bay Area. Vegetation may be exposed by the wind and damages as it is run over, especially where more hilly terrain could make rolligon use difficult. In a more temperate environment, vegetation might recover fairly quickly, but the intense cold and the freezing and thawing cycles of the arctic environment can make recovery rates much slower. However, there is no research to show whether this type of vegetational damage would affect foraging animals.[123]

The vegetation under ice roads and ice pads may be damaged, partly by compaction, but also by being delayed in its spurt of growth in the brief summer. Where all debris is removed and no spills have occurred, little effect has been observed.[124] Where insulation is used to maintain an ice pad over a single summer, damage appeared to be confined to areas around the edges of the pad, where some thawing had occurred but no sunlight had reached the plants; evidence of recolonization began to appear in two growing seasons.[125]

Port and Offshore Activity

The FLEIS assumed that 2 ports would be built to support development in the 1002 area. It is unclear whether that assumption is still likely. If water for ice roads is at a premium, port development could reduce the need for long ice roads from the west. If port facilities were carefully sited and built offshore, and connected to shore via causeways, and in turn to ice roads, they may prove attractive for the staging and movement of heavy equipment. Offshore facilities may also be considered by placement of heavy equipment such as water treatment plants, since such placement cold put them outside any 2,000 acre limit on surface occupancy (if Congress were to impose such a limit). The reduction in surface impacts would be traded for potential offshore impacts; in the FLEIS, the focus of impacts from causeways was on fish migration. If ports were to be located on Native lands, their regulation is unclear.

Aircraft Use

At Alpine, 6 to 8 aircraft, including large cargo planes, arrive daily.[126] Reliance on aircraft for summer transport is essential if connecting roads are to be eliminated. Effects on bird populations vary. Tundra swans appear to be affected only minimally by aircraft.[127] According to the FLEIS (p. 132), snow geese are "highly sensitive to aircraft disturbance" from flights at 100 ft. to 10,000 ft., and at 0.5 to 9 miles away. The geese appeared to habituate after several passes by helicopters or fixed wing aircraft. The report also noted evidence that snow geese are disturbed by traffic, noise, or other human activities and respond by taking Flight *en masse*. Regardless of source, sufficient disturbance would reduce available feeding time, weight gain, and resulting vigor for the fall migration. The FLEIS cited control of aircraft traffic as potential mitigation, but the development design examined n the FLEIS did not contemplate the heavy reliance on aircraft (and assumed that only 2 large permanent airfields would be built under full development) that would be essential if road mileage were substantially reduced.

---

[123] Gibbs, "The Arctic Oil and Wildlife Refuge."
[124] Jay D. McKendrick, "Vegetative Responses to Disturbance", in *The National History of an Arctic Oil Field*. p. 43.
[125] *Ibid*. p. 43.
[126] Gibbs, "The Arctic Oil and Wildlife Range", p. 68.
[127] Robert J. Ritchie and James G. King, "Tundra Swans," in *The Natural History of an Arctic Oil Field*, pp. 197-220.

Use of Resources by Non-Natives: Status and Effects[128]

The village of Kaktovik on Barter Island (see Figures 1 and 4) is the only currently occupied human settlement in the coastal plain of ANWR. Aside from Barter Island, topographic maps of the area[129] show that it also contains 5 cabins, 2 ruins, 2 landing strips, 2 towers, 1 grave site, and 6 tractor trails. Of these 18 features, all are within 5 miles of the coast, except for one trail. Some of these sites are the remains of facilities run by the Defense Department as part of the Distant Early Warning Line (DEWLine: see below). In addition, as discussed below, the remains of the drill pad and a protruding pipe mark the site of a closed exploratory well on lands of the Kaktovik Inupiat Corporation (KIC well; see *Alaska Native Lands and Rights*, below).

DEWLine and Kaktovik

Starting in the 1950s, the Defense Department constructed a system along the arctic coasts of Alaska and Canada to provide early warning of a Soviet attack.[130] Barrow served as a base for construction Kaktovik was designated as the site of a major installation, resulting in three relocations of the village to accommodate the military facility, and concentration of the previously more scattered Inupiat seeking jobs opportunities. Intermediate stations along the coast in what is now the ANWR 1002 area were constructed (from west to east) at Brownlow Point on the Staines River; Camden Bay, about 30 miles west-southwest of Kaktovik; and Beaufort Lagoon, about 30 miles southeast of Kaktovik.[131] Only the station at Kaktovik remained open in 1986. USGS maps (cited above) indicate one tower, one landing strip, and both a landing strip and tower at these three sites respectively. According to a 1986 report, "[a]bandoned materials include numerous rusting steel fuel drums located primarily at Camden Bay and Beaufort Lagoon, but also scattered along the coast and inland within the boundaries of ANWR."[132]

Recreation Visits

There have never been large numbers of recreational visits to this very remote Refuge. The peak was 886 visiting the entire Refuge in 1990, when development of the 1002 area was most recently broadly debated; visitor numbers for 2001 are also high.[133] Trips, starting from Fairbanks, usually cost $2,000-$3,000, and may last 1 or 2 weeks. Usually, small groups of visitors are ferried in light planes to a riverbank where they are dropped off, traveling with or without professional guides. Either way, they walk along or raft one of the many rivers flowing northward to the coast where another plane picks them up, often followed by a stop

---

[128] In addition, see *Use of Resources by Alaska Natives*, below.
[129] U.S. Dept. of the Interior, Geological Survey, maps for Demarcation Point, Mt. Michelson, Beechey Point, and Flaxman Island. Scale: 1:250,000.
[130] The following history is condensed from U.S. Dept. of the interior, Fish and Wildlife Service, *Final Report Baseline Study of the Fish, Wildlife, and Their Habitats*, Vol. II (Washington, DC: December, 1986), pp. 436-437.
[131] A fifth site in ANWR, Demarcation Point, lies between the 1002 area and the Canadian border.
[132] U.S. Dept. of the interior, Fish and Wildlife Service, *Final Report Baseline Study of he Fish, Wildlife, and Their Habitats*, Vol. II (Washington, DC: December, 1986), p. 437, citing a 1979 memo by A.S. Thayer.
[133] FWS statistics, cited by Sam Howe Verhovek, "Mention Drilling, and Tourists Rush to Alaska," *New York Times* (June 10, 2001), pp. 1 and 24.

in Kaktovik before returning south to Fairbanks. In the right season, the migrating caribou are part of the attraction and, in all seasons, so is the solitude. One outfitter stated, "Where else can you spend 10 days floating a river, and not see anyone at all?"[134] In 2001, with the increase in controversy over the Refuge's coastal plain, the number of visitors has increased, but statistics are not yet available. Under current conditions, given the remoteness of the Refuge's coastal plain, the solitude seems likely to remain one of the principal attractions for visitors. while migrating caribou and other species will attract others.

Migratory Birds: Hunting and Birdwatching

As noted below, birds are used by Inupiat subsistence hunters. Beyond the immediate ANWR area, use falls into 2 additional categories: direct taking by hunters in many states of a number of species, and "use" by birdwatchers in other states. It is difficult to assess the economic impact of such uses and tie them to populations breeding or staging for migration in the 1002 area specifically, since these species breed and stage in other places as well. The tremendous number of snow geese breeding elsewhere, but staging in the 1002 area, make the Refuge especially important to hunters of this species. (A map showing annual migration routes of some birds nesting in ANWR is at http://www.r7.fws.gov/nwr/arctic/birdpost.html.)

Use of Resources by Alaska Natives

Alaska's Natives are both participants in and subjects of the debate over ANWR. Alaska Natives include Eskimos (Inuit and Yupik), Aleuts, and American Indians, and make up over 15% of Alaska's population. Alaska Natives participate in the debate through many different groups and organizations. They are members of the state's 229 federally recognized Indian[135] tribes, may include both non-profit and for-profit corporations. (See box: *Corporations and Boroughs*, for a discussion of their origins.)

Among and within these groups and organizations, there is disagreement over whether to open ANWR and the 1002 area to oil and gas exploration and development.

One set of Alaska Native groups and organizations favors oil and gas development in the 1002 area. This set is centered around North Slope Inupiat, who are Alaskan Inuit. In northern Alaska, this pro-development set includes (1) Kaktovik, the only Native village in ANWR, and its municipal government; (2) Kaktovik Inupiat Corporation (KIC), the Native village corporation; (3) Arctic Slope Regional Corporation (ASRC), the Native regional for-profit corporation for North Slope Inupiat; and (4) the North Slope Borough government, the organized borough within which Kaktovik is located.

Another set of Alaska Native groups and organizations opposes oil and gas development in the 1002 area. This set is centered around a group of Gwich'in Indian villages. The Gwich'in (also known as Kutchin) are Athabaskan Indians and are situated in east-central Alaska and neighboring areas of northwestern Canada. The anti-development set includes (1) two Gwich'in villages, Venetie and Arctic Village, which are located in the Doyon region (an Athabaskan Indian Native region, which overlaps the southern portion of ANWR), and the two villages' tribal government, called the Native Village of Venetie Tribal Government; (2)

---

[134] *Ibid.* Carol Kasza, co-owner, Arctic Treks; quoted on p. 24.
[135] The federal government generally considers the terms *Indian and Indian tribe* to include Alaska Natives.

the Gwich'in Steering Committee, composed of Venetie, Arctic Village, and 13 other Gwich'in villages of Alaska and Canada; and (3) the Native regional non-profit corporation for the Doyon region, the Tanana Chiefs Conference, Inc. However, the Native regional for-profit corporation, Doyon, Ltd., favors oil and gas development of the 1002 area.[136] Unlike Kaktovik, the Gwich'in villages are not within an organized borough.

Corporations and Boroughs

The existence of Alaska Native corporations and boroughs, and their role in the Native debate, is the result of the intersection of the Alaska Native Claims Settlement Act of 1971 (ANCSA, P.L. 92-203, 85 Stat. 688, 42 Stat. 1601 *et seq.*) and Alaska state law. ANCSA was enacted to settle Alaska Natives' aboriginal land claims. The act established 12 for-profit Native regional corporations and several hundred for-profit or non-profit Native village corporations. Naives were to own shares in both regional village corporations. The regions were to be "composed as far as practicable of Natives having a common heritage and sharing common interests" and especially were to follow the regions represented by 12 existing Native associations. (Many of these 12 Native associations became today's non-profit regional corporations. At least one – the Inupiat Community of the Arctic Slope – became a federally recognized tribe. Other regional non-profits have been established since 1987.)

Both regional and village corporations were to own *surface* lands selected under ANCSA. Only regional corporations, however, could own *subsurface* interests in regional or village lands. Seventy percent of revenues flowing to regional corporations from subsurface rights (and timber) were to be shared with other regional corporations. ANCSA also abolished all but one of the few reservations that then existed in Alaska, but village corporations on these few reservations could opt to forego regional shareholders and instead take direct fee title to the surface and subsurface of their former reservations.

Today, many regional Native corporations have subsidiaries in the oil supplies and services industries, as well as in other industries. Successful Native corporations have been able to pass benefits on to their members in the form of employment and dividends.

Boroughs are county-like political units that originated from Alaska's state constitution and the state's Borough Acts of 1961 and 1963. These laws required that Alaska be divided into boroughs, which could be either "organized," with varying levels of powers, or "unorganized." In 1972, a year after the passage of ANCSA, the North Slope Borough was organized, with the power to levy property taxes. The North Slope Borough's subsequent tax income from oil and gas property has enabled it to carry out a borough-wide capital improvement program, constructing schools, utilities, housing, public buildings, and other facilities, and has also allowed it to provide extensive services and to become one of he largest employers on the North Slope. Since the Arctic Slope Native region nearly corresponds with the North Slope Borough, most Inupiat have benefited from North Slope Borough activities, and the Borough has been perhaps the major conduit for oil development benefits flowing to the Inupiat. The Gwich'in, however, have had no parallel source of benefits. Much of the Doyon Native region, including the Gwich'in area, is not in an organized borough; the unorganized borough has no taxing power and gets its services and public investment chiefly from the state.

---

[136] See [http://www.ANWR.org/people/akgroups.html], Nov. 1, 2001.

The pro-and anti-development sets of Alaska Natives are of course not monolithic. Not all Inupiat or North Slope Borough residents support oil and gas development in ANWR or the 1002 area, and not all Gwich'in or Athabaskans oppose it. Other local, regional, statewide, and national Native and Indian groups and organizations support the position of one set or the other. The Alaska Federation of Natives (AFN), the major statewide Alaska Native organization, favors oil and gas development in ANWR and the 1002 area. Some Native critics of the AFN position claim that the organization tends to represent the position of the for-profit Native corporations, who are generally more supportive of 1002 development. The National Congress of American Indians (NCAI), a major nationwide organization representing Indian tribes, opposes oil and gas development in ANWR, but many Alaska Native entities are not NCAI members.

The disagreement between the two sets of Alaska Natives often centers on the effects of energy development on subsistence resources, especially the Porcupine caribou herd. Both Kaktovik and the two Gwich'in villages make significant use of the PCH. (See also *Biological Resources: Status and Effects: Caribou*, above.) In both Inupiat and Gwich'in cultures, the millennia of dependence on subsistence animals have created a complex set of practices and beliefs linking well-being and identity to subsistence in general and to certain animals in particular. Threats to these animals may thus be seen as threats to the very basis of Inupiat and Gwich'in cultures.

The disagreement is also greatly affected by ANILCA, which had several provisions that ultimately allowed KIC to acquire surface lands – and ASRC to acquire subsurface rights under these KIC lands – in the 1002 area and elsewhere on the coastal plain within ANWR. (For fuller discussions, see *Alaska National Interest Lands Conservation*, above, and *Alaska Native Lands and Rights*, below.) An oil or gas discovery under KIC/ASRC land would enormously increase ASRC revenues and hence the material benefits to Inupiats.

Inupiat Use of ANWR and the 1002 Area

Kaktovik, the only Native village in ANWR, depends greatly for subsistence resources directly on the 1002 area, the coastal plain in general, and other parts of ANWR, as well as on marine resources off the coast of ANWR. Residents of the Inupiat village of Nuiqsut, about 175 miles west of ANWR, also make some subsistence use of the 1002 area. Nonetheless, Kaktovik is the only Alaska Native village whose residents depend so much on subsistence resources taken on the 1002 area. The FLEIS, citing studies from the late 1970s and early 1980s, found that most Kaktovik households depended on hunting, fishing, and gathering in ANWR for food, and that caribou, Dall sheep, and bowhead whales (taken off the coast of ANWR) were their chief sources of meat, although they also hunted numerous other types of mammals, birds, and fish. Whaling has such great cultural and subsistence importance among Inupiat – especially Kaktovik, which, under special rules for subsistence, is allowed to take one to three endangered bowhead whales a year – that they oppose offshore oil and gas exploration because they fear it may endanger their whaling. Kaktovik's take of caribou was estimated in the FLEIS to be about 100 caribou a year, 50-80% from the PCH and the rest from the Central Arctic Herde (CAH) to the west. Most Kaktovik caribou harvesting occurs in summer, during the PCH postcalving time, and much of the harvest is in the 1002 area.

Some recent observers have suggested that Kaktovik has become somewhat less dependent on subsistence hunting, even though the activity is still significant. They suggest that paid employment has become so important that it restricts time for subsistence hunting.[137] Statistics from the 1990 census show that 72% of Kaktovik's adults were in the labor force.[138] Like other Arctic Slope villages, Kaktovik has benefited from the North Slope Borough's programs, which has funded a modern high school, housing, street lighting, a community hall, a power plant, and other capital improvements.[139] Kaktovik also benefits from state government activities funded by North Slope oil development.

Many Kaktovik residents worry that a reduction in oil and gas development and production will reduce their present standard of living, and most of them favor oil exploration and development in the 1002 area.[140] Moreover, because they are shareholders in KIC and ASRC, because they would be the closest Native village to oil development in the 1002 area, and because exploration of the 1002 area may even reveal oil in lands where ASRC owns the subsurface rights, Kaktovik residents might be expected to benefit more than any other Alaska natives from 1002 oil and gas development. Moreover, through the actions by which ASRC acquired subsurface rights to KIC lands in ANWR (see *Alaska Native Lands and Rights,* below), ASRC was found by arbitration to be examined from ANCSA's requirement to share subsurface revenues with other regional corporations, so dividends to ASRC shareholders, including Kaktovik, might be even greater.

Kaktovik residents and other Inupiat supporting oil and gas development in the 1002 area argue that they are as concerned about the dangers to subsistence as the opponents, but that they are experienced in caring for wildlife and the environment and believe that development can be carried out without endangering subsistence animals, including especially the PCH. Alaskan Inupiat who support ANWR leasing have in their turn opposed or remained cool to offshore leasing on the grounds that it might harm or drive off the bowhead whales on which they depend for cultural and subsistence reasons.[141] That is, both sets of Natives have opposed leasing in areas commonly used by the resources on which they depend.

Gwich'in Use of ANWR and the 1002 Area

The Gwich'in do not hunt within the 1002 area. They take caribou from the Porcupine herd in areas south of the Brooks Range, inside and outside ANWR, during the fall, winter, and spring. According to the FLEIS, Arctic Village in Alaska and Old Crow in Canada are the two Gwich'in villages most involved in caribou harvesting (recent information suggests Fort McPherson in Canada may now have a larger harvest than Old Crow[142]). Other Alaska

---

[137] See, e.g., Impact Assessment, Inc., *Subsistence Resource Harvest Patterns: Kaktovik: Final Special Report* (Anchorage, AK: U.S. Dept. of the Interior, Minerals Management Service, Alaska Outer Continental Shelf Region, 1990); and Norman A. Chance, *The Inupiat and Arctic Alaska: An Ethnography of Development* (Fort Worth: Holt, Rinehart and Winston, 1990).

[138] Go to [http://factfinder.census.gov/servlet/BasicFactsTable?_lang=en&_vt_name=DEC_1990_STF3_DP3&_geo_id=16000US021560] for these statistics. The Census Bureau classifies persons who are either employed or unemployed but seeking work as being "in the labor force." Census respondents who list their occupation as "subsistence hunter" may be classified by the Bureau in its "hunters and trappers" occupational classification, but no persons were counted in this occupation in the Kaktovik data.

[139] Earl Lane, "Living to the Cold: Two Native Villages Differ on Oil Drilling; Both Share a Harsh Existence," *Seattle Times,* May 21, 2001), p. A3; and David Foster, "Mixing Oil and Wilderness," *Alaska* (August 2011), pp. 30-37.

[140] Foster, *Ibid.*

[141] Yereth Rosen, "Alaska Natives sue to block Phillips oil project." Reuters (Dec. 19, 2000) at [http://www.eenn.com/news/wire-stories/2000/12/12192000/reu_oil_40893.asp].

[142] [http://ww.taiga.net/caribou/pch/slides/pch6.html].

Gwich'in villages hunting PCH caribou are Venetie, Ford Yukon, and Chalkyitsik; some of these also trade for much of their caribou meat. These Gwich'in villages harvest more caribou than does Kaktovik. Caribou is the main food source for Arctic Village, Venetie, and other Gwich'in villages. Arctic Village, according to the FLEIS, harvested 200-1,000 caribou per year in the 1970s, as did Old Crow, while the other Alaskan Gwich'in villages together took 300-400 a year and the other Canadian villages 100-2,100 a year. The Gwich'in, in also harvest other animals as well as fish birds. For the Gwich'in, caribou are by far the most culturally important subsistence animal. They speak of themselves as "people of the deer," and traditionally the Gwich'in believed that people and caribou each had a bit of the other's heart in theirs.[143]

Arctic Village and Venetie have benefited from Alaska's oil and gas development, but to a much lesser extent than Kaktovik. Arctic Village and Venetie elected, under ANCSA, to forego regional corporation shareholdings and take private fee title to their 1.8-million-acre reservation. After 1971, the reservation was first held in joint ownership by the two villages' village corporations, but in 1979 the corporations transferred title to the villages' tribal government, the Native Village of Venetie Tribal Government (the land was not, however, restored thereby to the status of an Indian reservation). Hence, because they had no shareholdings in Doyon, Ltd., the regional for-profit corporation, Artic Village and Venetie residents have not shared in any dividends flowing to Doyon shareholders. Moreover, the Alaskan Gwich'in villages are not in an organized borough, so their benefits from North Slope development have come chiefly through state government activities. Their community facilities are less prosperous and extensive than those of North Slope Borough villages.[144] Paid employment in Arctic Village and Venetie is not as widespread as it is in Kaktovik. Census statistics for 1990 show that 54% of Arctic Village's adults and 48% of Venetie's adults were in the labor force.[145]

The Gwich'in argue that oil and gas development in the 1002 area will endanger the PCH by threatening the herd's calving areas, and that because of their dependence on the PCH they will suffer subsistence loss and harm to their culture. When critics from the pro-development set of Alaska Natives argue that Artic Village and Venetie in the 1980s sold oil development leases (ultimately unsuccessful) on their lands, and that the villages seemed unconcerned about endangering the PCH then, the Gwich'in respond that the lease areas were not calving or postcalving areas and thus were not as sensitive for the herd's survival.

Alaska Native Lands and Rights

Alaskan Natives have various property interests related to the issue of oil drilling in ANWR that may present complex legal issues for refuge management if the coastal plain is

---

[143] Richard Slobodin, "Kutchin," in *Handbook of North American Indians, Vol. 6, Subarctic,* June Helm, vol. Ed.; William C. Sturtevant, genl. Ed. (Washington: Smithsonian Institution, 1981), pp. 514-532.
[144] Lane, "Living in the Cold," *op.cit.*
[145] For these census statistics, go to [http://factfinder.census.gov/servlet/BasicFactsTable?_lang=en&_vt_name =DEC_1990_STF3_DP3&_geo_id=16000US020200] for Arctic Village and [http://factfinder.census.gov/servlet/BasicFactsTable?_lang=en&vt_name=DEC_1990_STF3_DP3&_geo_id= 16000US023480] for Venetie. As was the case with Kaktovik, no persons were counted in the "hunters and trappers" occupation in the Arctic Village and Venetie data.

opened to oil development.[146] In 1971, Congress enacted ANCSA to resolve all Native aboriginal land claims against the United States. ANCSA provided for monetary payments and also created village corporations that received the surface estate to approximately 22 million acres of lands. Village selection rights included the right to choose the surface estate in a certain amount of the lands within the National Wildlife Refuge System, in which case, under §22(g) of ANCSA, the lands were to remain subject to the laws and regulations governing use and development of the Refuge.[147] KIC received rights to three townships[148] along the coast of ANWR.

ANCSA also created regional corporations which could select subsurface rights to some lands and full title to others. Subsurface rights in National Wildlife Refuges were not available, but in-lieu selections to substitute for such lands were provided.

Section 1431 of ANILCA (1980) followed up on the previously enacted ANCSA and gave KIC rights to make certain selections and to enter into certain exchanges. ANILCA (§1002(b)) also defined the 1002 area by reference to a map dated August 1980, which has been interpreted as excluding the KIC lands. As a result, Kaktovik has its previous surface rights to three townships along the coast that are outside the 1002 area and one township inside that area. *Geographically*, the KIC lands are all on the coastal plain and are indistinguishable from surrounding lands in their important to wildlife. However, *all* of the Kaktovik lands are within the Refuge as a whole and hence are subject to the restrictions on oil and gas development §1003 of ANILCA and, under §22(g) of ANCSA and §1431(g) of ANILCA, they are subject to the laws and regulations governing the Refuge.

Section 1431(o) of ANILCA also authorized the Arctic Slope Regional Corporation (ASRC), whose shareholders are Inupiat, to obtain rights in the Refuge through exchanges, if lands in the National Petroleum Reserve-Alaska (NPR-A) or ANWR within a certain proximity to village lands were ever opened for commercial oil and gas development within 40 years of the date of ANILCA. However, under a different ANILCA exchange authority (§1302(h)), an exchange was executed on August 9, 1983, between then Secretary of the Interior James Watt and ASRC. Under this "Chandler Lake Agreement" the United States received certain ASRC lands in the Gates of the Arctic National Park and ASRC received the subsurface rights to the KIC lands – which, it will be recalled, are three townships within the Refuge on the coastal plain but outside the 1002 area, and one township within the 1002 area. Congress appears to have ratified the Agreement in later legislation (P.L. 98-377, §5; 98 Stat. 468, 470-471).

Also as part of the Chandler Lake Agreement, ASRC was given the contractual right to drill up to three exploratory wells on the KIC lands that are outside the 1002 area within a certain window of time. One test well was drilled, but the results of that well have been kept confidential.

In addition to the KIC and ASRC Native lands, there are also some individual Native "allotments" within the coastal plain. These are surface rights belonging to a particular individual. The conveyance of some lands has been completed; other lands have been applied for, but final rulings have not been made. BLM currently is compiling the exact locations and acreage of these allotments, but preliminary data indicate that these allotments and

---

[146] See CRS Report RL31115, *Legal Issues Related to Proposed Drilling for Oil and Gas in the Artic National Wildlife Refuge.*
[147] See 50 C.F.R. Parts 25 and 26.
[148] A *township* is about 36 square miles – roughly 23,000 acres.

applications appear to be clustered along to the coast and near Sadlerochit Spring, both of which are important wildlife areas. (See *Special Areas*, below.) Allotments already conveyed total over 10,000 acres. Use of allotments appears not to be subject to §22(g) ANCSA controls, nor to other restrictions or regulations unless Congress enacts same.

The 1983 Agreement and its appendices address oil exploration and development on the KIC/ASRC lands and their terms will govern the development and oil production on those lands unless they are superseded by statutory provisions. Appendix 2, part 9 of the 1983 Agreement states that development and production activities undertaken on ASRC lands "shall be in accordance with the substantive statutory and regulatory requirements governing oil and gas exploration, including exploratory drilling, and development and production that are designed to protect the wildlife, its habitat, and the environment of the coastal plain, or the ASRC Lands, or both." Other provisions in the Agreement purport to survive subsequent legislation (which is to say they likely would unless Congress acts to expressly negate them), and would affect the applicability of any environmental controls Congress might otherwise enact. If Congress repeals the current prohibition against oil development in the Refuge, development could occur on the more than 100,000 acres of Native lands that are comprised of KIC/ASRC lands and individual Native allotments.

Canadian Interests in Traditional Native Rights

The Canadian government has consistently opposed development in the 1002 area, citing risks to the PCH and consequently to the Gwich'in people found on both sides of the international border.[149] It also points to a 19878 U.S.-Canada "Agreement on the Conservation of the Porcupine Caribou Herd" under which each nation agreed to protect the PCH and its habitat. If one country plans to carry out an activity that may result in significant long-term adverse impacts on the PCH, the other is to be notified, and given the opportunity to consult before any final decision. Canada cities evidence of its commitment to the herd in its creation of Ivvavik and Vuntuk National parks on the Canadian side, which prevent development in important calving and migration areas on its side of the border. The embassy website notes: "... the 1002 Area of ANWR contains the core of the critically important calving area for the Porcupine Caribou Herd, and Canada is convinced that only permanent protection of the plain will assure the herd's long-term sustainability."[150]

Development proponents often claim that the Canadian position borders on hypocrisy, since a significant portion of the PCH range in Canada was leased for oil and gas development in decades past. But commercial quantities of hydrocarbons were not found, and leases have been allowed to lapse. Thus, this argument goes, Canadian opposition arose only after it became clear that commercial quantities of oil were not found in the PCH range in Canada. In response, Canadians (and Gwich'in on both sides of the border) argue that the portion of the calving area on the U.s. side is the most frequently used, and that at the time the Canadian leases were offered, the importance of the proposed leasing areas to caribou was

---

[149] Canada could also be affected by a proposed natural gas pipeline route from the North Slope (whether the gas was from the1002 area or not). Two of the three main options for the route would pass through Canada before reaching U.S. markets. Canada has generally supported a gas pipeline through its territory. (See Figure 5 and *Natural Gas Pipeline from North Slope*, above.)

[150] From Statement by Canadian Environment Minister David Anderson on Arctic National Wildlife Refuge on August 3, 2001; cited on [http://www.ec.gc.ca/Press/2001/010803_s_e.htm].

unclear. Indeed, some Canadian industry officials now complain of government hostility to development in the northern areas of the country, based on what they perceive as overzealous environmental concerns.

Reclamation Issues After Development

If the 1002 area were opened to exploration, and if energy development did occur, then even the most stringent requirements for environmental protection, a major question would remain: what should be done after the oil and/or natural gas are depleted? The FLEIS seemed to be of two minds. It speaks of "rehabilitation"[151] and says which effects on wildlife could be "very long-term [but] would not be considered irreversible once the life of the producing fields in the 1002 area was over."[152] Yet it also speaks of "the long-term commitment of this area to industrial use based on oil and gas development"[153] and of "long-term changes in the wilderness environment, wildlife habitats, and native community activities currently existing, resulting instead in an area governed by industrial activities."[154] And it notes that "complete restoration [of disturbed sites] may not be possible, inasmuch as construction activities dramatically alter surface features which determine plant species composition in the natural habitat."[155] These comments raise the question as to whether the 1002 area, upon initiation of development, remains an integral part of a wildlife refuge with a temporary (albeit long) interlude of industrial activity, or an area whose fundamental purpose has changed, but continues to lie within the boundaries of a national wildlife refuge.

Whatever development might be permitted, should it be seen as essentially *temporary* – serving immediate energy needs and then being removed, followed by restoring the 1002 area habitat to a condition as near as possible to its predevelopment state? The answers to questions about rehabilitation of the 1002 area, and the confidence in the response, will crucially affect not only any development of the area, but also will likely affect view son whether the 1002 area should be opened to exploration and production in the first place.

Conditions for Rehabilitation

Total rehabilitation after development could be defined as restoration to a state that a trained ecologist could not distinguish from the original ecosystem. So defined, total rehabilitation of the 1002 area might require centuries and could be impossible, since it might be confounded by other long-term changes: global warming, changes in sea level, expansion or contraction of the polar ice cap, changes in the northern polar hole in the ozone layer or in CO_2 levels, etc. On the other hand, if "substantial" rehabilitation were defined as restoration of the area to a state approximately the original, with a full complement of pre-development species (if not all at pre-development population levels), so that at least untrained observers could not easily or frequently detect human influences, then such a level might be an achievable but very difficult goal. Such a goal would probably required not merely the

---

[151] For example, pp. 86, 114, 116, and 139.
[152] FLEIS, p. 164.
[153] FLEIS, p. 165.
[154] FLEIS, p. 165.
[155] FLEIS, p. 116.

removal of structures and equipment and stringent pollution control, including the safe disposal of hazardous and other wastes, but also the return to pre-development human population levels, the removal of gravel roads, and the restoration of native vegetation.

As yet no major operating oil fields anywhere are known to have been shut down permanently, and many have kept producing long beyond initial expectations, due to enhanced recovery techniques. Thus there is little relevant experience to guide a total closure of potential 1002 area development. Interestingly, in 1988 ARCO Alaska said with respect to Prudhoe Bay that "Large scale rehabilitation/restoration is neither currently practical nor required by Federal or State regulations."[156] Thus, rehabilitation and restoration could be an important feature in congressional debate concerning the 1002 area.

Human Population Levels

In an oil field, human population levels reach a peak during the construction phase, once a producible field has been confirmed. In 1987, the FLEIS estimated 1,500 workers at the peak of construction.[157] After major construction projects are completed, personnel levels drop to those needed for operations – perhaps a few hundred workers – or for smaller construction projects such as the action of new frill pads.

Once energy production ceases, it is hard to imagine what incentives would hold workers in the 1002 area, since few other industries seem likely to seek the high cost of North Slope operations. An import exception would be Alaska Natives, presumably those in Kaktovik especially. With an increasing reliance on a monetary economy, both for personal and local government income, there may be pressure to maintain development to support (possibly subsidized) alternative local industries, including tourism. The North Slope Borough has stated that its support for 1002 development stems partly from a concern over declining Prudhoe Bay revenues, which are used for schools, fire stations, and other facilities. Over the years little debate has focused on the post-development status of permanent human populations – a reflection, in part, of a lack of debate on the long-term fate of the 1002 area in general.

Removal of Road and Gravel Structures

There is a striking distinction between the access policies around development areas in the North Slope versus those in the 1002 area as it is currently managed. In the former, a road network provides relatively easy transportation, but its use is largely restricted to authorized persons. In the latter, the lack of roads requires aircraft for most ravel, but the journey is relatively unrestricted. If Congress decides to authorize 1002 area development, the fate of roads could have far-reaching environmental effects.

Under the scenario for development based on current technologies, fewer roads would be built with older technology. However, if oil prices fall, or operating costs rise, the cost of reliance on expensive aircraft might make construction of haul roads seem attractive, especially for movement of heavy equipment. In addition, it is unclear whether any

---

[156] ARCO Alaska, Inc. *NRDC/Trustees for Alaska/National Wildlife Federation Report "Oil in the Arctic: The Environment Record of Oil Development on Alaska's North Slope – Comments and Critique.* 1988. P. 21.
[157] FLEIS, p. 85. Considerable advances in technology have occurred since then, so this number should probably be considered a maximum; no newer local employment figures are known.

restrictions on road construction would apply to Native lands, and still less whether requirements for road removal would apply on Native lands. In any event, under all current scenarios, it is likely that at least some roads would be built. If these are in unconnected small segments, as at Alpine, their effects on human access would probably be quite small. Experience in national park, national forests, and national wildlife refuges has shown that reducing human access can benefit sensitive species, in such matters as preventing illegal hunting, or reducing disturbance of nesting sites, calving areas, or spawning streams.

Removing millions of tons of gravel from roads (and pads) – some of it contaminated with oil or other toxins – would be expensive, but so would continued gravel maintenance to preserve culverts and other flow control measures. Costs would likely prevent either the total removal of roads once production ceased, or the indefinite maintenance of the full network. Unless otherwise specified or required, rehabilitation of gravel structures would likely include removal of culverts and bridges to ensure natural drainage, grading and scoring of the road or pad surfaces, and seeding of grasses and forbs. Care would be required to minimize erosion, sedimentation, and ponding. Probably, only if there were a need for gravel elsewhere would some portion of the gravel be removed form abandoned roadbeds.

Thus, if leasing is allowed and production is achieved, there appear to be several options, depending on the gravel structure and congressional policy. First, some may wish to see certain useful structures retained even if all production ceases. Examples of such structures are water treatment plants and some airfields. Others, such as drill pads, seem unlikely to be useful in a post-production setting, and would likely be priority candidates for removal. Finally, for roads, there appear to be two basic options: maintain some roads while rehabilitating rights of way for the rest; or abandon all of the roads and rehabilitate the rights of way in an effort to return to predevelopment conditions. If development were to result in increased tourism (e.g., visitor centers or visitor cabins), there might be considerable pressure to keep at least some roads open, especially if tourism were seen as a continuing source of income for Natives after developed ceased. Continuing access would be expected to prolong habitat disturbance and delay rehabilitation.

Restoration of Naïve Vegetation

Once production ceased, restoration of the correct species and adequate numbers of native plants would be a key factor in restoration of animal populations. There is a key distinction between the 1002 area and the developed areas to the west: the rolling hills of much of the 1002 area support more shrubby, woody vegetation, while the wetlands of the developed areas are dominated by herbaceous vegetation. Thus, restoration experience around Prudhoe Bay and environs may provide useful techniques for only part of the 1002 area. Moreover, recent research has shown that "none but the smallest and wettest patches on level ground ... recovered unassisted to something approaching their original state in the medium term (20-75 years)."[158] In larger, drier, or more sloping sites, revegetation (where it occurred) often resulted in a species composition that differed from the original state. "A wide range of small disturbances resulted in alternative vegetation states with reduced species diversity."[159]

---

[158] Bruce C. Forbes, James J. Ebersole, and Beate Strandberg," Anthropogenic Disturbance and Patch Dynamics in Circumpolar Arctic Ecosystems", *Conservation Biology*, Vol. 15 (August, 2001), p. 966. (Hereafter referred to as "Forbes, et al.")

[159] Forbes, et al., p. 966.

If roads and other gravel structures were not removed, revegetation on these structures would be particularly difficult, due to drying, loss of seeds, and erosion. On the other hand, revegetation at the edges of the pads would be less difficult, due to wetter conditions and protection from wind.

Site Phase-Out

The requirement to remove all facilities and to rehabilitate the site is generally a term or condition of a lease sale. Thus far, there is relatively limited experience in the arctic from which to judge the effectiveness of this requirement. North Slope fields that have been developed are still active and only a relatively small number of drilling sites have been abandoned. These abandoned sites include a few artificial drilling islands in the Beaufort Sea and a number of onshore sites, several of which are in the NPR-A. At the abandoned island sites, facilities and slope protection have been removed and the artificial islands were left to erode away. The NPR-A example is particularly relevant to ANWR development.

Site Cleanup in the NPR-A

Before the recent return to NPR-A prospects, there were two rounds of drilling in the NPR-A. The most recent was between 1974 and 1981, when 28 wells were drilled in a federal program under the supervision of USGS. In that round, each exploratory site included a drill pad, airstrip, and source of water supply. Buildings and equipment were located on the drilling paid, often on pilings to prevent thawing of the permafrost. The pad design included a fuel storage pit, a reserve pit for drilling fluids and cuttings, and a flare pit.

Cleanup included removing miscellaneous debris, cutting off pilings below ground level, and filling the pits by grading off and contouring the gravel pads. Then revegetation of the sites was attempted using grass seed mixtures and fertilizer. The program for revegetating the pads met with mixed success. Generally, the least success was found at some coastal sites where pads were constructed of relatively brine-rich clay silts excavated from the reserve pits. Considering the somewhat experimental nature of the revegetation program and the variability of individual sites, revegetation was thought to progress at reasonable to excellent rates by 1986.[160] In the interim, pad construction techniques elsewhere on the North Slope have evolved, and exploration pads such as those in the USGS program at NPR-A would be built of ice.

However, as with roads, the return of vegetation is not identical to recovery of the tundra to its previous condition. Even if organic matter is left intact after a disturbance, "significant and essentially permanent change [in] both vegetation and soils" may still occur.[161] Nonetheless, a manger may be satisfied if a site simply returns to a plant-covered, stable surface.[162]

---

[160] Phillip D. J. Smith, "Final Wellsite Cleanup on National Petroleum Reserve – Alaska." U.S. Geological Survey Contract no. 14-08-001-21787. Anchorage Alaska: Nuera Reclamation Company, 1986. Vol. 1, p. 43.
[161] Forbes, et al., p. 965.
[162] [I]f a manager simply wants a green, stable surface, then a measure of vascular cover – usually provided by graminoids [grass-like plants] – may be all that is feasible under the most severe conditions." Forbes, et al., p. 960, citing 1999 work by Forbes and Jeffries.

Site Development and Facility Removal

Facility removal really begins as soon as drilling a well is finished. At that point, the drill rig is removed, leaving only pipe valves and gages for each well and any operational facilities on the pad. When a field is depleted or a well is abandoned, the well is plugged with cement plugs at various points and at the surface. Surface facilities are removed, and that pad would be graded and revegetated. The FLEIS full development scenario estimated that 5,650 acres scattered around the 1.5 million acre 1002 area would be physically covered with gravel (less than 0.4%). As noted previously (see *Land and Gravel Use*, above), somewhat less would probably be covered with the use of modern technologies, though these features would still be scattered in various spots around the 1002 area. Until the affected areas wee restored and revegetated, the impacts would remain visible (at least as long as they were not concealed by snow and darkness). As different requirements for rehabilitation might apply to Native lands, their inholdings might retain various structures or pads might remain for a considerably longer period.

Retention of Facilities: The Other Option

The alternative to removing all drilling pads, roads, buildings, airstrips, and other facilities would be a judgment that some of the development may be of longer term and/or broader benefit than the oil and gas development in the immediate area. In remote regions of a hostile environment, emergency shelters can be lifesavers. A building or other recognizable structure, such as a road or airstrip, in a featureless region can serve as a visual aid to navigation, which can also save lives. In addition, if it were necessary to redevelop a location, it would likely be less disruptive to the environment to reopen a closed facility than to construct a new one. In any event, carrying out the actual restoration requirements in ANWR would probably not arise for many years; thus a tension might exist between those preferring that a goal of restoration be made a condition of development and those preferring that the decisions on some facilities be considered on a case-by-case basis later. In the later case, it could be difficult to enforce a cleanup measure that was not originally specified as regulation, or a term or condition of the lease.

LEGISLATIVE ISSUES

The ANWR debate has continued for such a long time that most issues have a long history of debate. Some of the issues that have been raised most frequently are described briefly below.

Alternatives to Developing 1002 Area

Opponents of energy development in ANWR argue that a variety of other options could provide the energy equivalent of most projections of ANWR oil production, especially if one assumes the high energy prices necessary to reach the most generous assumptions regarding Refuge resources. More succinctly, the high-energy prices that would make Refuge oil economic would make a variety of other energy options attractive as well. Recognizing the great importance of oil in the transportation market, opponents most frequently mention increases in fuel economy for cars and light trucks, and production of ethanol from cellulose.[163] Increase in efficiency in other sectors (heating and cooling especially) are also mentioned. Others have argued that developing ANWR oil, thereby continuing a national reliance on TAPS, is harmful to U.S. energy security, especially with respect to terrorist attacks. One author called TAPS "among the gravest threats to U.S. energy security," due to the vulnerability of the pipeline, lack of alternatives if it were seriously damaged, and the difficulty of repairing the aging pipeline.[164] Addition of any ANWR oil would continue that risk, in this line of reasoning.

Consequently, for not only environmental, but also economic and security reasons, opponents of ANWR oil development believe that other options (especially in the transportation sector) are preferable to development of the Refuge. Proponents downplay the economic rationale and practicality of the alternatives, but have only recently begun to focus on continued reliance on TAPS as a security argument.

Exploration Only

Some have argued that the 1002 area should be opened to exploration first, before a decision is made on whether to proceed to leasing. Those with this view hold that with greater certainty about the presence or absence of energy resources, a better decision could be made about whether to open the coastal plain for full leasing. This idea has had relatively little support over the years. For those opposed to energy development, the reasons are fairly clear: if there were economic discoveries, support for further development might be unstoppable. And even if exploration resulted in no or insufficient economic discoveries, any damage from exploration (e.g., soil compaction, erosion, or altered drainage patterns) would remain.

Those who support leasing see unacceptable risks in such a proposal. First, who would be charged with carrying out exploration, who would pay for it, and to whom would the results be available? Second, if no economic discoveries were made, would that be because the "best" places (in the eyes of whatever observer) were not examined? Third, might any small discoveries become economic in the future? Fourth, if discoveries did occur, could industry still be foreclosed from developing the area, or might sparse but promising data elevate bidding competition to unreasonable levels? Fifth, if exploration were authorized, what provisions should pertain to Alaska Native lands? In short, various advocates see insufficient gain from such a proposal. In the 107th Congress, no bill supporting exploration only has been introduced.

---

[163] For an analysis of energy alternatives, see CRS Report RL 31033. *Energy Efficiency and Renewable Energy Fuel Equivalents to Potential Oil Production from the Artic National Wildlife Refuge (ANWR),* by Fred Sissine.

[164] Amory B. Lovins and L. Hunter Lovins, "Frozen Assets? Alaskan Oil's Threat to National Energy Security", RMI Solutions, Spring, 2001. [http://www.rmi.org/sitepages/art1051.php].

Compatibility with Refuge Purposes

As a general rule, activities may be allowed in federal wildlife refuges if they are compatible with the *major* purposes of the National Wildlife Refuge System and with the purposes of any particular unit of that System.[165] Long-term uses of refuge may be allowed if compatibility with all of the purposes of the particular refuge and the System.[166] The mineral leasing laws apply to lands within the System to the same extent they applied prior to October 15, 1966 (the date of the first general refuge management statute), unless lands are subsequently withdrawn.[167]

A new compatibility policy and new regulations were published on October 18, 2000, effective November 17, 2000.[168] "Compatible use" is defined as "a proposed or existing wildlife-dependent recreational use or any other use of a national wildlife refuge that, based on sound professional judgment, will not materially interfere with or detract from the fulfillment of the National Wildlife Refuge System mission or the purpose(s) of the national wildlife refuge." Lands within Alaska refuges are subject to the regulations on compatibility.

More specifically as to mineral leasing, Public Land Order 2214, which withdrew lands to create the original Range, withdrew the lands from operation of the mining laws, but not the mineral leasing laws. Congress, of course, in §1003 of ANILCA reserved to itself the decision of whether to lease the coastal plain area. Any legislation that ultimately permitted oil and gas leasing in that area would answer the question of compatibility by authorizing leasing, and probably would expressly address the compatibility of that leasing, and might set limits on such activities.

Compliance with NEPA

Some question whether the existing FLEIS, prepared in 1987 in compliance with the National Environmental Policy Act (NEPA), is adequate to support development, or whether an updated or new EIS needs to be prepared. A court in a declaratory judgment action in 1991[169] held that the Department of the Interior should have prepared a Supplemental Environmental Impact Statement (SEIS) at the time to encompass new information about the 1002 area in connection with the Department's recommendation that Congress legislate to permit development. Therefore, it is likely that either on SEIS or a new EIS would have to be prepared before development, unless Congress changed or waived this requirement.

Environmental Direction

Congress could choose to leave environmental matters to administrative agencies under existing laws. Alternatively, Congress could impose a higher standard of environmental

---

[165] 16 U.S.C. 668dd(d)(1)(1A) (emphasis added).
[166] 16 U.S.C. 668dd(d)(1)(B).
[167] 16 U.S.C. 668dd(c).
[168] 65 Federal Register 62484 and 65 Federal Register 62458, respectively. See 50 C.F.R. §§25 and 26 for compatibility materials.
[169] NRDC v. Lujan, 68 F.Supp.870 (D.D.C. 1991)

protection because the area is in a national wildlife refuge or because of the fragility of the arctic environment, or it could legislate a lower standard to facilitate development. One issue would be the use of gravel an water resources essential for oil exploration and development. Other potential legislative issues include extend and regulation of gravel structures, gravel mines, or other development; limitations on miles of roads or other surface occupancy; the adequacy of existing air and water pollution standards; research needs; monitoring; prevention and treatment of spills; the adequacy of current waste disposal requirements; prohibitions on landfills; aircraft overflights; reclamation; and concerns over shared liability that can made consolidation of facilities unattractive to oil companies.

Of the various bills introduced over the years, few had provisions that mandated specific technologies. Rather, the focus was on requirements to use 'best available" or "best practicable" technologies or similar phrases. In recent debates on the issue, limitations on surface occupancy have been also considered. These limitations are generally focused on those features covered by gravel structures (e.g., drill pads, runways, and connector roads). Debates over surface occupancy have tended to omit features that require no laying of gravel or could be built offshore, e.g., gravel mines, pipelines (as opposed to pipeline piers supports), culverts, altered drainage patters, water treatment plants, ports, causeways, and the like.

Special Areas

Congress could decide to set aside certain special areas for their ecological or cultural values. This could be done either by designating the areas specifically, in legislation, or by authorizing the Interior Secretary to set aside areas to be selected after enactment. A few bills have named specific areas (especially Sadlerochit Spring) within the 1002 area for set-asides. A number of bills in the past have chosen the latter course, with a cap of around 45,000 acres in which surface occupancy (a term not usually defined) could be limited. Depending on the meaning of "surface occupancy," such areas might be open to seismic exploration (which requires no roads of any type) or to (temporary) ice roads. Such areas could also still be accessible for leasing, if developed from drill pads outside these areas. The four special areas named in the FLEIS together total more than 52,000 acres, so some choices would be necessary if the set-aside acreage available to the Secretary were too low to accommodate the identified areas.

Expedited Judicial Review

Leasing proponents urge that any ANWR leasing program to put in place promptly; expediting judicial review may be one means to that goal. Judicial review can be expedited through procedural changes such as time limits within which suits must be filed, or by avoiding some level of review. The scope of the review also could be curtailed, or the burden imposed on a challenger could be increased. Bills before congress have combined all of these elements.

Project Labor Agreements

A continuing issue in federal and federally-funded projects is whether project owners or contractors effectively should be required, by "agreement," to use union workers. In the past 10 years, President George Bush, President Bill Clinton, and President George W. Bush have issued executive orders pertaining to the question, with President Clinton favoring their use and Presidents Bush opposing their use. Members of Congress have become involved when they objected to a presidential action. In the 107th Congress, the issue has come up in the context of proposed oil and gas development of ANWR.

Project labor agreements (PLAs) are agreements between a project owner or main contractor and the union(s) representing the craft workers for a particular project. PLAs establish the terms and conditions of work that will apply for the particular project. The agreement may also specify a source (such as a union hiring hall) to supply the craft workers for the project. Typically, the agreement is binding on all contractors and subcontractors working on the project, and specifies wage rates and benefits, discusses procedures for resolving labor and jurisdictional disputes, and includes a no-strike clause.

Proponents of PLAs argue that they ensure a reliable, efficient labor source and help keep costs down. Opponents contend that PLAs inflate project costs and decrease competition. There is little independent information and data to sort out these conflicting assertions and demonstrate whether PLAs contribute to lower or higher project costs. Construction and other unions and their supports strongly favor PLAs because they believe that PLAs help ensure access for union members to federal and federally funded projects. Nonunion firms and their supporters believe that PLAs unfairly restrict their access to federally-funded projects.[170]

Revenue Disposition

A recurring issue in the ANWR debate is that of disposition of possible revenues, not only from oil but also from sale of gravel or water resources. There are two parts to the disposition question: (a) how would revenues be split between the federal government and the state; and (b) how would the federal portion be used?

Federal/State Split

The Mineral Leasing Act (MLA)[171] governs the leasing of oil and gas and certain other minerals from federal public lands. Under §35 of the MLA, certain western states receive directly 50% of revenues received. An additional 40% goes to those states indirectly through the construction and maintenance of irrigation projects under the Reclamation Act of 1902.[172] Before 1976, these percentages wee 37½% and 52½% respectively. Because the territory of Alaska did not benefit from the Reclamation Act, it received only a 37½ % share of federal leasing revenues. Before enactment of the Alaska Statehood Act, Congress amended the

---

[170] For discussion of PLAs, see CRS Report 98-965 E, *Project Labor Agreements in Federal Construction Contracts; An Overview and Analysis of Issues*, by Gail McCallion (Aug. 24, 1999). 8 p.

[171] Act of February 25, 1920, ch. 85, 41 Stat. 450, 30 U.S.C. 191.

[172] This money is available only if Congress subsequently appropriates it from the Reclamation Fund – it is not permanently appropriated.

MLA to provide that the territory would receive an additional 52½% share, thereby putting Alaska on the same footing as the other states.[173] Section 28(b) of the Alaska Statehood Act again amended the MLA to change the references from territory to State of Alaska.[174] Section 317 of the Federal Land Policy Management Act of 1976 amended the revenues section of MLA to direct payment of 90% to Alaska, rather than the separate percentages previously stated.[175] The committee report accompanying the 1976 change states that the action was intended to clarify that Alaska was to continue to receive 90% of the mineral revenues taken in from federal lands in Alaska.[176]

Alaska has asserted that the 90% total referenced in the Statehood Act cannot be changed and must always be paid to the state because the Statehood Act is a compact between the prospective state and the federal government. Others assert that the Statehood Act provision was a technical one, meant to recognize that Alaska should receive a share comparable to that of other states *under the MLA*, but does not preclude the Congress from changing the MLA or at times making special provision for leasing certain areas under a different regimen.

Alaska sued in the U.S. Court of Federal Claims, asserting that because the United States had an obligation under the Statehood Act both to maximize mineral leasing in Alaska and to always pay a 90% share of gross receipts to Alaska, the United States had either breached the contract established by the Statehood Act, or "taken" property of Alaska by withdrawing some lands in Alaska from leasing (notably ANWR) and by dedicating administrative costs prior to the disbursement of the 90% revenues to the State. The court found that the Statehood Act and the previous statute providing the territory of Alaska with the same shares as the other states "simply plugged [Alaska] into the MLA, along with the other States."[177] Therefore, Congress could amend the MLA, e.g., to provide a different way of calculating receipts, and the changes would lawfully pertain to Alaska. Furthermore, the court concluded that the United States did not promise in the Statehood Act to make federal mineral lands produce royalty revenues for the State, and that the United States therefore retained discretion over leasing decisions.[178] Because of these findings, the court also granted the government's motion for summary judgment on the Takings claim, dismissing Alaska's claim.

If the Statehood Act simply means that Alaska will be treated like other states under the MLA, the question may be asked whether Congress may legislate specifically as to ANWR and prescribe different revenue-sharing provisions. Congress has done so in the past, e.g., with respect to the National Petroleum Reserves, in which situation all of the revenues go into the federal Treasury,[179] except for the National Petroleum Reserve in Alaska, in which instance the revenue sharing is 50/50.[180] Therefore, arguably Congress has flexibility in legislating regarding oil and gas leasing in the Refuge, including providing for the disposition of revenues from any such leasing.

---

[173] P.S. 85-88, 71 Stat. 282 (1957). The 37½% was to be spent for the construction and maintenance of public roads or for the support of public schools or other public educational institutions as the legislature of the territory may direct. The 57½% was to be paid to the territory to be disposed of as the legislature directed in general.
[174] P.L. 85-508, 71 Stat. 339, 351.
[175] P.L. 94-579, 90 Stat. 2743, 2770-2771.
[176] H.Rept. 94-1724, p. 62 (1976).
[177] Alaska v. United States, 35 Fed. Cl. 685, 701 (1996).
[178] *Ibid.*, at 706.
[179] 10 U.S.C. 7433.
[180] P.L. 96-514, 94 Stat. 2964.

Uses for Federal Share of Revenues

Proponents of opening ANWR for oil production point out that the federal share of any revenues could be made available for various conservation purposes, including ameliorating impacts, providing funds for research on renewable energy sources, or assisting other refuges and conservation areas. While additional funding for these purposes would undoubtedly cheer many environmental groups, it is difficult to name any such group whose views on ANWR development have been swayed by such proposals.

Wilderness Designation

In each Congress since 1980, bills have been introduced in both House and Senate statutorily to designate the coastal plain of the Refuge as wilderness. Energy development is not permitted in wilderness areas, unless there are pre-existing rights or unless Congress specifically allows it or later reverses the designation. Development of the surface and subsurface holdings of Native corporations would be precluded inside wilderness boundaries (although compensation might be owed). This choice would preserve existing recreational opportunities and jobs, as well as the existing level of protection of subsistence resources, including the Porcupine Caribou Herd, while of course foregoing any energy resources that might be available.

Not Action Alternative

Because current law prohibits development unless Congress acts, this option also prevents energy development. Those supporting delay often argue that not enough is known about either the probability of discoveries or about the environmental impact if development in permitted. Others argue that oil deposits should be saved for an unspecified "right time."

GLOSSARY: KEY FEATURES, TERMS, ACRONYMS, AND ABBREVIATIONS

1002 area –
A portion of the coastal plain of ANWR north of the Brooks Range along the Beaufort Sea. Section 1002 of the ANILCA defined the area with respect to a "map dated August 1980" but the area was later defined by a published description.

1002 report –
See *FLEIS*.

ADEC –
Alaska Department of Environmental Conservation; regulates nonhazardous and RCRA-exempts solid wastes and underground injection wells.

ADF&G –
Alaska Department of Fish and Game.

ADNR –
Alaska Department of Natural Resources.

AFN –
Alaska Federation of Natives; the major statewide Alaska Native organization.

Alaska Natives –
Eskimos (Inuit and Yupik), Aleuts, and American Indians in Alaska, who together make up over 15% of Alaska's population. Included by the federal government in the terms *Indians* and *Indian tribe*.

Alpine Corporation Oil Field –
A 40,000 acre oil field originally owned by ARCO Alaska, Inc., and now owned by Phillips Petroleum Co. Originally permitted at 98 acres for development, its current footprint is slightly smaller. It is situated west of the Kuparuk Oil Field, and is accessible only by aircraft or winter ice road. Oil development facilities here are considered state-of-the-art arctic (energy) technology.

ANCSA –
Alaska Native Claims Settlement Act of 1971 (P.L. 92-203). Provides for selection and conveyance of property title and monetary award to Alaska Natives in settlement of their aboriginal claims; authorizes establishment of native regional and village corporations; also contains various provisions regarding federal land management in Alaska.

ANGTS –
Alaska Natural Gas Transportation System (surface pipeline).

Angun Plains –
One of several "special areas" in ANWR defined in the FLEIS, where evidence of Pleistocene glaciation is considered special. It comprises about 36 square miles.

ANILCA
Alaska National Interest Lands Conservation Act of 1980 (P.L. 96-487): Among other things, it expanded the boundaries of ANWR, designated the 1002 area, prohibited energy development in the Refuge unless authorized by Congress, and established numerous federal conservation system units (National Parks, Wildlife Refuges, etc.) on federal lands in Alaska; amended several provisions of ANCSA and included various provisions regarding federal land and resource management in Alaska.

ANWR –
Arctic National Wildlife Refuge; also called "the Refuge."

AOGCC –
Alaska Oil and Gas Conservation Commission. The state agency regulates extraction of oil and gas on non-federal lands. It also has primary responsibility for regulation of

subsurface injection of fluids brought to the surface from oil and gas production operations or liquid hydrocarbons, which are stored underground through a permit program under the Safe Drinking Water Act (SDWA). AOGCC's responsibilities under the SDWA are split with EPA. (See SDWA.)

ARCO Alaska –
Formerly a subsidiary of Atlantic Richfield Company; operated the eastern half of the Prudhoe Bay field until April 2000, when the company's Alaska businesses were bought by Phillips Petroleum Co. ARCO Alaska was the original developer of the Alpine field near the border of the NPR-A; like other ARCO Alaska holdings, Alpine is now owned by Phillips Petroleum.

Arctic Power –
A consortium of proponents of energy development in ANWR, whose members include, among others, petroleum industry representatives, the State of Alaska, and various Native corporations.

ASRC –
Arctic Slope Regional Corporation. Established under ANCSA, a Native regional corporation for essentially all of the Alaskan North Slope. ASRC owns the subsurface rights beneath the lands within the coastal plain of ANWR owned by the Kaktovik Inupiat Corporation.

BACT –
Best Available Control Technology, required to be imposed on major sources of specified pollutants in areas subject to the Prevention of Significant Deterioration Program of the Clean Air Act. BACT requirements would apply to ANWR.

Barter Island –
A coastal island within ANWR; the site of the Native Village of Kaktovik and a DEWLine station. Currently, only occupied human habitation on the coastal plain of the Refuge.

bbl –
Barrel; barrels (of oil); 42 gallons.

BEA –
Bureau of Economic Analysis; part of the U.S. Department of Labor.

Beaufort Lagoon –
A small lagoon on the eastern edge of the 1002 area.

Beaufort Sea –
Portion of the Arctic Ocean adjacent to central and eastern Alaska (including ANWR), as well as northwestern Canada.

BLS –
Bureau of Labor Statistics; part of the U.S. Department of Labor.

BLM –
Bureau of Land Management in DOI. Among other responsibilities, BLM administers the federal mineral estate, including oil leases, on federal lands.

BMP –
Best Management Practices. In petroleum energy development, those development plans which focus on pollution prevention rather than end-of-pipe discharge limits through specification of structural and operational controls, maintenance, and inspections.

Bonus bids –
The up-front payment made by a successful bidder to the federal government for tract of federal land on which to explore, and if any energy reserves are found, to produce it. The size of this payment is the vehicle by which companies compete to obtain a federal energy lease.

BPAlaska –
Formerly a division of British Petroleum Company, it became a major North Slope operator in 1968. BPAlaska was sold to Standard Oil Co. (Ohio) in 1978. In 1987, British Petroleum Company acquired complete control of Standard Oil Co., its U.S. associate. British Petroleum Company became BP Amoco p.l.c. after 1998, and then became BP p.l.c. in May 2001, and it currently operates in the western half of the Prudhoe Bay field, as well as other parts of the North Slope, and it is vested in the Trans-Alaska Pipeline.

Brooks Range –
An east-west trending mountain range in northern Alaska, running from the Chukchi Sea eastward into northwestern Canada; north of this Range, water drains to the Arctic Ocean; southward, to the Yukon River in Central Alaska.

btu –
British Thermal Unit. The amount of heat required to raise the temperature of a pound of water one degree Fahrenheit.

CAH –
Central Arctic Herd; caribou whose range is partly in the developed areas, including Prudhoe Bay, west of the Refuge; they occupy an area about one-fifth the size of the Porcupine Caribou Herd (PCH).

CEPR –
Center for Economic and Policy Research. An economic and social welfare policy research organization, aimed at promoting debate on economic social issues through conducting research and presenting the findings of its own and others' studies. (In September 2001, CEPR reanalyzed the 1990 WEFA study of the economic impact of the possible development of ANWR.

Chandler Lake Agreement –
The 1983 land exchange agreement between DOI and ASRC, and under which the U.S. received lands in Gates of the Arctic National Park and ASRC received subsurface rights to KIC lands in ANWR in return.

Coastal Plain –
When used in lower case, the relatively flat area between the foothills of the Brooks Range and the north coast of Alaska; much of it is wetland, especially around Prudhoe Bay. When used with upper case ("Coastal Plain"), the term is used as defined pursuant to §1002 of ANILCA and excludes Native lands in the coastal area.

COE –
U.S. Army Corps of Engineers. Approves permits affecting wetlands subject to EPA guidelines.

Compatible Use –
Defined as "A proposed or existing wildlife – dependent recreational use or any other use of a National Wildlife Refuge that, based on sound professional judgment, will not materially interfere with or detract from the fulfillment of the National Wildlife Refuge System mission or the purpose(s) of the National Wildlife Refuge." (50 C.F.R. §25.12). Lands within Alaska refuges are subject to the regulations on compatibility in 50 C.F.R. §§25 and 26.

Corps –
See COE.

CWA –
Clean water Act; among other things, the CWA requires permits for oil and gas operations in the arctic that typically require the use of best management practices to protect water resources. The CWA also requires a state certification that energy development activities requiring federal permits or licenses will comply with state water quality standards.

CZMA –
Coastal Zone Management Act. Among other things, requires certification by states that projects to be located in a state's coastal zone are consistent with the state's coastal zone management program. For ANWR, this would apply to oil exploration and development on the coastal plain (ANILCA §1002).

Deadhorse –
The oldest support center for oil exploration in the Prudhoe Bay field; includes offices, depots, repair and service facilities, and housing for employees.

Denning –
The act of a wild, usually predatory animal taking to its lair or taking shelter. Often associated with bears and other animals which hibernate during the winter, and with females of the species when they are giving birth.

DEWLine –
Distant Early Warning Line. Series of stations used by U.S. and Canadian military for detection of possible national security threats from the former Soviet Union; usually a surveillance post and telecommunications relay at each station. In the case of ANWR,

one is situated on Barter Island just off the north coast of Alaska, adjacent to the village of Kaktovik.

DOI –
U.S. Department of the Interior.

Doyon, Ltd.
Regional for-profit Native corporation for central Alaska Natives (chiefly Athabascan Indian), established under ANCSA.

Economically Recoverable Oil –
Estimated amount of oil that could be feasibly extracted under the assumption of a particular level of crude oil prices. If Congress were to allow for energy development in ANWR, the price of oil would come into play in the decision to explore for and develop resources in the extreme conditions of the North Sloe. *(See technically recoverable oil and oil in place.)*

EIA –
The Energy Information Administration in DOE. Responsible for inventorying and forecasting U.S. Energy Resources.

Endicott –
Small oil field located offshore from Prudhoe Bay; contains 375,000 barrels of recoverable oil. Formerly operated by Standard Alaska Production Company; acquired as part of Standard Oil Co. (Ohio) holdings by British Petroleum Company in 1987; now belongs to BP p.l.c.

EOR –
Enhanced Oil Recovery. A technique used to increase petroleum recovery from known deposits, e.g., permeability of rocks may be increased by deliberate fracturing, using explosives or water under very high pressure; carbon dioxide gas under pressure can be used to force out more oil; and hot water or steam may be pumped underground to warm thick, viscous oils so that they flow more easily and be extracted more completely.

EPA –
Endangered Species Act; 16 U.S.C. 1531ff.

Exxon-Mobil –
A major oil company with substantial North Slope holdings, including oil fields in Prudhoe Bay

FLEIS –
Final Legislative Environmental Impact Statement; in the ANWR context, the final report published under §1002 of ANILCA on April 1987 by FWS/DOI on alternatives for preserving, managing, and/or developing the 1002 area. Also called *1002 report*.

Footprint –
The area within the outline of any structures on the surface of the land as these features might be shown on an ordinary two dimensional map. On the case of arctic energy development, there is debate over exactly what features might be counted in assessing the total size of the footprint.

FWS –
Fish and Wildlife Service in DOI. Among other things, manages federal wildlife refuges, including ANWR.

GDP --
Gross Domestic Product. Main indicator of total output in the economy used by the U.S. Department of Commerce; before 1991, GNP was used.

Gwich'in –
Athabaskan Indians, situated in east-central Alaska and neighboring areas of northwestern Canada.

Infrastructure –
Physical facilities. In oil development, these include roads, pipelines, drilling pads and structures associated with wells, pumps, facilities for handling the oil and gas, housing and offices, gravel mines, airports, docks, waste disposal facilities, support services and others.

INGAA Foundation –
A Foundation of the Interstate Natural Gas Association of America; the official name of this foundation uses the acronym. I reported original cost estimates of developing a natural gas pipeline for Alaska (the Trans-Alaska Pipeline).

Inholdings –
Non-federal lands within a federal area. For ANWR, inholdings include Native lands such as those owned by such Native corporations as the Kaktovik Inupiat Corporation and the Arctic Slope Regional Corporation.

Inupiat –
Eskimo (specifically, Inuit) people of the Alaska North Slope and bordering areas.

Jaco River –
Large north-flowing river in the eastern third of the 1002 area.

Kaktovik –
Native village (population between 200 and 300) located in ANWR on Barter Island; part of the North Slope Borough. Also the site of a U.S. DEWLine station.

Kaktovik Inupiat Corporation
Native Village Corporation of Kaktovik. (KIC)

KIC –
Kaktovik Inupiat Corporation.

Kongakut River –
River that lies between the 1002 area and the Canadian Border in the ANS frontier and flows into the Beaufort Lagoon.

Kuparuk –
Large oil field located west of Prudhoe Bay. Field formerly operated by ARCO, now by Phillips Petroleum. Also, Kuparuk Oil Industrial Center.

LNG –
Liquefied natural gas.

Milne Point –
Oil Field located northwest of Prudhoe Bay, operated by BP exploration (Alaska) Inc., a subsidiary of BP p.l.c. Drilled and operated briefly by Conoco, Inc; once shut-in because of low world oil prices, and now reopened.

MLA –
Mineral Leasing Act. Federal law that generally governs the leasing of oil and gas and certain other minerals from federal public lands and revenue sharing from these resources. However, Congress has authorized leasing some federal lands under other statutory provisions.

NAAQS –
National Ambient Air Quality Standards. Heath-based standards established by EPA for concentrations of ozone, sulfur dioxide, nitrogen oxides, particulate matter, carbon monoxide, and lead in outdoor air.

National Petroleum Reserve-Alaska (NPR-A) –
Reserve of approximately 37,000 square miles located on the North slope, west of Prudhoe Bay, and originally set aside to provide oil for federal military use. Early exploration did not reveal any potential commercial oil resources, and exploration sites were abandoned. Recently reopened to leasing with most recent lease sale held May 1999, and 130 bids totaling $105 million accepted. This name replaced the earlier "Naval Petroleum Reserve No. 4."

Native –
When capitalized, used synonymously with "Alaska Native."

Native Corporation –
Any regional, village, urban, or group corporation established under ANCSA. (See also Regional And Village Corporation.)

Native Village –
Any tribe, band, clan, group, village, community, or association in Alaska composed of Alaska Natives. (Here, also includes "Native Groups", defined in ANCSA as having less

than 25 Natives.) The Bureau of Indian Affairs in DOI recognizes over 220 such Native villages, irrespective of population.

NCAI –
National Congress of American Indians; major nationwide organization representing Indian tribes.

NEPA –
National Environmental Policy Act. Requires that certain analyses of possible environmental effects of proposed federal actions be completed. Preparation of an updated version of the FLEIS or Supplemental Environmental Impact Statement under NEPA might be necessary before energy developing in ANWR could proceed, unless Congress specified otherwise.

North Slope –
A geographic area of Alaska on the north side of the Brooks Range, exceeding 100,000 square miles (64,000,000 acres) and including foothills and the relatively flat coastal plain, where the waters drain to the Chukchi and Beaufort Seas. Reaches from roughly Point Lisburne on the Chukchi Sea across NPR-A, oil development areas, the 1002 area, and east into Canada.

North Slope Borough –
Local North Slope government established in 1972 under Alaska state law; boundaries are roughly similar to those of the North Slope itself. Equivalent to a county, it has power to tax property.

NO_x –
Nitrogen oxides, one of the principal air pollutants likely to be emitted by oil field operations in ANWR.

Ocean Dumping Act –
Title I of the Marine Protection Research and Sanctuaries Act (also known as the Ocean Dumping Act). Requires the COE to issue a permit for the disposal of dredged material at designated sites in any ocean waters including the (U.S.) territorial seas, e.g., for disposal of material dredged in the construction of channels in open seas needed to get oil/gas tankers to shore facilities.

OECD –
Organization for Economic Cooperation and Development.

OPEC –
Organization of Petroleum Exporting Countries.

Oil in place –
The amount that might be present or "in place" in a given field or area. This figure is just a starting point, since it is not possible to extract all of the oil in a field. Estimates are almost always given as a range of numbers and probabilities. (See *economically recoverable oil* and *technically recoverable oil*.)

PCH –
Porcupine (River) Caribou Herd. Herd of caribou (variable population levels – from about 120,000 to over 180,000) that winters in central Alaska and Canada and migrates to ANWR in spring and summer; in most years PCH calving is concentrated in the 1002 area; foothills, plain, and coast of 1002 area are used for feeding and insect relief. The PCH herd is estimated to be about five times as large as the Central Arctic (caribou) Herd (CAH).

Phillips Petroleum –
Major operator on North Slope (in addition to BP). Operates the eastern half of the Prudhoe Bay field as well as other North Slope fields (e.g., Alpine).

PLAs –
Project labor agreements. Agreements between a project owner or main contractor and the union(s) representing the craft workers for a particular project that establish the terms and conditions of work that will apply

PLO –
Public Land Order. An administrative action relating to public lands taken by the Secretary of the Interior. PLO 2214 withdrew federal lands in the territory of Alaska to create the original Arctic National Wildlife *Range*. Although it withdrew the lands from operation of the mining laws, it did not withdraw the lands from mineral leasing.

Prospect –
In petroleum exploration, a site which is believed to have the potential for containing a petroleum accumulation of sufficient size to be of commercial interest.

Prudhoe Bay –
Bay on north coast of Alaska, between the 1002 area and the NPR-A. Also, the adjacent on-shore site of the largest oil field ever found in the U.S. Originally estimated to contain 9.6 billion bbl of proven reserves, then revised upward to 13 billion bbl; an estimated 3 billion bbl of reserves are through to remain. This field is operated by Phillips Petroleum and BP. (The term often is used loosely to refer to all developed areas on the North Slope.)

PSD –
Prevention of Significant Deterioration: a regulatory program established by the Clean Air Act to protect air quality in areas that meet National Ambient Air Quality Standards.

RCRA –
Resource Conservation and Recovery Act. Governs the generation, storage, transportation and disposal of hazardous wastes; in Alaska the program is carried out by the U.S. EPA.

Regional Corporations –
Alaska Native Regional Corporation established under ANCSA and the laws of the State of Alaska. After 1971, the DOI Secretary divided Alaska into 12 geographic regions, as

defined in §1606 of ANCSA, with each region composed as far as practicable of Natives having a common heritage and sharing common interests.

Reinjection –
Process by which most of the natural gas produced so far on the North Slope has been put back into the ground by oil field operators to maintain pressure in the oil reservoir zones.

Rent –
The annual payment made by a lessee to the federal government for the right to a tract obtained for energy production under the Mineral Leasing Act of 1920. Rates are $1.50 per acre per year for the first 5 years and $2.00 per acre per year thereafter.

Riparian –
Areas alongside streams and rivers; in the 1002 area these are often vegetated with low brush that is attractive habitat to a number of species. Frequently serve as corridors for wildlife movement.

Rolligon –
Large vehicles with enormous soft tires that spread their weight evenly across the surface.

Royalty –
A payment by a lessee to the federal government under the Mineral Leasing Act of 1920 for oil or gas produced on federal land. Currently, the royalty rate is set at 12.5%.

Sadlerochit Spring –
A "special area' in the southernmost part of the 1002 area. During the section 1002 study, 4,000 acres around the spring were closed to exploration. The spring maintains a flow of water at 50°-58°F year-round, and keeps the river open for nearly 5 miles downstream, even in winter. It represents the extreme northern range of some plants and birds, and provides wintering habitat for fish; muskoxen frequent the area.

SDWA –
Safe Drinking Water Act. Manages a permit program to protect underground sources of drinking water (USDWs) from contamination by injection through wells. In Alaska, U.S. EPA has primary responsibility to issue permits authorizing subsurface injection of nonhazardous industrial wastes associated with oil exploration and development. The Alaska Oil and Gas Conservation Commission shares regulatory authority over underground injection wells. (See AOGCC).

SEISS
Supplemental Environmental Impact Statement; in a declaratory judgment action in 1991, a judge held that DOI should have prepared a SEIS at that time to encompass new information about the 1002 area in connection with the Department's recommendation that Congress legislate to permit development.

Special Area –

Areas of natural beauty or prolific wildlife areas, habitats, and ecosystems in the 1002 area. Five special areas were specifically named in the FLEIS as potential set-asides; these total more than 52,000 acres.

TAGS –

TransAlaska Gas System. Proposed subsurface pipeline delivery system to supply natural gas to LNG processing facilities on the North coast of Alaska.

TAPS –

TransAlaska Pipeline System. Transports oil Prudhoe Bay to Valdez, a port on Alaska's south coast. The pipeline was completed and opened in 1977.

tcf –

Trillions of cubic feet, e.g., of natural gas.

Technically recoverable oil –

Oil which has been successfully prospected and may be extracted given the scientific and technological know how, resources, infrastructure, etc.; however, its extraction is limited by such factors as the market price of oil, which is related to its supply and demand. (See *economically recoverable oil and oil in place.)*

Trans-Alaska Pipeline Authorization Act –

Federal law which authorized construction of TAPS and by granting a right of way over federal lands (P.L. 93-153, 87 stat. 584, 43 U.S.C. 1651 et seq.). In addition, federal law had generally prohibited the export of oil transported through pipelines which had been granted a right of way over federal lands (30 U.S.C. §185(u)). However, an amendment enacted in 1996 permits oil shipped through the pipeline to be exported though only under certain very restrictive conditions (30 U.S.C. §185(s)).

Tundra –

Major ecological community of the arctic and high elevation alpine areas, characterized by usually waterlogged soil sitting on permafrost, and by low growing plants such as mosses, lichens, and dwarf forms of wood plants.

USGS –

U.S. Geological Survey. A DOI agency that, among other things, conducts mineral and energy resource assessments of the U.S. and the world; advises on prospecting and extraction of petroleum and mineral resources on federal lands; evaluates national water resources.

Village Corporation –

Alaska Native Village Corporation organized under ANCSA and the laws of the State of Alaska as a business corporation (for profit or non-profit) to hold, invest, and/or distribute lands, property, funds, and other rights and assets on behalf of a Native village (as defined in ANCSA).

WEFA Group, The –
Economic consulting group, now merged with "DRI" (not an acronym), forming DRI-WEFA. In 1990, published a study of the economic impact of the possible development of ANWR (See also CEPR.)

Wellhead Price –
The price paid a producer in the producing field. It is often calculated based on the delivered or first sale price, less the cost of associated transport. Transport tariffs are generally related to pipeline length. In the case of North Slope oil (or gas) – where there pipeline cost is (or would be) substantial, the implied price at the wellhead would be commensurately low.

Chapter 2

ARCTIC NATIONAL WILDLIFE REFUGE: LEGISLATIVE ISSUES

M. Lynne Corn, Bernard A. Gelb and Pamela Baldwin

MOST RECENT DEVELOPMENTS

On February 15, 2002, the Senate began floor consideration of S. 517, to which Senator Daschle offered S. Amdt.2917, an omnibus energy bill. No development language was in the amendment, but such an amendment to the bill is widely expected when the Senate resumes work on the measure in March 2002. Cloture votes are expected. On December 3, 2002, the Senate failed to invoke cloture on a motion by Senator Lott to amend H.R. 10 (yeas 1, nays 92, Roll Call no. 344). The Lott motion included, among a number of provisions, language to open ANWR development. ANWR provisions were among several features that were cited in opposition to the amendment. (See discussion below.) The national security threat, budgetary considerations, and maintenance of the investment in the Alaskan oil infrastructure are key factors in the renewal interest in energy development in short term in countering calls for new production. Action on an energy bill is scheduled in the Senate for mid-February.

BACKGROUND AND ANALYSIS

The Arctic National Wildlife Refuge (ANWR) consists of 19 million acres in northeast Alaska. It is administered by the Fish and Wildlife Service (FWS) in the Department of the Interior (DOI). Its 1.5 million acre coastal plain is currently viewed as one of the most likely U.S. onshore oil and gas prospects. Together, the fields on this federal land could hold as much economically recoverable oil as the giant field at Prudhoe Bay, found in 1967 on the state-owned portion of the coastal plain west of ANWR, now estimated to have held 11-13 billion barrels.

At the same time, the Refuge, and especially the coastal plain, is home to a wide variety of plans and animals. The presence of caribou, polar bears, grizzly bears, wolves, migratory birds, and many other species in a nearly undisturbed state has led some to call the area

"America's Serengeti." The Refuge and two neighboring parks in Canada have been proposed for an international park, and several species found in the area (including polar bears, caribou, migratory birds, and whales) are economic and geological factors that have triggered new interest in development, followed by the philosophical, biological, and environment quality factors that have triggered opposition to it.

The conflict between high oil potential and nearly pristine nature creates a dilemma; should Congress open the area for oil and gas development or should the area's ecosystem be given permanent protection from development? What factors should determine whether to open the area? If the area is opened, how can damages be avoided, minimized, or mitigated? To what extent should Congress legislate special management of the area (if it is developed) and to what extend should Congress legislate special management of the area (if it is developed) and to what extent should federal agencies be allowed to manage the area under existing law?

HISTORY OF THE REFUGE

The energy and biological resources of northern Alaska have raised controversy for decades, from legislation in the 1970s, to a 1989 oil spill, to more recent efforts to use ANWR resources to address energy needs or to help balance the federal budget. In November 1957, an application for the withdrawal of lands in northeastern Alaska to create an "Arctic National Wildlife Range" was filed. The first group actually to propose to Congress that the area become a national wildlife range, in recognition of the many game species found in the area, was the Tanana Valley (Alaska) Sportsmen's Association in 1959. On December 6, 1960, after statehood, the Secretary of the Interior issued Public Land Order 2214 reserving the area as the "Arctic National Wildlife Range."

In 1971, Congress enacted the Alaska Native Claims Settlement Act (ANCSA) TO RESOLVE ALL Native aboriginal land claims against the United States. ANCSA provided for monetary payments and also created Village Corporations that received the surface estate to approximately 22 million acres of lands in Alaska. Village selection rights included the right to choose the surface estate in a certain amount of lands within the National Wildlife Refuge System Under §22(g) of ANCSA, the chosen lands were to remain subject to the laws and regulations governing use and development of the particular Refuge. Kaktovik Inupiat Corporation (KIC, the local corporation) received rights to three townships along the coast of ANWR. ANCSA also created Regional Corporations, which could select subsurface rights to some lands and full title to others. Subsurface rights in National Wildlife Refuges were not available, but in-lieu selections to substitute for such lands were provided.

In 1980, Congress enacted the Alaska National Interest Lands Conservation Act (ANILCA, P.L. 96-487, 94 Stat. 2371), which included several sections about ANWR. The Arctic Range was renamed the Arctic National Wildlife Refuge, and was expanded, mostly southward and westward, to include an additional 9.2 million acres. Section 702(3) of ANILCA designated much of the original Refuge as a wilderness area, but not the coastal plain.[1] Instead, Congress postponed decisions on the development or further protection of the coastal plain. Section 1002 of ANILCA directed a study of the "coastal plain" (which therefore is often referred to as the "1002 area") and its resources be completed within 5 years and 9 months of enactment. The resulting 1987 report was called the *1002 report* or the Final Legislative Environmental Impact Statement (FLEIS). ANILCA defined the "coastal plain" as the lands on a specified map – language that was interpreted as excluding most Native lands, even though these lands are *geographically* part of the coastal plain.

Section 1003 of ANILCA prohibited oil and gas development in the entire Refuge, or "leasing or other development leading to production of oil and gas from the range" unless authorized by an Act of Congress.

In recent years, Congress attempted to authorize the opening of ANWR in the FY1996 reconciliation bill (H.R. 2491, §§5312-5344), but the measure was vetoed. President Clinton cited the ANWR sections as one of his reasons for vetoing the measure.

While bills were introduced, the ANWR issue was not debated in the 105th Congress. In the 106th Congress, bills to designate the 1002 area of the Refuge as wilderness and others to open the Refuge to energy development were introduced. Assumptions about ANWR revenues were included in the FY2001 budget resolution (S.Con.Res. 101) as reported by the Senate Budget Committee on March 31, 2000. An amendment to remove the language was tabled. However, conferees rejected the language. The conference report on H.Con.Res. 290 did not contain this assumption, and the report was passed by both Houses on April 13. S.2557 was introduced May 16, 2000; it included a title to open the Refuge to development.

Only three recorded votes relating directly to ANWR development occurred from the 101st to the 106th Congress. All were in the Senate:

- In the 104th Congress, on May 25, 1995, there was a motion to table an amendment that would have stripped ANWR development titles from the Senate version of H.R. 2491. The motion passed (Roll Call #190).
- In the same Congress, on October 27, 1995 there was another motion to table a similar amendment to H.R. 2491. This motion also passed (Roll Call #525).
- In the 106th Congress, the vote to table an amendment to strip ANWR revenue assumptions from the budget resolution (S.Con.Res. 101; see above) was passed (April 6, 2000, Roll Call #58).

Legislation in the 107th Congress

One energy bill, H.R. 4, containing ANWR development provisions passed the House on August 2, 2002. Title V, Division F, was the text of H.R. 2436 (H.Rept. 107-160, Part I; yeas 240, nays 189; Roll Call No. 320). The measure would open ANWR to exploration and development. The previous day, an amendment by Representative Sununu to limit specified surface development to 2,000 acres was passed (yeas 228, nays 201; Roll Call No. 316). Representatives Markey and Johnson (CT) offered an amendment to strike the title; this was defeated (yeas 206, nays 223; Roll Call No. 316).

In the Senate, Title V of S. 388 would open the Refuge as well; its provisions are similar to those of H.R. 4, but not identical. The bill has not been voted out of the Committee on Energy and Natural Resources. However, the vehicle for Senate floor consideration is S. 517,

---

[1] Newer portions of the Refuge were not included in the wilderness system.

which concerns energy technology development. On February 15, 2002, Senator Daschle offered an amendment (S.Amdt. 2917), an omnibus energy bill. It did not contain provisions to develop the Refuge, but such an amendment is widely expected to be offered, probably late in the debate, in March 2002. Press reports indicate that the Administration is considering support for an amendment to open the westernmost portion of the 1002 area to development, but no specific language has been unveiled at this point.

ANWR development proponents support speedy Senate consideration of a bill to open the Refuge. In the first session, Senator Lott (on behalf of himself and Senators Murkowski and Brownback) offered an amendment (No. 2171) to an amendment on pension reform (No. 2170) to H.R. 10, a bill also on pension reform. Their amendment included, among other energy provisions, the ANWR development title in H.R. 4, as passed by the House (discussed above). Their amendment also included provisions prohibiting cloning of human tissue. A cloture motion was filed on the Lott amendment, and the Senate failed to invoke cloture (1-94, Roll Call No. 344) on December 3, 2001. Instead, the Senate voted the same day in favor of invoking cloture on the underlying amendment (No. 2170), by a vote of 81-15 (Roll Call No. 345). Because cloture was invoked on the underlying amendment, Senate rules required that subsequent and pending amendments to it be germane. The Senate's presiding officer subsequently sustained a point of order against the Lott amendment, which was still pending, on the grounds that it was not germane to the underlying amendment, and thus the amendment fell.

Finally, H.R. 770 and S. 411 would designate the 1002 area as wilderness, but no action has been taken on either bill. As the second session opens, a key obstacle to Senate passage of ANWR development legislation, at least as an amendment to an omnibus energy bill, is the probability of a filibuster. The issues most commonly arising in the current legislative debate are described below under *Major Legislative Issues in the 107th Congress*, along with the treatment of these issues by these four bills (H.R. 4, S. 388, S. 411, and H.R. 770).

THE ENERGY RESOURCE

Parts of Alaska's North Slope (ANS) coastal plain have proved abundant in oil and gas reserves, and its geology holds promise for ANWR. The oil-bearing strata extend eastward from structures in the National Petroleum Reserve-Alaska past the Prudhoe Bay field, and may continue into and through ANWR's 1002 area.

Oil

Estimates of ANWR oil potential, both old and new, depend upon limited data and numerous assumptions about geology and economics. The most recent government study of oil and natural gas prospects in ANWR, completed in 1998 by the U.S. Geological Survey (USGS),[3] found that there is an excellent chance (95%) that at least 11.6 billion barrels of oil are present on federal lands in the 1002 area. There also is a small chance (5%) that 31.5

---

[3] U.S. Dept. of the Interior, Geological Survey. *The Oil and Gas Potential of the Arctic National Wildlife Refuge 1002 Area, Alaska.* U.S.G.S. Open File Report 98-34. (Washington, DC, 1999). Summary and Table EA4.

billion barrels or more are present. USGS estimates there is an excellent chance (95%) that 4.3 billion barrels or more are technically recoverable (costs not considered); and there is a small change (5) that 11.8 billion barrels or more are technically recoverable. But the proportion that would be economically recoverable depends upon the price of oil. The USGS estimated that, at $24/barrel (in 1996 dollars), there is a 95% chance that 2.0 billion barrels or more could be *economically* recovered and a 5% chance of 9.4 billion barrels or more.

Oil prices, geologic characteristics such as permeability and porosity, cash flow, and any transportation constraints, would be among the most important factors affecting the development rates and production levels that would be associated with given volumes of oil resources. The Energy Information Administration estimated that at a faster development rate, production would peak 15-20 years after the start of development, with maximum daily production rates of roughly 0.00015 (0.015%) of the resource. Production associated with the slower rate would peak about 25 years after the start of development at a daily rate equal to about 0.000105 (0.0105%) of the resource. Peak production associated with a technically recoverable resource of 5.0 billion barrels (bbls) at the faster development rate would be 750,000 bbls per day. U.S. petroleum consumption is about 19 million bbls per day.

Natural Gas

Substantial quantities of natural gas are estimated to be in the 1002 area as well. However, as with the abundant natural gas discovered at Prudhoe Bay, there is currently now way to deliver this gas to market. There has been considerable recent interest in construction of a pipeline to transport natural gas directly to North American markets and/or a warm-water port for shipment in tankers. Either option could enhance the commercial prospects of the 1002 area – and the rest of the ANS. The prospect of being able to sell its abundant gas would also enhance Prudhoe Bay economics – oil as well as gas. Until recently, estimated costs of transporting the gas precluded serious consideration of pipeline construction.

Advanced Technologies

As development has proceeded since the discovery of Prudhoe Bay, North Slope oil field operators have developed less environmentally intrusive ways to develop arctic oil, primarily through innovations in technology.

Field exploration has benefited from new seismic technology. Advanced analytical methods generate high-resolution images of geologic structures and resolve hydrocarbon accumulations. And improved ice-based transportation infrastructure serves remote areas during exploration drilling on newly developed insulated ice pads. More powerful computers allow the manipulation of vastly more data, yielding more precise well locations and, consequently, reduce the number of wells needed to find hydrocarbon accumulations.

Recent advances in drilling also lessen the footprint of petroleum operations. New drilling bits and fluids and advanced forms of drilling – such as extended reach, horizontal and "designer" wells – permit drilling to reach laterally far beyond a drill platform, with the current record being seven miles at one site in China. Other advances reduce the space needed for a drilling rig, reduce equipment volume and weight, and lessen the generation of drilling waste. Modules that perform many functions also make production facilities more compact. Production drilling techniques using slim-hole technology such as coiled tubing and multilateral drilling also decrease the footprint, reduce waste, and increase recovery of hydrocarbons per well.

Proponents of opening ANWR note that these technologies could mitigate the environmental impact of petroleum operations, but no eliminate it. Opponents maintain that a facility of any size would still be an industrial site and change the character of the Refuge. They argue that whether environmental impacts would be minimized would depend in part on the wording of legislation, and that there still would be the need for gravel and the scarce water resources of the 1002 area; and permanent roads, port facilities, and airstrips would follow the initial roadless construction. They also note that spills may occur.

THE BIOLOGICAL RESOURCES

The FLEIS rated the Refuge's resources highly: "The Arctic Refuge is the only conservation system unit that protects, in an undisturbed condition, a complete spectrum of the arctic ecosystems in North America" (p. 46). It also said "The 1002 area is the most biologically productive part of the Arctic Refuge for wildlife and is the center of wildlife activity" (p. 46). The biological value of the 1002 area rests on the very intense productivity in the short arctic summer; many species arrive or awake from dormancy to take advantage of this richness, and leave or become dormant during the remainder of the year. Caribou have long been the center of the debate over the biological impacts of Refuge development, but other species have also been at issue. Among the other species most frequently mentioned are polar bears, musk oxen, and the 135 species of migratory birds that breed or feed there.

The species which has drawn the most attention in this debate is the caribou. The Porcupine Caribou Hert (PCH) calves in or near the 1002 area in most years [http://www.r7.fws.gov/nwr/arctic/pchmaps.html], and winters south of the Brooks Range in Alaska or Canada; it is the subject of a 1987 executive Agreement Between the United States and Canada on the Conservation of the Porcupine Caribou Herd. The herd is currently estimated at 130,000, but caribou population numbers fluctuate markedly. In both countries it is an important food source to Native people and others – especially since other meat is either expensive or unavailable. Some scientists cite studies that show a reduction in density of cows with calves near roads and developed areas around Kuparuk (Nellemann and Cameron, 1998). They fear that development and production in the 1002 area could cause cows to calve in less desirable locations or prevent the herd's access to sites where they can escape from the voracious insects common in early summer.

Based on the Prudhoe Bay experience, it appears that individual animals, especially adult males, habituate to the disturbance, and sometimes seek out gravel pads and roads, where insect attacks may be less severe. However, cows with young calves appear to be more sensitive, and during the first few weeks after calving, avoid roads and other human disturbance for distances of a mile or more. The calving area of ANWR is more confined than that of Prudhoe Bay and vicinity, and nearby areas of similar habitat may not be available.

When cows are slowed by late thaws or heavy snows, they may not reach the 1002 area. This displacement, though natural, can have severe consequences. For example, in 2000, when heavy snowfall delayed cows in reaching the 1002 area before calving, the June calf survival rate and the July calf to cow ratio were the lowest ever recorded. This reduced calving success served to highlight the importance of the preferred area. In the narrow coastal plain of the 1002 area, any cows displaced southward would calve in or nearer the Brooks Range, where bears, golden eagles, and wolves (all calf predators) are more abundant than on the plain.

Effects on polar bear dens in the Refuge have been an issue. Modern winter exploration technology, while an improvement on environmental impact over previous technologies in many respects, would be more likely to affect polar bears' winter dens, or conversely, the mitigation required to protect bear dens could increase the cost of exploration, development and product. Polar bears are the subject of the international Agreement on the Conservation of Polar Bears, to which the United States is a party. Musk oxen, snow geese, and other species have also featured in the ANWR debate.

For opponents of development, the central issue is whether the area should be maintained as an intact ecosystem – off limits to development – not whether development can be accomplished in an environmentally sound manner. In terms that emphasize deeply held values, supporters of wilderness designation argue that few places as untrammeled as the 1002 area remain on the planet, and fewer still on the same magnificent scale. Any but the most transitory intrusions (e.g., visits for recreation, hunting, fishing, subsistence use, research, etc.) Would, in their view damage the "sense of wonder" they see the area as instilling. The mere knowledge that a pristine place exists, whether one ever visits it, can be important to those who view the debate in this light.

MAJOR LEGISLATIVE ISSUES IN THE 107TH CONGRESS

The primary issue in the 107th Congress is whether to approve energy development in the Arctic National Wildlife Refuge (ANWR) in northeastern Alaska, and if so, under what restrictions, or whether to continue to prohibit energy development in order to protect the area's biological resource and wilderness values. Some of the issues that have been raised most frequently in the current ANWR debate are described briefly below. In addition to the issue of whether development should be permitted at all, key aspects of the current debate include specifications that might be provided in legislation, including the physical size, or footprint, of development; the activities that might be permitted on Native lands; the disposition of revenues; labor issues; oil export restrictions; compliance with the National Environmental Policy Act, and other matters. (References below to the "Secretary" refer to the Secretary of the Interior, unless stated otherwise.)

Environmental Direction

Congress could choose to leave environmental matters to administrative agencies under existing laws. Alternatively, Congress could impose a higher standard of environmental protection because the area is in a national wildlife refuge or because of the fragility of the arctic environment, or it could legislate a lower standard to facilitate development. The degree of discretion given to the administering agency could also affect the stringency of environmental protection. For example, Congress could include provisions requiring use of "the best available technology" or "the best commercially available technology" or similar general standards; alternatively it could limit judicial review of environmental standards. One issue would be the use of gravel and water resources essential for oil exploration and development. Other legislative issues include limitations on miles of roads or other surface occupancy; the adequacy of existing pollution standards; prevention and treatment of spills; the adequacy of current environmental requirements; and aircraft overflights, among other things.

H.R. 4 (§6507(a)) requires the Secretary to administer the leasing program so as to "result in no significant adverse effect on fish and wildlife, their habitat, subsistence resources, and the environment, ...including.... requiring the application of the best commercially available technology...." S. 388 (§503(a)) both also require that this program be done "in a manner that ensures the receipt of fair market value by the public for the mineral resources to be leased." It is unclear how the two goals of environmental protection and of fair market value relate to each other (e.g., if environmental restrictions might make some fields uneconomic). H.R. 4 (§6506(a)(3) and (95)) and S.388 (§508(15) and (17)) require lessees to be responsible and liable for reclamation of lands within the Coastal Plain to support pre-leasing uses or to a higher use approved by the Secretary. There are requirements for mitigation (§6506(b)),development of regulations and other measures to protect the environment (§6506(c) and (d)). These include prohibitions on public access to service roads and other transportation restrictions. S. 388 (§509) requires bonding or other financial sureties to ensure reclamation of lands and waters; the bonds are to continue until the Secretary determines specified requirements have been met. Other provisions may also affect environmental protection. H.R. 770 and S. 411 have no such environmental provisions and would designate the area as wilderness, as discussed below.

The Size of the Footprint

H.R. 4 (§6507(d)(7)) and S. 388 (§508(14)) both provide for consolidation of leasing operations; among other things, consolidation would tend to reduce environmental impacts of development. H.R. 4 (§6507(a)(3)) would further require, "consistent with the provisions of §6503" (which include ensuring receipt of fair market value), that the Secretary administer the leasing program to "ensure that the maximum amount of surface acreage covered by production and support facilities, including airstrips and any areas covered by gravel berms or piers for the support of pipelines, does not exceed 2,000 acres on the Coastal Plain." This floor amendment was passed on August 1, 2001 (yeas 228, nays 201; Roll Call No. 316). The terms used have not been defined in the bill (nor discussed in the committee report), and therefore the full set of structures on Native lands would be included under this provision). Floor debate focused on the extent to which the facilities covered in the amendment would be widely distributed around the Refuge. In this light, it is noteworthy that one single compact facility of 2,000 acres (3.1 square miles) would not permit full development of the 1002 area, since current technology under optimum circumstances permits directional drilling at most 7 miles from the wellhead. The result would be that at most about 11% of the Coastal Plain could be developed. Instead, full development of the 1002 area would require that facilities (even if limited to 2,000 acres total) be more widely dispersed around the Coastal Plain. Also, the acreage limitation appears not to apply to Native lands.

Native Lands

The Alaska Native Claims Settlement Act (ANCSA) of 1971 resolved aboriginal claims against the United States by (among other things) creating Village Corporations that could select lands to which they held the surface estate, and Regional Corporations that could select surface and subsurface rights as well. The surface lands (approximately three townships) selected by Kaktovik Inupiat Village (KIC) are along the coastal plain of ANWR (but were administratively excluded from being considered as within the "1002 Coastal Plain"). These lands and a fourth township that is within the defined Coastal Plain are all within the Refuge and subject to regulations of the Refuge. The Arctic Slope Regional Corporation (ASRC) obtained subsurface rights beneath the KIC lands pursuant to a 1983 land exchange agreement. In addition, there are currently more than 100,00 acres of conveyed and individually owned Native allotments in the area of the Refuge that are not subject to Refuge regulations.

Both H.R. 4 and S. 388 would repeal the ANILCA prohibition on oil and gas development. Once oil and gas development is authorized for the federal lands in the Refuge, development can occur on the more than 100,000 acres of Native lands, arguably free of any acreage limitation applying to development on the federal lands. The extent to which the Native lands could be regulated to protect the environment is uncertain, given the status of allotments and some of the language in the 1983 Agreement with ASRC.

Revenue Disposition

Another issue that has arisen during debates over leasing in the ANWR is that of disposition of possible revenues – whether Congress may validly provide for a disposition of revenues formula other than the 90/10 percent split mentioned in the Alaska Statehood Act. A court in *Alaska v. United States* (35 Fed. Cl. 685, 701 (1996) seems to have indicated that the language in the Statehood Act means that Alaska is to be treated like other states under the Mineral Leasing Act (MLA), which contains (basically) a 90/10 split. However, Congress can establish a non-MLA leasing regimen -- for example, the separate leasing arrangements that govern the National Petroleum Reserve-Alaska – where the revenue sharing formula is 50/50.

Section 514 of S. 388 would provide that Alaska receive the same share as under the NPR-Alaska statute (presumably 50%). Other parts of § 514 would direct that all revenues received by the federal government as bonus bids go into a special fund known as the Renewable Energy Research and Development Fund. It is not clear whether the bonus bid revenues go into this Fund before or after the state share is taken out, or how the amount received as bonus bids is to be earmarked during the process.

Several sections of H.R. 4 relate to revenues. Section 6512 would provide that 50% of adjusted revenues be paid to Alaska. Then 50% of revenues from bonus payments go into a Renewable Energy Technology Investment Fund; and 50% from rents and royalties go into a Royalties Conservation Fund. It is not clear whether the basis for the shared revenues is to be gross or net receipts. More fundamentally, under §6503(a), the Secretary is to establish and implement a leasing program under the *Mineral Leasing Act*, yet §6512 directs a revenue sharing program different from that in the MLA. Establishing a leasing program under the MLA, yet providing for a different revenue disposition may again raise validity questions. If the alternative disposition were struck down and the revenue provisions were determined to be severable, it is possible that Alaska could receive 90% of the revenues from ANWR.

Project Labor Agreements

A recurring issue in federal and federally funded projects is whether project owners or contractors effectively should be required, by "agreement," to use union workers. Project labor agreements (PLAs) are agreements between a project owner or main contractor and the union(s) representing the craft workers for a particular project that establish the terms and conditions of work that will apply for the particular project. The agreement may also specify a source (such as a union hiring hall) to supply the craft workers for the project. Typically, the agreement is binding on all contractors and subcontractors working on the project, and specifies wage rates and benefits, discussed procedures for resolving labor and jurisdictional disputes, and includes a no-strike clause. Proponents argue that PLAs ensure a reliable, efficient labor source and help keep costs down. Opponents contend that PLAs inflate project costs and decrease competition. There is little independent information and data to sort out these conflicting assertions and demonstrate whether PLAs contribute to lower or higher project costs. Construction and other unions and their supporters strongly favor PLAs because they believe that PLAs help ensure access for union members to federal and federally funded projects. Non-union firms and their supporters believe that PLAs unfairly restrict their access to federal and federally funded projects.

One of the lease conditions of § 508 of S. 388 requires project labor agreements "to the extent feasible that will ensure productivity and consistency recognizing a national interest in both labor stability and the ability of construction labor and management to meet the particular needs of and conditions of projects to be developed..." H.R. 4, § 6506 is more specific: the Secretary is directed to require lessees "to negotiate to obtain a project labor agreement." The Secretary would do so "recognizing the Government's proprietary interest in labor stability and the ability of construction labor and management to meet the particular needs and conditions of projects to be developed..."

Oil Export Restrictions

Export of North Slope oil in general, and any ANWR oil in particular, has been an issue, beginning at leans with the authorization of the TransAlaska Pipeline and continuing into the current ANWR debate. Much of the pipeline's route is on federal lands and the Mineral

Leasing Act of 1920 prohibits export of oil transported through pipelines granted rights-of-way over federal lands (16 U.S.C. 185(u)). The Trans-Alaska Pipeline Authorization Act (P.L. 93-153, 87 Stat. 584, 43 U.S.C. 1651 *et seq.*), signed November 16, 1973, specified that oil shipped through it could be exported only under very restrictive conditions. Subsequent legislation strengthened the export restrictions further.[4] Exports of North Slope oil became effectively banned. Oil began to be shipped through the pipeline in increasing amounts as North Slope oilfield development grew. With exports effectively banned, much of North Slope oil went to West Coast destinations; the rest was shipped to the Gulf Coast via the Panama Canal or overland across the isthmus. In the early and mid-1990s, the combination of Californian and federal offshore production, North Slope oil, and imports resulted in such large quantities relative to demand that crude oil prices in California fell below those elsewhere in the United States, eliciting complaints from Californian and North Slope producers. By 1995, three or four year of low world oil prices and relative calm in the Mideast had reduced concern about petroleum.

However, market forces eventually created pressure to change the law. On November 28, 1995, P.L. 104-58 (109 Stat. 557) was enacted, Title II of which amended the Mineral Leasing Act to provide that oil transported through the Pipeline may be exported unless the President finds, after considering stated criteria, that is *not* in the national interest. The President may impose terms and conditions; and authority to export may be modified or revoked. Beginning with 36,000 bbl/d in 1996, ANS exports rose to a peak of 74,000 bbl/d in 1999, representing 7% of North Slope production. ANS oil exports ceased voluntarily in May 2000.

H.R. 4, § 6506 (a)(8) would require the prohibition of the export of oil produced under a lease in the 1002 Area as a condition of a lease; S. 388 leaves current law in place.

NEPA Compliance

The National Environmental Policy Act (NEPA) requires the preparation of an environmental impact statement (EIS) to examine the effects of major federal actions on the environment. These last full EIS examining the effects of leasing development in ANWR was completed in 1987 and some observers assert that a new EIS is needed to support development now. Both bills address the issue.

Section 505 of S. 388 states that the Congress finds the 1987 EIS adequate to satisfy the legal and procedural requirements of NEPA with respect to the promulgation of regulations for the ANWR leasing program, the first lease sales, and grants of rights of way. The bill language does not prohibit completion of studies; it eliminates the legal requirement to do so with respect to these actions. Section 503(c) directs the Secretary to impose terms and conditions on leases to ensure that oil exploration and development in the 1002 area will result in no significant adverse effect on fish and wildlife, etc. These terms and conditions may be difficult to develop without current scientific information, which arguably may be developed with typical NEPA documents.

---

[4] The Energy Policy and Conservation Act of 1975 (P.L. 94-163), the 1977 amendments to the Export Administration Act (P.L. 95-52 and P.L. 95-223), and the Export Administration Act of 1979 (P.L. 96-72), which replaced the Export Administration Act of 1969.

Section 6503(c) of H.R. 4 deems the 1987 EIS adequate with respect to actions by the Secretary to develop leasing regulations, yet requires the Secretary to prepare an EIS with respect to other actions, some of which might usually require only a (shorter) "environmental assessment." Consideration of alternatives is to be limited to two choices, a preferred option and a "single leasing alternative." (Generally, an EIS analyzes several alternatives, including a "no action" alternative.)

Compatibility with Refuge Purposes

Under current law for the management of national wildlife refuges (16 U.S.C. § 668dd), an activity may be allowed in a refuge only if it is compatible with the purposes of the particular Refuge and with those of the Refuge System as a whole. Both §503(c) of S. 388 and §6503(c) of H.R. 4 state that the oil and gas leasing program and activities in the coastal plain are deemed to be compatible with the purposes for which the ANWR was established and that no further findings or decisions are required to implement this determination. This language appears to answer the compatibility question and to eliminate the usual compatibility determination processes. The general statement that leasing "activities" are compatible arguably encompasses necessary support activities such as construction and operation of port facilities, staging areas, personnel centers, etc.

Judicial Review

The current bills contemplate prompt action to put a leasing program in place. Toward that end, both S. 388 and H.R. 4 have sections on expedited judicial review, which are alike in several respects. Both require that judicial review be sought within 90 days from the date of the action being challenged or the date the complainant knew or reasonably should have known of the grounds for the complaint. Section 6508(a)(1) and (a)(2) of H.R. 4 appear to contradict each other as to where suits are to be filed and it is possible part of a sentence may be omitted. Section 511 of S. 388 provides for suits generally to be filed in any appropriate district court of the United States except that a complaint seeking review of an action of the Secretary in promulgating regulations may only be filed in the United States Court of Appeals for the District of Columbia (i.e., skipping district court).

H.R. 4 (§ 6508(a)(3)) would also limit the scope of review by stating that review of a Secretarial decision, including environmental analyses, shall be limited to whether the Secretary complies with the terms of Division F of H.R. 4, be based on the administrative record, and that the Secretary's analysis of environmental effects is "presumed to be correct unless shown otherwise by clear and convincing evidence to the contrary." This standard in this context arguably would make overturning a decision more difficult.

Special Areas

Some have raised the possibility of setting aside certain special areas described in the FLEIS for their ecological or cultural values. This could be done either by designating the areas specifically in legislation, or by authorizing the Secretary to set aside areas to be selected after enactment. Development of such areas could be forbidden and/or surface occupancy could be limited. H.R. 4 (§ 6503(e)) allows the Secretary to set aside up to 45,000 acres of special areas, and names one specific area to be included in which leases, if permitted, would forbid surface occupancy. S. 388 (§ 503(f)) has similar provisions, but names no specific areas. The FLEIS identified four special areas, which together total more than 52,000 acres, so the Secretary would be required to select among these areas or any others that may seem significant. H.R. 770 and S. 411 would designate the entire 1002 area as wilderness.

Non-Development Options

Several options would either postpone or forbid development, unless Congress were later to change the law. These options are allowing exploration only, designating the 1002 area as wilderness, and taking no action.

Exploration Only

Some have argued that the 1002 area should be opened to exploration first, before a decision is made on whether to proceed to leasing. Those with this view hold that with greater certainty about the presence or absence of energy resources, a better decision could be made about whether to open the coastal plain for full leasing. This idea has had relatively little support over the years. For those opposed to energy development, the reasons are fairly clear if exploration results in no or insufficient economic discoveries, any damage from exploration would remain. If there were economic discoveries, support for further development might be unstoppable. Those who support development see unacceptable risks in such a proposal. First, who would be charged with carrying out exploration, who would pay for it, and to whom would the results be available? Second, if no economic discoveries are made, would that be because the "best" places (in the eyes of whatever observer) were not examined? Third, might any small discoveries become economic in the future? Fourth, if discoveries did occur, could industry still be foreclosed from development, or might sparse but promising data elevate bidding to unreasonable levels? Fifth, if exploration is authorized, what provisions should pertain to Native lands? In short, various advocates see insufficient gain from such a proposal. While an exploration bill has been mentioned in the past, none has been introduced in the 107th Congress.

Wilderness Designation

Energy development is not permitted in wilderness areas, unless there are pre-existing rights or unless Congress specifically allows it or later reverses the designation. Development of the surface and subsurface holdings of Native corporations would be precluded inside wilderness boundaries (though compensation might be owed). It would also preserve existing recreational opportunities and jobs, as well as the existing level of protection of subsistence resources, including the Porcupine Caribou Herd. H.R. 770 and S. 411 would designate the 1002 areas as wilderness.

No Action

Because current law prohibits development unless Congress acts, this option also prevents energy development. Those supporting delay often argue that not enough is known about either the probability of discoveries or about the environmental impact if development is permitted. Other argue that oil deposits should be saved for an unspecified "right time."

LEGISLATION

H.R. 4 (Tauzin)

Division F. Title V, contains the provisions of H.R. 2436, with the inclusion of a new provision for a 50:50 federal:state revenue split. Introduced July 27, 2001; referred to Committees on Energy and Commerce, Science, Ways and Means, Resources, Education and the Workforce, Transportation and Infrastructure, the Budget, and Financial Services. August 1, 2001, House passed Sununu amendment to limit specified surface development to 2,000 acres (yeas 228, nays 201; Roll Call No. 316) and defeated Markey-Johnson (CT) amendment to strike Title V defeated (yeas 206, nays 223; Roll Call No. 317). Passed House August 2, 2001 (yeas 240, nays 189; Roll Call No. 320).

H.R. 39 (D. Young)

Repeals current prohibition against ANWR leasing; directs Secretary to establish competitive oil and gas leasing program; specifies that the 1987 FLEIS is sufficient for compliance with the National Environmental Policy Act; authorizes set-asides up to 45,000 acres of Special Areas that restrict surface occupancy; sets minimum for royalty payments and for tract sizes; and for other purposes. Introduced January 3, 2001; referred to Committee on Resources.

H.R. 770 (Markey)

Designates Arctic coastal plain of ANWR as wilderness. Introduced February 28, 2001; referred to Committee on Resources.

H.R. 2436 (Hansen)

Title V repeals current prohibition against ANWR leasing; directs Secretary to establish competitive oil and gas leasing program; specifies that the 1987 FLEIS is sufficient for compliance with the National Environmental Policy Act; authorizes set-asides up to 45,000 acres of Special Areas that restrict surface occupancy; sets minimum acreage for the first lease sale and minimum royalty payments; prohibits ANWR oil export; specifies project labor agreements; and for other purposes. Introduced July 10, 2001; referred to Committee on Resources and on Energy and Commerce. Reported (amended) by Resources on July 25 (H.Rept. 107-160, Part I) and discharged by Energy and Commerce on July 25, 2001. Provisions incorporated into H.R. 4.

S. 388 (Murkowski)

Title V opens the 1002 area to energy leasing; provides for the timing and size of lease sales; specifies that the 1987 FLEIS is sufficient for compliance with the National Environmental Policy Act. requires posting of bonds for reclamation; requires expedite judicial review; authorizes set-asides up to 45,000 acres of Special Areas that restrict surface occupancy; provides for a 50:50 revenue split with the State; requires on-site inspections, provides for use of any federal revenues; and other purposes. Introduced February 26, 2001; referred to Committee on Energy and Natural Resources.

S. 411 (Lieberman)

Designates Arctic coastal plain of ANWR as wilderness. Introduced February 28, 2002; referred to Committee on Environment and Public Works.

S. 517 (Bingaman)

Authorizes a program for technology transfer in the Department of Energy. Introduced March 12, 2001; referred to Committee on Energy and Natural Resources. Reported June 6, 2001 (S. Rept. 107-30). February 15, 2002, laid before Senate by unanimous consent. February 15, 2002, S. Amdt. 2917 (Daschle) proposed; authorizes an omnibus energy program. (Amendment lacks ANWR development provisions, but an ANWR development amendment to it is widely expected.)

S. 1766 (Daschle)

Alters national energy programs in a variety of ways; lacks provisions to open ANWR. Introduced Dec. 5, 2001; not referred to Committee.

For Additional Reading

Nellerman, C. and R. D. Cameron. Cumulative Impacts of an Evolving Oil-field Complex on the Distribution of Calving Caribou. Canadian Jour. Of Zoology. 1998. Vol. 76, p. 1425.

Revkin, Andrew C. Hunting for Oil: New Precision, Less Pollution. New York Times. January 30, 2001. P. D1-D2.

U.S. Department of the Interior. Bureau of Land Management. Overview of the 1991 Arctic National Wildlife Refuge Recoverable Petroleum Resource Update. Washington, DC, April 8, 1991. 8p., 2 maps.

U.S. Department of the Interior. Fish and Wildlife Service, Geological Survey, and Bureau of Land Management. Arctic National Wildlife Refuge, Alaska, Coastal Plain Resource Assessment. Report and Recommendation to the Congress of the United States and Final Legislative Environment Impact Statement. Washington, DC, 1987, 208 p.

U.S. Department of the Interior. Geological Survey. The Oil and Gas Resource Potential of the Arctic National Wildlife Refuge 1002 Area, Alaska. 1999. 2 CD set. USGS Open File Report 98-34.

U.S. General Accounting Office. Arctic National Wildlife Refuge: An Assessment of Interior's Estimate of an Economically Viable Oil Field. Washington, DC. July, 1993. 31 p. GAO/RCED-93-130.

Chapter 3

LEGAL ISSUES RELATED TO PROPOSED DRILLING FOR OIL AND GAS IN THE ARCTIC NATIONAL WILDLIFE REFUGE

Pamela Baldwin

INTRODUCTION

Congress is currently considering whether to permit drilling for oil and gas in the coastal plain of the Arctic National Wildlife (ANWR), to designate the area as wilderness, or to retain the status quo.[1] Current law prohibits the production of oil and gas in the Refuge, but high prices for oil and natural gas have renewed debate over whether to open the Refuge to development. H.R. 4, of which Title V of Division F would authorize oil development in ANWR, passed the House of Representatives on August 2, 2001. Title V, Of S. 388 also would direct oil and gas development in the Refuge. At this time, these are the principal bills addressing oil and gas development in ANWR.[2] The land ownerships and laws relevant to possible development in the Refuge are complex, and the policy choices controversial.[3] The environmental protections provided in the bills and the effects on the Refuge and its wildlife that might result from oil and gas development are central to the debate on whether to open the Refuge to drilling. Several legal issues that relate to possible development of the Refuge and the current provisions in these bills are discussed in this report. This report will be updated or revised as circumstances warrant.

---

[1] See CRS Report RL31278, *Arctic National Wildlife Refuge: Background and Issues.*, M. Lynne Corn, coordinator.
[2] No committee reports are available for either bill as of the date of this report.
[3] See CRS Issue Brief IB10073, *The Arctic National Wildlife Refuge: The Next Chapter*, by M. Lynne Corn, Bernard A. Gelb, and Pamela Baldwin.

BACKGROUND

The Arctic National Wildlife Refuge is managed by the United States Fish and Wildlife Service (FWS) and consists of approximately 19 million acres located at the Northeast corner of Alaska directly adjacent to Canada. The coastal plain of the Refuge on the Beaufort Sea is approximately 1.5 million acres and is the part of the Refuge that is richest in wildlife and migratory birds, including the Porcupine caribou herd, polar bears, musk oxen, eagles, snow geese, and many others. The coastal plain is directly east of Prudhoe Bay, a state-owned oil field that has provided a large volume of oil, and many experts believe that significant deposits of oil and natural gas may exist under the Refuge as well. The presence of biological and wilderness values together with the potential for large hydrocarbon deposits results in the current controversy over whether to allow oil drilling in the Refuge.

In November, 1957, an application for the withdrawal of lands to create an Arctic Wildlife Range was filed to protect the area's wealth of wildlife and migratory birds. Under the regulations in effect at that time, this application "segregated" the lands in question, removing them from disposal. This fact was important because on July 7, 1958, the Alaska Statehood Act was passed and on January 3, 1959, Alaska was formally admitted to the Union. On December 6, 1960 (after statehood), the Secretary of the Interior issued Public Land Order 2214, reserving the area as the Arctic National Wildlife Range.[4]

The Supreme Court has held that the initial segregation of lands before statehood was sufficient to prevent the passage of ownership of certain submerged lands within the Refuge to the State of Alaska at statehood.[5] If this ruling had been in favor of Alaska, certain lands beneath the rivers in the coastal plain might have belonged to the state, which could have developed the resources in them, including the oil, gas, gravel, and water.

In 1971, Congress enacted the Alaska Native Claims Settlement Act (ANCSA)[6] to resolve Native claims against the United States. This Act provided the opportunity for the selection and conveyance of lands to Native groups – usually either the surface estate of lands to Native Village Corporations, or the subsurface estate to Native Regional Corporations, associated with the Village Corporations within each Region. Usually, the Regional Corporations could receive the lands beneath the Village Corporations in their area, but subsurface lands beneath refuges were not available, and in-lieu lands were substituted for them. Under § 22(g) of ANCSA, surface lands selected in refuges were subject to the regulations applicable to the particular refuge of which they were a part.

In 1980, Congress enacted the Alaska National Interest Lands Conservation Act (ANILCA),[7] which, among other things, renamed the Range[8] to be the Arctic National Wildlife Refuge, and expanded the Refuge to include an additional 9.2 million acres, mostly to the south.[9] Section 702(3) of ANILCA designated much of the original Range as a wilderness area, but did not include the coastal plain. Instead, Congress postponed decisions

---

[4] 25 Fed. Reg. 12598 (December 6, 1960). Other actions have changed the boundaries of the Refuge, but are not relevant to this analysis of leasing on the coastal plain.
[5] United States v. Alaska, 521 U.S. 1 (1997).
[6] Pub. L. No. 92-203, 85 Stat. 688, 43 U.S.C. §§ 1601 *et seq.*
[7] Pub. L. No. 96-487, 94 Stat. 2374, 16 U.S.C. §§ 3101 *et seq.*
[8] President Carter by Proclamation 4729 of February 29, 2980 had renamed the Range "The William O. Douglas Arctic Wildlife Range." ANILCA did not address this proclamation, but renamed the lands comprising the original Range and the added lands as the Arctic National Wildlife Refuge.
[9] Section 303(992).

on the development or further protection of the coastal plain. Section 1002 of ANILCA designated a part of the coastal plain of the Refuge for study. (As a result, this part of the plain is sometimes referred to as the "1002 area" or the "Coastal Plain.") In an ambiguous series of actions, this 2003 area was administratively articulated as excluding the three townships of land belonging to the Kaktovik Inupiat Corporation (KIC), a Village Corporation.[10] However, these lands *geographically* are on the coast of ANWR, and are very important to the wildlife and scenic resources of the area. Pursuant to a land exchange under § 1431(g) of ANILCA, KIC was entitled to receive additional lands within the Coastal Plain. Section 1003 prohibited oil and gas development in the Refuge as a whole, and "leasing or other development leading to production of oil and gas from the range" unless authorized by an Act of Congress.[11]

In 1983 the United States and the Arctic Slope Regional Corporation (ASRC), a Native Regional Corporation, executed an agreement ("the 1983 Agreement") embodying an exchange of lands under which ASRC would receive title to the subsurface estate beneath the KIC surface lands. Normally, ASRC would not have received these lands because they were in a refuge. The ASRC lands in ANWR cannot be developed unless Congress opens ANWR to oil development. Conversely, if Congress opens ANWR, then the more than 92,000 acres of Native lands (KIC surface/ASRC subsurface) in the four townships within the Refuge could be developed. These extensive Native holdings would be affected by the authorization of oil and gas development on the coastal plain, and, in turn, could also affect the Refuge and its resources. In addition, there are individually owned Native allotments within the Refuge that might be developed if oil and gas drilling is allowed. All types of Native lands within the Refuge total more than 100,000 acres.

As interest in the possible leasing of the coastal plain has increased, review of several legal aspects of possible drilling in the Refuge appears timely.

ISSUES

I. Environmental Constraints

One of the most controversial aspects of any consideration of possible leasing in the Refuge is what the environmental effects of leasing are likely to be. There have been vigorous assertions on both sides – either that the bills are highly protective of the environment, or that

---

[10] Section 1002(b) of ANILCA defines the "coastal plain" as the area identified as such in the map entitled ' Arctic National Wildlife Refuge', dated August 1980." The Refuge map published in the Federal Register Notice of the legal description of the boundaries of the Refuge does not show the native lands as excluded. (48 Fed. Reg. 7980 (February 24, 1983)). We are having trouble obtaining a copy of the original map of the Refuge certified in August, 1980 (the map referenced in the statute). One copy shows the boundaries of the KIC lands with the boundaries crossed out by hand, but without any explanation of when and by what authority these marks appeared or what their significance was intended to be with respect to the coastal plain. Maps certified in August, 1980 exist labeled Refuge and Wilderness, but we have not been successful in obtaining any map of that date that depicts the coastal plain (excluding KIC lands then conveyed) were published on April 19, 1983 (48 Fed. Reg. 16838), the introductory material assets: "By virtue of the map referred to in section 1002(b)(1), lands in which the surface estate has already been conveyed to Kaktovik Inupiat Corporation ...are excluded from the coastal plain...."

[11] It is not clear whether this language was intentional, but it may have been intended to allow preliminary activities in the additional lands that were added to the Refuge.

they are not. Hence the environmental aspects of the current bills are of particular interest. Some of the most critical elements in an analysis of the environmental provisions of the bills are: 1) the agency that would administer the leasing program; 2) the compatibility of leasing with the purposes of the Refuge; 3) the standard for environmental protection and how might it function in practice; 4) the level of industrial technology required; 5) the protections that would be statutorily provided with respect to the wildlife resources of the Refuge; and 6) the extent to which administrative decisions and actions implementing a leasing program were judicially reviewable. This last item will primarily be discussed later in this report under the heading "Judicial Review."

(A). Administration of Leasing

Under the National Wildlife Refuge System Administration Act ("Refuge Administration Act") on the management of the National Wildlife Refuge System, it is the Secretary of the Interior acting – "through the United States Fish and Wildlife Service" – who is to administer Refuge lands.[12] This language was added by Congress in 1976 to clarify that management of refuges could not be administratively assigned to other agencies.[13] Under current law, when evaluating whether to approve an activity in a refuge, the Director of the FWS (or an FWS officer to whom the duties are delegated) may approve an activity only if it is compatible with the *major* purposes for which the System and the particular unit were created. Longer-term uses must be compatible with all the purposes, major or otherwise, of both the System and the particular unit.[14] The Refuge Administration Act does not close refuges to possible oil and gas leasing, but many individual units are withdrawn and leasing is allowed on very few.

Although the Bureau of Land Management (BLM), another agency also in the Department of the Interior, is generally the mineral development manager for the Untied States,[15] the Mineral Leasing Act does not specify that the Secretary of the Interior is to administer leasing through that agency. Current mineral leasing regulations recognize the authority of FWS over the wildlife resources on refuge lands and reserve considerable authority to the Director of FWS with respect to oil and gas leasing in Refuges:

> (a)... Sole and complete jurisdiction over such lands for wildlife conservation purposes is vested in the Fish and Wildlife Service even though such lands may be subject to prior rights for other public purposes or, by the terms of the withdrawal order, may be subject to mineral leasing.
> (b)... [there is to be no drilling or prospecting under any mineral lease heretofore or hereafter issued on lands within a wildlife refuge except with the consent and approval of the Secretary with the concurrence of the Fish and Wildlife Service as to the time, place and nature of such operations in order to give complete protection to wildlife populations and wildlife habitat on the areas leased, and all such operations shall be conducted in accordance with the stipulations of the Bureau on a form approved by the Director [of the National Wildlife Refuge System].[16]

---

[12] 16 U.S.C. § 668dd(a)(1).

[13] Pub. L. No. 94-223, 90 Stat. 199.
[14] 16 U.S.C. 668dd(d).
[15] See Secretarial Order 3087, December 2, 1982, as amended February 7, 1983 (48 Fed. Reg. 8983).
[16] 43 C.F.R. § 3101.5-1.

This protective posture is repeated in another regulation that provides:

> Leases shall be issued subject to stipulations prescribed by the Fish and Wildlife Service as to the time, place, nature and condition of such operations in order to minimize impacts to fish and wildlife populations and habitat and other refuge resources on the areas leased. The specific conduct of lease activities on any refuge lands shall be subject to site-specific stipulations prescribed by the Fish and Wildlife Service.[17]

Given that there are no statutory requirements that mineral leasing be through the BLM, and that since 1976 there is a statutory requirement that management of refuges be by the Secretary through the FWS, it is not clear by what authority BLM is the lead agency with respect to leasing in refuges. Even if the Refuge Administration Act could be interpreted as only addressing the surface management of refuges, it can be asked whether the approval of the Secretary of Leasing in refuges must be given through FWS, which is to say with the concurrence of the Director of FWS. We are not aware of any Departmental interpretation of these issues.

Under current procedures, refuges in Alaska that are open to leasing are not to be available until the FWS has first completed compatibility determinations.[18] A new compatibility policy and new regulations were published on October 18, 2000, and became effective November 17, 2000.[19] "Compatible use" is defined as a "proposed or existing wildlife-dependent recreational use or any other use of a national wildlife refuge that, based on sound professional judgment, will not materially interfere with or detract from the fulfillment of the National Wildlife Refuge System mission or the purposes(s) of the national wildlife refuge."[20] Native lands in Alaskan refuges that are subject to certain restrictions under § 22(g) of ANCSA are expressly subject to the regulations on compatibility in 50 C.F.R. 25 and 26.[21]

PLO 2214, which withdrew lands to create the original Arctic National Wildlife Range, withdrew the lands from operation of the mining laws, but not from the mineral leasing laws. Congress in § 1003 of ANILCA reserved to itself the decision of whether to lease the coastal plain area.[22] The current bills would authorize oil and gas leasing and address both management and compatibility.

H.R. 4 states in § 6503(a) that leasing is to be under the Mineral Leasing Act (MLA)[23] and administered by the Secretary – which term is defined in § 6502(2) as the Secretary of the Interior or the Secretary's designee. As noted above, generally leasing under the MLA is conducted by the BLM, with conditioning authority in FWS when the leasing is in a refuge. Because there is no reference to the usual powers of the Director of FWS, and because, under § 6507 of H.R. 4, the Secretary is to impose the environmental stipulations through new leasing regulations, the role of the FWS is ambiguous.

However, in 1981, a court found the administrative assignment of responsibility for studying the coastal plain area under §1002 of ANILCA to the United States Geological

---

[17] 43 C.F.R. § 3101.5-4.
[18] 43 C.F.R. § 3010.5-3.
[19] 65 Fed. Reg. 62484 and 65 Fed. Reg. 62458, respectively.
[20] 50 C.F.R. § 25.12(a) and see 16 U.S.C. § 668ee, which is nearly identical.
[21] 50 C.F.R. § 25.21(b).
[22] 16 U.S.C. § 3143.
[23] This language also raises issues in connection with the revenue-sharing provisions. See "Revenues" below.

Survey rather than to F' S to be unlawful because the Refuge Administration Act requires that the Refuge System be administered by the Secretary of Interior through FWS, absent a clearly expressed legislative intent to the contrary.[24] H.R. 4 does not expressly assign leasing responsibilities to the BLM, although that result is implied by the reference to leasing being under the MLA. The bill also does not expressly modify the usual authority of FWS to manage and protect the Refuge resources and to condition mineral leases. Therefore, an argument can be made that FWS retains that authority, and would develop the environmental constraints on surface disturbance in the leasing regulations. However, the intent of Congress is not clear in light of the fact that H.R. 4 directs the Secretary to develop environmental constraints but omits the direction that the Secretary act "through the Fish and Wildlife Service." As the legislation evolves, the respective jurisdictions of BLM and FWS in this context may be clarified.

Section 503(a) of S. 388 expressly states that BLM, rather than the FWS, is to manage the leasing program. That section directs the Secretary, "acting through the Bureau of Land Management *in consultation with* the Fish and Wildlife Service and other appropriate Federal offices and agencies," (emphasis added) to establish and implement an oil and gas leasing program that is to ensure that oil and gas production will result in no significant adverse effect on the wildlife and environment. Section 503(d) further states that the title (Title V) is to be the "sole authority" for leasing in the Refuge. These provisions more clearly place BLM in charge of both supervising leasing and developing and carrying out environmental constraints, a departure from the current posture of the law. The scope of authority left to the FWS to protect the wildlife resources of the Refuge from the effects of oil drilling is not clear, but appears to be less than under current law and regulations, where as discussed above, the FWS can impose terms and conditions on leases.

Arguably, placing BLM in charge of the leasing program for ANWR and evidently reducing the otherwise applicable role of FWS could divorce the mineral development aspects from the biological/wildlife purposes and the expertise of FWS personnel, and may result in the coastal plain of ANWR receiving less protection than lands in other refuges do under current law and regulations.

Both the 1983 Agreement and many past bills in Congress continued responsibility for ANWR leasing with the FWS, subject to congressionally enacted direction. Pursuant to §1002 of ANILCA, the FWS adopted regulations (see 50 C.F.R. Part 37) governing the exploratory activities that took place in the Refuge.

(B). Compatibility

Both § 503(c) of S. 388 and § 6503(c) of H.R. 4 state that for purposes of the Refuge Administration Act, *the oil and gas leasing program and activities* in the coastal plain are deemed to be compatible with the purposes for which the Arctic National Wildlife Refuge was established, and that no further findings or decisions are required to implement this determination. (Emphasis added.) This provision both answers the compatibility question and appears to eliminate the usual compatibility determination processes. Arguably too, it raises additional ambiguities as to FWS authority to impose conditions on leases and as to what extent and by whom impacts resulting from activities occurring on Native lands may be

---

[24] Trustees for Alaska v. Watt, 524 F. Supp. 1303 (D. Ak. 1981), *aff'd* 690 F. 2d 1279, 1307 (9th Cir. 1982).

regulated. (See Native Lands section below.) The general statement that leasing "activities" are compatible arguably may encompass a great many actions such as construction and operation of pot facilities, staging areas, personnel centers, etc.

(C). Environmental Standard

Both bills use "no significant adverse effect" on fish and wildlife, their habitat, subsistence resources, and the environment as the standard that is to guide leasing.[25] This phrase is not defined in either bill, but has been used in the past. It was used in § 1002 of ANILCA as the standard for the limited exploration allowed under that section, throughout the 1983 Agreement, and in past bills that authorized leasing.[26] Arguably, it could be seen as analogous to the standard used in the National Environmental Policy Act (NEPA), which is "significant effect on the quality of the human environment." (In practice this has been interpreted as addressing only significant *adverse* effects.) Although the contexts are different, judicial interpretation of NEPA may provide guidance in applying the standard contained in the ANWR bills.

The standard of significant adverse effects might allow considerable environmental harm before the threshold is crossed. Although the standard has been used before, Congress has also chosen other, more protective, language at times. For example, the language Congress used with respect to exploration in environmentally sensitive areas of the National Petroleum Reserve-Alaska was to "assure the maximum protection of such surface values consistent with the requirements of this Act for the exploration of the reserve."[27] Another example of other language Congress has used is the Wilderness Act of 1964, which requires that mineral leases in wilderness areas "shall contain such reasonable stipulations as may be prescribed by the Secretary of Agriculture for the protection of the wilderness character of the land consistent with the use of the land for the purposes for which they are leased, permitted, or licensed.[28] A statute that addresses already existing mining rights in national parks requires that mining rights by "subject to such regulations prescribed by the Secretary of the Interior as he deems necessary or desirable for the preservation and management of those areas.[29] In ANWR, Congress would be authorizing new leasing and hence would have greater latitude to impose a protective standard without infringing upon existing rights.

(D). Technology Standard

Both bills require the use of the "best commercially available technology for oil and gas exploration, development, and production, on all new exploration, development, and production operations, and whenever practicable, on existing operations, ..." This means that the best commercially available technology will be required for initial installation and

---

[25] See, e.g., § 503(a) of S. 388 and § 6503(a)(2) of H.R. 4.
[26] See H.R. 1320 and S. 1220, 102d Congress. H.R. 1320 defined the term as follows: "The term ' significant adverse effects' means those effects on habitat quality or availability which, despite the reasonable application of mitigation measures involving appropriate technology, engineering, and environmental control measures, including siting and timing restrictions, are likely to result in widespread long-term reductions in the natural abundance or distribution of a species of fish or wildlife on the coastal plain."
[27] 42 U.S.C. § 6504(b).
[28] Act of September 3, 1964, 78 Stat. 890, 893, 16 U.S.C. § 1133(d).
[29] Pub. L. No. 94-429, 90 Stat. 1342, 16 U.S.C. § 1902.

production, and should be phased into on-going operations, if practicable, as new technology develops. A computer search indicates that the phrase "best commercially available technology" is not currently used in the U.S. Code, and does not have any available judicial interpretation.[30] Because it refers to technology that already is more widely available, it may be a more lenient standard than "best available technology economically achievable," or "best practicable control technology" – both of which standards are used in the Clean Water Act.[31]

(E). Specific Protections

Both bills contain provisions that would provide specific environmental protections. Many of these provisions leave much to the discretion of the Secretary. The evaluations of environment effects made by the Secretary, and the particular actions taken by the Secretary in the exercise of the Secretary's discretion would be insulated under the House bill by the stringent provisions on judicial review. (See "Judicial Review" below.) This fact – that the Secretary's environmental choices could be difficult to overturn – is relevant to many of the provisions discussed in this part.

Section 503 of S. 388 and § 6503(e) of H.R. 4 provide that the Secretary, "after consultation with the State of Alaska, City of Kaktovik, and the North Slope Borough," is authorized to designate up to a total of 45,000 acres of the 1002 area as "special Areas" and close such areas to leasing if the Secretary determines that they are of "such unique character and interest so as to require special management and regulatory protection." However, closure is discretionary and designated areas may be leased if the Secretary limits or conditions surface use and occupancy by lessees.[32] This provision does not require consultation with the FWS, and the Secretary may implement the advice of state and local entities as to designation, special protection, and possible closure of unique and special areas.

The above-cited sections would impose an acreage limit of 45,000 acres (out of the 1.5 million coastal plain acres) that could be designated as Special Areas for optional special protection or closure. The House bill contains additional details, such as the direction in §6503(e)(1) that the Secretary designate the Sadlerochit Spring area, comprising approximately 4,000 acres, as a Special Area, and §6503(e)(2) that Special Areas be managed so as "to protect and preserve the area's unique and diverse character including its fish, wildlife, and subsistence resource values."

Both bills state that the closure authority in the bill is the sole source of closure authority.[33] This may eliminate any separate authority under the Refuge Administration Act to close areas, and also raises the question of whether closure is an available option if it is determined to be necessary to avoid jeopardizing a species under the Endangered Species Act. Possibly ESA-necessitated closures could exhaust the acreage available for closure, making

---

[30] Several provisions in current law use the phrase "commercially available technology" and at least two provisions call for technological improvements above that standard. See 42 U.S.C. § 5906(b)(1) re non-nuclear energy research; 42 U.S.C. §§ 13331 and 13352 re clean coal technology.

[31] 33 U.S.C. § 1311.

[32] The House Bill also contains a paragraph (4) entitled "directional Drilling," which permits "horizontal drilling" under Special Areas. Although the two terms are similarly in common usage, directional drilling may be the broader term and the same term should be used in both the caption and substance of the section. Section 503(f) of S. 388 also refers to horizontal drilling.

[33] See §§ 6503(f) in H.R. 4 and 503(g) in S. 388.

that tool unavailable where closure is merely desirable to avoid harm, rather than crucial to survival of a species.

Section 6505(a)(2) of H.R. 4 and § 508(7) of S. 388 provide that the Secretary may close, on a seasonal basis, portions of the Coastal Plain to *exploratory* drilling activities as necessary to protect caribou calving areas and other species of fish and wildlife. There is no express authority for seasonal closures during the production phases of oil development in the Senate bill. However, § 6507(d)(2) of H.R. 4 authorizes "[s]easonal limitations on exploration, development, and related activities, where necessary, to avoid significant adverse effects during periods of concentrated fish and wildlife breeding, denning, nesting, spawning, and migration." It is not clear what would need to be shown to demonstrate the *necessity* of seasonal closures, or to demonstrate effects sufficiently significant and adverse to justify closure. It also is not clear whether seasonal closure areas count toward the acreage limitation on closures.

Under both bills, the Secretary is to develop regulations to govern the leasing of the coastal plain. These leasing regulations are to be developed within 14 months under § 504(a) of the Senate bill and within 15 months under § 6503(g)(1) of H.R. 4. Under § 6504(e)(1) of the House bill, the first lease sale is to be held within 22 months after enactment and under § 506 of the Senate bill the deadline is within 20 months of enactment. See the heading "NEPA Compliance" below for a discussion of the fact that other bill provisions would eliminate comprehensive new environmental studies in order to achieve this accelerated leasing schedule.

The leasing regulations required under the House bill must include regulations that relate to the protection of the fish and wildlife, their habitat, subsistence resources, and the environment of the Coastal Plain.[34] Both bills would direct the Secretary to impose terms and conditions on leases to address environmental concerns, but there is little detail under the Senate bill. The environmental provisions would undoubtedly provide some protections, but the net import of some of the provisions is unclear.

For example, the reclamation standard in §§ 6506(a)(5) of H.R. 4 and 508(17) of S. 388 requires reclamation to a condition capable of supporting the uses which the lands were capable of supporting prior to exploration or development or "upon application by the lessee, to a higher or better use as approved by the Secretary." Under general zoning law, "higher or better" uses are those that "bring the greatest economic return."[35] Uses that are 'higher and better' than undeveloped wildlife habitat could include many conditions.

Under §§ 6506(a)(6) and 508(18), environmental conditions may be a part of a lease "as *required*" pursuant to previous sections. (Emphasis added.) This language may mean only as required to avoid "significant adverse effects." There is no express authority to impose conditions that embody a margin of safety and it is not clear whether a court would read in that authority.

Section 6507(d) requires that the proposed regulations and lease conditions comply with all applicable provisions of Federal and State environmental law, which would include a broad range of requirements. However, the applicable laws governing management of refuges may be modified by the instant legislation, as indicated.

---

[34] Section 6503(g)(1) and § 6507(c).
[35] Black's Law Dictionary (6th ed. 1990).

Section 6507(d)(1) of H.R. 4 requires protective standards "at least as effective as the safety and environmental mitigation measures set forth in items 1 through 29 at pages 167-169 of the "Final Legislative Environmental Impact Statement" (April 1987) on the Coastal Plain." These measures also include many beneficial items, but some of the measures, by regulating certain activities may basically condone those activities – e.g. the provisions that address roads and other permanent infrastructure facilities, incinerators, marine facilities, docks, causeways, etc. Although the legislated language requires the new ANWR leasing standards to be "at least as effective as" the 1987 measures and therefore would allow more stringent measures, additional statutory requirements and guidance might provide clarity regarding some of those important infrastructure topics and to guide development on both the federal and the Native Lands in the Refuge.

Section 6507(a)(3) of the House bill would require that the Secretary ensure that:

> the maximum amount of surface acreage covered by production and support facilities, including airstrips and any areas covered by gravel berms or piers for support of pipelines, does not exceed 2,000 acres on the Coastal Plain.

This provision would require that oil development facilities not occupy more than 2,000 acres on the Coastal Plain. The reference to surface acreage "covered by" production and support facilities may exclude facilities that are not touching the ground, e.g. the pipes in elevated pipelines. Two thousand acres is a small amount relative to the 1.5 million acre plain. However, given that under both bills the Secretary is required to lease not less than 200,000 acres in the first lease sale,[36] a greater footprint may prove necessary. Also, it is likely that oil development facilities will not be in a single, consolidated footprint, but scattered over a much larger area and connected by pipelines and possibly roads. Equally important, if oil and gas were discovered in commercial qualities, it appears that support and development facilities could be constructed on Native lands, and such construction arguably is not constrained by the 2,000 acre limitation.[37] If not, then more than an additional 23,000 acres within the coastal plain and over 100,000 acres of Native lands within the Refuge as a whole might be available for surface occupancy associated with oil development. (See "Native Lands," below.)

The House bill in § 6507(b)(1) requires a site-specific analysis of the probable effects, if any, that drilling or related activities will have on fish and wildlife, their habitat, and the environment. (See the discussion of NEPA compliance below.) Section 6507(b)(2) requires that a plan be implemented to avoid, minimize, and mitigate (in that order and to the extent practicable) any significant adverse effect identified under paragraph (1). This preference of avoiding adverse effects is clearly a protective posture. However, under § 6507(b)(3) this plan is to be developed "after consultation with" the agency or agencies having jurisdiction over matters mitigated by the plan. This last reference would be to the FWS, which has the authority under current law to develop and approve of such plans and activities, rather than to consult regarding them.

---

[36] See §6504(d) in H.R. 4 and § 506 of S. 388.
[37] The leasing program addresses leasing of the federal lands. Under the 1983 Agreement discussed in the following section of this report, the Arctic Slope Regional Corporation agreed that the terms of that agreement governing oil development on its lands could be modified by subsequent legislation on oil development in ANWR, but there is no indication in the House bill that the 2,000 acre limit on surface use in the coastal plain is intended to apply to the Native lands

Section 6507(d)(3) requires that *exploration* activities be limited to the winter and be conducted by ice roads or other means that buffer the tundra, but then also provides that the Secretary may allow other exploration if special circumstances exist and the Secretary finds such exploration will have no significant adverse effect on the fish and wildlife, their habitat, and the environment of the Coast Plain.

Similarly, § 6507(d)(4),(95),(7), and (12) relate to potential controls of roads, transportation, and air traffic disturbance, but no specific controls are enacted. Here too, the regulations will depend on the Secretary' s interpretation. This is also true with respect to the requirements for "appropriate" controls on explosives, sand and gravel extraction, etc.

The Senate bill does not elaborate on the terms and conditions to protect the environment, except to direct that leases may contain terms and conditions "as required" by § 503(a) of the bill – i.e., to avoid significant adverse effects.

It may also be asked what penalties would be available to enforce the environmental protections and other lease requirements. H.R. 4 does not specifically address penalties for violation of lease terms by a lessee. The bill does state that leasing in the Refuge would be under the MLA. The MLA provides for cancellation of leases for infractions,[38] and the MLA leasing regulations also provide civil and criminal penalties for leasing violations, including failure to comply with lease terms.[39] Because of the ambiguity about the role of FWS regarding the leasing activities, it is not clear whether the penalties usually available for infractions on refuge lands would continue to apply in this context. If so, these include fines and imprisonment.[40]

Under § 513 of S. 388, the Secretary is to diligently enforce all regulations and lease terms and under § 508(10), if a lessee of a non-producing lease fails to comply with any provisions of the act or any other law or leasing regulation, the lease may be canceled by the Secretary after 30 days notice. Under § 508(11) of S. 388, a producing lease may be forfeited and canceled by any appropriate proceeding brought by the Secretary in any United States district court having jurisdiction under the provisions of that title.

Because § 503(d) states that it is the sole authority for leasing in the 1002 area, arguably the penalties available under the Refuge Administration Act would not be available for environmental infractions by a lessee.

To whatever extent only cancellation is available as a penalty for violation of lease terms, the absence of a gradation of penalties could make adequate enforcement of environmental protections difficult. Penalties for a specific violation of another law, such as the Clean Air Act, arguably would still be available under that law.

(F). Possible Effects on International Polar Bear Agreement

Beginning in the sixties, concern grew regarding the protection of marine mammals, including the polar bear. In 1972, the Marine Mammal Protection Act (MMPA) was enacted. In 1973, the United States, Canada, Denmark, Norway and the former Union of Soviet

---

[38] 30 U.S.C. § 188.
[39] 43 C.F.R. Subpart 3163.
[40] 16 U.S.C. 668dd(f) and (g).

Socialist Republics developed an international agreement on polar bear conservation.[41] This Agreement was ratified by the United States in 1976.

The Agreement prohibits the "take" of polar bears, which term is defined as "hunting, killing and capturing."[42] Article III sets out five exceptions to the taking prohibition, which a party to the Agreement may allow. These exceptions include several relating to traditional take by a party's nationals; take for scientific purposes, for conservation purposes, or to prevent serious disturbance of the management of other living resources.

Article II of the Agreement requires certain actions to protect habitat of the bears. Parties are to:

1) take "appropriate action to protect the ecosystem of which polar bears are a part;"
2) give "special attention to habitat components such as denning and feeding sites and migration patterns;" and
3) manage polar bear populations in accordance with "sound conservation practices" based on the best available scientific data.

Recently, some critics have asserted that oil and gas development in the Arctic may be inconsistent with or violate the Agreement in that such development could result in the death of polar bears. A draft report to Congress raised questions in this regard.[43] One of the principal issues raised is that the MMPA permits the unintentional taking of polar bears incidental to other lawful activities. The draft report asserts that such take would be inconsistent with the Agreement because there is no exception for such take in Article I or III and "if a lethal take were to occur during activities conducted under incidental take authority, the United States arguably could be considered to not be in compliance with the Agreement."[44]

However, the argument can be made that all references to killing or taking polar bears in the Agreement, whether in the prohibition or the exceptions sections, are to intentional take. Given this fact, the argument could continue, it is not inconsistent with the Agreement for an implementing law to permit but regulate incidental take. That this could be an appropriate interpretation is bolstered by the wording of the discussion accompanying the recommendation to ratify the Agreement, which also discusses only intentional takes – whether through hunting, or for other specified reasons.[45] Furthermore, the State Department, in presenting the Agreement to the President for transmission to the Senate for its advice and co sent, took the position that the MMPA provided adequate domestic legislation to implement the terms and provisions set forth in the Agreement.

However, a more generalized argument could be made that the combination of the MMPA and the opening of ANWR to leasing, with concomitant development of the Native coastal lands, either per se or as such development progressed in actuality, could violate the pledge by the United States to protect the ecosystem upon which the bears depend. In such an

---

[41] Agreement on the Conservation of Polar Bears, T.I.A.S. No. 8409, 27 U.S.T. 3918 (Nov. 15, 1973) [hereinafter Polar Bear Agreement].
[42] *Id.*, art.I(2).
[43] Draft Report to Congress on Status of United States Implementation of the 1073 International Agreement on the Conservation of Polar Bears, Prepared by U.S. Fish and Wildlife Service, Alaska Region, October, 1997.
[44] *Id.*, at 9.
[45] Executive Rep. No. 94-34(1976).

eventuality recourse would be available only to the other parties to the Agreement, but the argument exists as a policy argument against such leasing activities, and at least one commentator asserts that such leasing might result in an inconsistency with the Agreement, such that either the Agreement or the MMPA should be amended.

> The Polar Bear Agreement does not authorize incidental take within the polar bear protection zone. Such takes are authorized under section 101(a)(5) of the MMPA. Because the Agreement does not now prohibit harassment, an inconsistency exists only to the extent such takes would be lethal, involve the capture of bears, or be a product of habitat degradation or destruction. Because there is potential for polar bears to be lethally taken incidental to activities such as oil and gas operations, it is necessary to either amend the Agreement or to amend the MMPA to prohibit such takes if consistency with the Agreement is the goal. Takes by harassment could still be allowed under the MMPA, consistent with the Agreement[46].

(G). Discussion

There are few specific requirement6s in either bill that address particular items of environmental concern, such as port and support facilities, airstrips, disposal of wastes, gravel mining, water sources, etc. Many details of the environmental constraints would be left to the leasing regulations that are to be developed by the Secretary with very little advance study and little statutory guidance other than the avoidance of significant adverse effects. The role of the FWS is ambiguous, but appears to be less than under its current authority. Many decisions relating to the protection of the fish and wildlife resources of the Refuge and the protection of the environmental in general would be committed to the discretion of the Secretary, whose choices would be difficult to challenge under the strict standards for judicial review in the House bill. A gradation of penalties for wrongdoing by a lessee may not be available. The Senate bill provides only for a judicial cancellation of a producing lease as the recourse; the House bill provides for cancellation, but penalties under the MLA may also be available. It is unclear whether the currently available penalties for violations in refuges would be available. And, arguably, the reclamation standard provides that at the end of the potentially lengthy period of mineral leasing activity, restoration of lands to current wildlife uses would not necessarily be requested.

II. Native Lands

Both bills would repeal § 1003 of ANILCA, thereby permitting oil and gas development on both the federal Refuge lands and on the Native lands within the Refuge.[47] These Native lands total over 100,000 acres, and although some of the most important elements in assessing the possible impacts of opening ANWR to leasing involve the property interests of Native-Americans in the Refuge, this aspect of permitting leasing has been little discussed. Both Native individuals and Native Village and Regional Corporations have various interests relevant to the issue of oil drilling in ANWR.

---

[46] Donald C. Baur, Reconciling Polar Bear Protection under United States Laws and the International Agreement for the Conservation of Polar Bears, 2 ANIMAL LAW 9, 85 (1996) (footnote omitted).

[47] Section 403(b) of S.388; § 6503(b) of H.R. 4. See Native Lands section below.

(A). The Nature and History of Native Rights in ANWR

In 1971, Congress enacted the Alaska Native Claims Settlement Act (ANCSA) to resolve Native aboriginal claims against the United States. ANCSA provided for monetary payments and also created Village Corporations that received the right to select the surface estate to approximately 22 million acres of lands in close proximity to villages. A village located in or adjacent to a refuge could select a certain amount of surface lands within the refuge,[48] thereby maintaining traditional ways of life. Under § 22(g) of ANCSA, lands chosen in pre-ANCSA refuges were subject to the laws and regulations governing the use of the refuge of which they were a part.[49] The Kakovik Inupiat Corporation (KIC), a Village Corporation in the Refuge, received selection rights to three townships under ANCSA.[50]

ANCSA also created Regional Corporations, which could receive subsurface rights to some lands and full title to others. The Regional Corporations typically were entitled to lands beneath the Village Corporation lands with which they were associated. However, subsurface rights in National Wildlife Refuges were not available, but in-lieu selection rights were provided to substitute for such lands.[51] Even though the shareholders of a Village Corporation shared in the profits of the relevant Regional Corporation, the interests of a Regional Corporation in maximizing the economic development of its subsurface estate may not always coincide with the interests of a Village Corporation in possibly using the surface estate for subsistence hunting and other traditional uses.

The 1980 ANILCA contained many provisions that followed up on ANCSA. Section 11002 of ANILCA designated the "coastal plain" of the Refuge as "the area identified as such in the map entitled 'Arctic National Wildlife Refuge,' dated August, 1980." The Refuge map published in the Federal Register Notice of the legal description of the boundaries of the Refuge does not show the native lands as excluded.[52] We have not been able to obtain a copy of the original map of the Refuge certified in August, 1980 (*i.e.* the map referenced in the statute). One copy shows the boundaries of the KIC lands with the boundaries crossed out by hand, but without any explanation of when and by what authority these marks appeared or what their significance was intended to be with respect to the coastal plain. Maps exist that were certified in August, 1980 and labeled Refuge and Wilderness, but we have not been successful in obtaining any map of that date that depicts the coastal lain labeled as such. Yet, when the legal description of the boundaries of the coastal plain (excluding KIC lands then conveyed) were published on April 19, 1983, the introductory material asserts: "By virtue of the map referred to in section 1002(b)(1), lands in which the surface estate has already been conveyed to Kaktovik Inupiat Corporation .... are excluded from the coastal plain ..."[53] However, geographically the KIC lands are on the coastal plain and are important to the wildlife of the area.

Under § 1431(g) of ANILCA, KIC was authorized to exchange certain of its land interests and obtained the rights to a fourth township within the 1992 area. As a result, KIC has surface rights to three townships along the coast of ANWR that are outside the 1002 area,

---

[48] Section 12(a)(1); 43 U.S.C. § 1611(a)(I).
[49] Section 22(g), 43 U.S.C. §1621(g).
[50] A "township" is a unit of the federal surveying system that is a block of land 6 miles on a side, divided into 36 mile-square sections, each of which contains 640 acres. Therefore, a township consists of 23,040 acres.
[51] 43 U.S.C. §1611(a)(1).
[52] 48 Fed. Reg. 7980 (February 24, 1983).
[53] 48 Fed. Reg. 16838, 16869 (April 19, 1983).

and one township inside that area, totaling approximately 92,160 acres. However, all of the KIC lands are within the Refuge as a whole and hence are subject to: 1) the restrictions on oil and gas development in § 1003 of ANILCA; and 2) under § 22(9g) of ANCSA and § 1431(g) of ANILCA, to the laws and regulations governing the Refuge.

Section 1431(o) of ANILCA also authorized the Arctic Slope Regional Corporation (ASRC), whose shareholders are Inupiat Eskimos, to obtain subsurface rights beneath lands belonging to villages in the National Petroleum Reserve-Alaska or ANWR, if parts of those two areas within a certain proximity to Native village lands were opened for commercial oil and gas development within 40 years of the date of ANILCA. Under this authority, ASRC would not have been authorized to obtain the subsurface beneath the KIC lands in the Refuge until ANWR was opened for commercial development, and any development would've been subject to protective regulations. However, under §1302(h) of ANILCA, a separate exchange authority, an exchange was agreed to on August 9, 1983 between then Secretary of the Interior James Watt and ASRC. Basically, under the 1983 Agreement, the United States received the surface rights to certain lands in the Gates of the Arctic National Park and ASRC received the subsurface rights to the KIC lands. Congress appears to have ratified the agreement (known as the "Chandler Lake Agreement" or "the 1983 Agreement"),[54] although Congress also later specified that the Secretary could not actually convey by exchange or otherwise, lands or interests in lands within the coastal plain of ANWR without the prior approval of Congress.[55]

Section 1431(o)(4) of ANILCA provides that the Secretary may promulgate regulations regarding the subsurface estates acquired *pursuant to that subsection* to protect the environmental values of the Reserve or Range consistent with regulations governing the development of those lands within the Reserve or Range which have been opened for purposes of development, including § 22(g) regulations. However, that subsection of ANILCA did not apply to the ASRC exchange in ANWR since a different exchange authority was utilized. Instead, the 1983 Agreement contained considerable detail relating to exploration and environmental issues, thereby making those features a matter of contract law. ASRC also agreed in the 1983 Agreement that § 22(g) – and hence Refuge regulations – would apply to its lands, but with significant additional terms. This point will be discussed further below.

On March 17, 1993, lands were withdrawn by Public Land Order 6959 to allow KIC to make its final selections to complete its four townships in the Refuge.[56] Pursuant to § 22(h)(2) of ANCSA and § 1410 of ANILCA, the Order made more lands available than was KIC's entitlement, thereby providing some flexibility as to choices. This larger quantity of lands desired by KIC had been identified initially in an agreement effective January 22, 1993, before the PLO was issued. Those lands were withdrawn and, under the terms of the January agreement, KIC was then to have filed a selection application and simultaneously submitted a prioritization of land choices from which conveyances could be completed up to the amount of the entitlement. However, BLM advises us that it appears that no final prioritization list has yet been submitted. Therefore, the exact location of the last of the KIC (and hence ASRC) lands is not yet known.

---

[54] *See* Pub. L. No. 98-366, 98 Stat. 468, 471.
[55] Pub. L. No. 100-395, 102 Stat. 981, amending § 1302(h) of ANILCA; 16 U.S.C. § 3192(h)(2).
[56] 58 Fed. Reg. 14323 (March 17, 1993).

Also as part of the Chandler Lake Agreement, ASRC was given the contractual right to drill, within a certain window of time, up to three exploratory wells on the KIC lands outside the 1002 area. One test well was drilled within the specified time, but the results of that well have been kept confidential. However, full oil and gas development of the ASRC lands was prohibited until and unless Congress opened the Refuge for such development. Conversely, if Congress opens the Refuge, the Agreement provides that ASRC may proceed with development of its subsurface interests.

In addition to the KIC and ASRC Native lands, there are also individual Native "allotments" within the coastal plain and elsewhere in the Refuge. Approval and conveyance of some allotments have been completed; other lands have been applied for, but may not be approved. BLM currently is compiling the exact locations, acreage, and status of these allotments and applications. It appears, based on a preliminary mapping, that allotments and applications for allotments are clustered primarily along the coast and near Sadlerochit Spring, both of which are considered vital wildlife areas. BLM reports that allotments range in size up to 160 acres each and that approximately 9,797 acres have been conveyed, with an additional 1,719.66 acres approved but still pending.

If allotments are conveyed under the provisions of ANCSA, they are expressly for the surface estate only. However, if a claimant qualified for and opted for a conveyance under previous statutes, the status of the mineral estate of a particular allotment would have to be checked. Nonmineral lands (in the sense of "hardrock" minerals such as gold, silver, etc.) Were not to be available for selection, and typically the United States reserved any oil and gas.[57]

(B). Current Bill Provisions and Issues
(1). Final Conveyances to KIC

Both bills have identical language in § 6510 of H.R. 4 and § 503(h) of S. 388 that authorizes the conveyance of final land selections to KIC. It will be recalled that congressional authorization to complete the conveyances is required by the 1988 amendment to ANILCA. More than sufficient lands for identification of selections were made available in PLO 6959, as identified by KIC in the agreement effective January 22, 1993. (The bill provisions refer to section 2 of the PLO as setting out the available lands, but the correct reference is paragraph 1.) Neither bill directs that conveyance of the selected lands be in accordance with the January 22, 1993 Agreement, nor requires a prioritization by a date certain in order to clarify which lands will ultimately leave federal ownership. Consequently, unless language were added to impose a timetable on the finalization of selections, the final location of these lands could remain uncertain.

(2). Environmental Constraints on Native Lands

As discussed above, both bills addressed oil development activities in the coastal plain/1002 area, and provide some environmental controls. It is unclear to what extent the

---

[57] 43 U.S.C. § 1617(a). BLM advises that all of the allotments are pursuant to the Act of May 17, 1906, ch. 2469, 34 Stat. 197, amended August 2, 1956, ch. 891, 70 Stat. 954, in which case they may be subject to restrictions on alienation. Oil and gas on all of these allotments is reserved to the United States. Other allotments are listed as approved pursuant to ANILCA; however, the status of the title of particular allotments and applications may not be clear at this time.

Native lands will be subject to the same or similar controls – whether whatever constraints are placed on the federal Refuge lands would also pertain to the Native lands within the Refuge, or, if not, what other constraints on environmental effects and development facilities might apply to the Native lands. These issues are vitally important to understanding the possible overall effects of oil development on the Refuge.

In considering this question, the various Native property interests must be considered separately: 1) the interests of KIC in the surface estate of lands, within the coastal plain and the Refuge as a whole; 2) the interests of ASRC in the subsurface (and related use of the surface), within the coastal plain and the Refuge; and 3) individual allotments in the coastal plain and Refuge.

As discussed above, one section of KIC lands is in the 1002/coastal plain; three sections are outside the coastal plain; all are within the Refuge as a whole.

(3). ASRC Lands and the 1983 Agreement

Currently ASRC has rights to the subsurface beneath the KIC lands, both within and outside the coastal plain. It is important to note that the 1983 Agreement and its appendices address oil exploration and development on the ASRC subsurface estate and provide that its terms will govern the development and oil production on those lands unless they are superseded by statutory provisions. Appendix 2, part 9 of the Agreement states that development production activities undertaken on "ASRC lands" will be subject to statutory constraints. Specifically ASRC development:

> shall be in accordance with the substantive statutory and regulatory requirements governing oil and gas exploration, including exploratory drilling, and development and production that are designed to protect the wildlife, its habitat, and the environment of the *coastal plain*, or the ASRC Lands, or both. (Emphasis added.)

Other provisions of the 1983 Agreement also pertain to environmental effects. Appendix 1 provides that the grant of lands to ASRC is subject to:

1. the requirements of the second sentence of § 22(g) of ANCSA, (which requires compliance with the regulations of the Refuge).
6. the covenant that ASRC will use the lands "in conformance with the 'Land Use Stipulations" attached as Appendix 2.
7. the covenant that ASRC "shall not use those lands, or the surface of those lands, in any manner that significantly adversely affects the fish and wildlife, their habitats, or the environment of those lands of Arctic National Wildlife Refuge lands....."

Therefore, it appears that as a general matter, the environmental constraints of the bills applicable to the coastal plain arguably would apply to development of all ASRC lands, both within the coastal plain and outside it.[58] The same standard – the avoidance of significant adverse effects – is used in the 1983 Agreement and in both bills.

However, absent express new statutory language that addresses the relationship of the new legislation to the 1983 Agreement and to particular management and land use

---

[58] See Paragraph 4, p. 10 of the Agreement that states that Appendix 1 applies to the lands to be conveyed to ASRC, thereby incorporating by reference Paragraph 1 of Appendix 1 that applies 22(g) to ASRC lands and Paragraph 6 of Appendix 1, which requires compliance with the Land Use Stipulations of Appendix 2.

considerations, issues may arise. Both bills currently speak in general terms on environmental constraints, leaving much to be fleshed out by the Secretary of the Interior in new leasing regulations for the Refuge. The 1983 Agreement contemplates that subsequent legislation and regulations may supersede its provisions. Yet, arguably, the current bills do not accomplish this, in that they postpone many decisions and aspects of oil and gas development to possible coverage in the leasing regulations that are to be developed. To whatever extent the congressional acts and administrative regulations do not clearly supersede the 1983 Agreement, its terms will govern oil development on the ASRC lands. And other provisions of the 1983 Agreement may still operate despite the general legislated environmental constraints with respect to ASRC oil development.

For example, the 1983 Agreement qualifies its general statement that statutory language on oil development in the coastal plain will supersede the Agreement, by stating in Paragraph B.9 of Appendix 2 (pp. 28-29) that certain provisions in Paragraph B.3(c) - (m) – that set out an approval process for a "plan of operations" for oil development – will remain in effect.[59] This provision may mean that Congress would have to expressly address and change this plan approval process, or the terms of the Agreement may still govern. The referenced Paragraph B.3(c)-(m) provisions provide a special process for approval of a plan of operations for ASRC development under which if the Regional Director of Fish and Wildlife Service and ASRC disagree as to whether a part of a proposed plan would significantly adversely affect the wildlife, habitat, or environment of the ASRC lands or Refuge lands or would otherwise be inconsistent with any provision of the Agreement, ultimately (after some prescribed exchanges of written points of view and negotiations) the United States must obtain a *court order* restraining implementation of the plan of operations, or else ASRC will have the right to implement the plan of operations as originally proposed or as subsequently modified. In other words, the opinion of ASRC as to harm will prevail unless the United States obtains the agreement of a court with its views in every instance.

Should ASRC assert that this provision remains in effect even if the Director of BLM, rather than the Regional Director of FWS is the responsible leasing official, this language appears to impose a difficult burden on the United States to assert and control adverse effects of leasing on Native lands. This burden, combined with the fact that the current bills do not address the 1983 Agreement and which of its terms are superseded, and do not contain specific environmental controls that would supersede the provisions of the Agreement, may result in some Agreement provisions that were intended as "state of the art" environmental constraints in 1983 becoming less than desirable standards today, in light of technological changes since 1983. For example, provisions in Appendix 2 of the Agreement speak to "reserve pits" and ponds as means for the disposal of wastes on the surface of the Refuge, while current practice is to reinfect wastes underground, rather than using reserve pits. Other provisions in the Agreement also address environmental considerations in ways that might not be considered acceptable today. The Agreement specifically addresses, for example, the use of explosives, aircraft, fires, disposal of gray water on the surface of the Refuge, removal of water from streams, incineration, fuel pits, extraction of sand and gravel, and the type and location of support facilities. Depending on the specificity of the oil development regulations

---

[59] The agreement refers to "such" plans. This could refer either to exploration plans in Paragraph B.3, or it could refer to all plans – exploration or development – that are the subject of Paragraph B.9. A reading of B.9 as a whole would seem to indicate that the latter interpretation is more likely the correct one. Given the importance of this issue, Congress may wish to clarify this point.

that the Secretary is to develop, some of these provisions of the Agreement that are not expressly superseded may ultimately function to permit pollution and the siting and use of facilities that might not be permitted under current practices.

S. 388 as introduced provides in § 503(d) that the title on ANWR leasing "shall be the sole authority for leasing on the 1002 Area." It is not clear how this statement relates to the 1983 Agreement – whether it applies only to leasing of the federal lands, or totally supersedes the 1983 Agreement with respect to oil development activities on ASRC lands.[60] If it does, then what constraints might apply to development of the ASRC holdings in the coastal plain is unclear. If the 1983 Agreement does not apply, then arguably neither its stipulations, nor § 22(g) apply. While § 503(h) of S. 388 mentions the 1983 Agreement with respect to conveyance of the remainder of KIC and ASRC lands, it does not otherwise address the Agreement or issues relating to the Native holdings.

Some bills in previous Congresses have specifically address oil development-related activities on Native lands within the Refuge and expressly set out development limitations and specifications, together with expedited judicial review of possible Native claims for breach of contract or "takings" under the 5th Amendment of the Constitution. See *e.g.,* H.R. 3601 in the 100th Congress and H.R. 1320 in the 102d Congress, which limited port facilities and other development support activities and directed the promulgation of Refuge-wide regulations within a specified time. While both current bills repeat many of the provisions of bills from the 102d Congress that relate to what should be covered in leasing regulations, they omit other provisions that related to specific environmental constraints, development of the ASRC lands and expedited review of Native claims.

(4). Section 22(g) Constraints

Both the KIC and ASRC lands are currently subject to § 22(g) of ANCSA, and hence to regulations governing ANWR; the KIC lands by the terms of that Act, and ASRC lands by the terms of the 1983 Agreement. Before the development of compatibility regulations that spoke to lands subject to § 22(g), several exchanges, including the ASRC exchange, had contained land-use stipulations to attempt to clarify what could and could not be done on the lands. Some current regulations shed light on how § 22(9g) might apply to ANWR lands generally. Because § 22(g) requires compliance with the regulations of the particular refuge of which the Native lands are a part, the law enacted to lease ANWR and the Refuge regulations could impose some constraints on inholdings. However, some of the general regulations that apply allow a considerable range of activities on Native lands in refuges.

43 C.F.R. § 2650.4-6 states that regulations governing the use and development of refuge lands conveyed pursuant to § 14 of ANCSA "shall permit such uses that will not materially impair the values for which the refuge was established." This appears to be a standard that would allow a considerable range of activities.

The new compatibility regulations address § 22(g) lands and state that compatibility determinations for those lands are to be made in compliance with the requirements stated in the regulations, several of which are relevant to this report. Notably, the regulations state, for example, that only the effects on refuge lands that result from a use made on Native lands, not

---

[60] Section 503 of the bill refers to the 1983 Agreement, but only with reference to confirming the subsurface rights ASRC is to take beneath lands that section directs be conveyed to KIC.

the use on the Native lands itself, will be considered, and that the Refuge management plan will not include the Native lands:

(1)(i) Refuge managers will work with 22(g) landowners in implementation of these regulations. The landowners should contact the Refuge Manager in advance of initiating a use and request a compatibility determination. After a compatibility determination is requested, refuge managers have no longer than ninety (90) days to complete the compatibility determination and notify the landowner of the finding by providing a copy of the compatibility determination or to inform the landowner of the specific reasons for delay. If a refuge manager believes that a finding of not compatible is likely, the Refuge Manager will notify the landowner prior to rendering a decision to encourage dialog on how the proposed use might be modified to be compatible.
(ii) Refuge managers will allow all uses proposed by 22(g) landowners when the Refuge Manager determines the use to be compatible with refuge purposes.
(iii) Compatibility determinations will include only evaluations of how the proposed use would affect the ability of the refuge to meet its mandated purposes. The National Wildlife Refuge System mission will not be considered in the evaluation. Refuge purposes will include both pre-ANILCA purposes and those established by ANILCA, so long as they do not conflict. If conflicts arise, ANILCA purposes will take precedence.
(iv) A determination that a use is not compatible may be appealed by the landowner to the Regional Director. The appeal must be submitted in writing within forty-five (45) days of receipt of the determination. The appeals process provided for in 50 C.F.R. 36.41(e)(3) through (5) will apply.
(v) Compatibility determinations for proposed uses of 22(g) lands will only evaluate the effects of the use on the adjacent refuge lands, and the ability of that refuge to achieve its purposes, not on the effects of the proposed use to (sic) the 22(g) lands.
(vi) Compatibility determinations for 22(g) lands that a use is compatible are not subject to re-evaluation unless the use changes significantly, significant new information is made available that could affect the compatibility determination, or if requested by the landowner.
(vii) Refuge comprehensive conservation plans will not include 22(g) lands and compatibility determinations affecting such lands will not be automatically re-evaluated when the plans are routinely updated.
(viii) Refuge special use permits will not be required for compatible uses of 22(g) lands. Special conditions necessary to ensure a proposed use is compatible may be included in the compatibility determination and must be complied with for the use to be considered compatible.

....

(g) Except for uses specifically authorized for a period longer than 10 years (such as rights-of-ways), we will re-evaluate compatibility determinations for all existing uses other than wildlife-dependent recreational uses when conditions under which the use is permitted change significantly, or if there is significant new information regarding the effects of the use, or at least every 10 years, whichever is earlier. In addition, a refuge manager always may re-evaluate the compatibility (sic) of a use at any time.
(H) For uses in existence on November 17, 2000 that were specifically authorized for a period longer than 10 years (such as rights-of-ways), our compatibility re-evaluation will examine compliance with the terms and conditions of the authorization, not the authorization itself. We will frequently monitor and review the activity to ensure that the permitted carries out all permit terms and conditions. However, the Service will request modifications to the terms and conditions of these permits from the permitted if the Service determines that such changes are necessary to ensure that the use remains compatible. After November 17, 2000 no uses will be permitted or re-authorized, for a period longer than 10 years, unless the terms and conditions for such long-term permits specifically allow for modifications to the terms and conditions, if necessary to ensure compatibility. We will make a new compatibility determination prior to extending or renewing such long-term uses at the expiration of the authorization. When we prepare a compatibility determination for re-authorization of an existing right-of-way, we will

base our analysis on the existing conditions with the use in place, not from a pre-use perspective.[61]

These regulations, and the 1983 Agreement, could allow a considerable range of development on the KIC and ASRC lands, unless superseded or elaborated on by new statutory and regulatory leasing provisions. Both H.R. 4 (§ 6503(c) and S. 388 (§ 503(c)) provide that oil and gas leasing in the Refuge is found to be compatible with the purposes of the Refuge and no further findings or decisions are required to implement this determination. The exact effect of this statutory finding on the scope of possible regulation under § 22(g) is not clear.

(5). Allotments

Allotments, it will be recalled, are lands the surface of which are owned by the individuals. Even if the United States retained the oil and gas rights beneath allotments, the surface is in non-federal ownership and can be developed. Allotments within the refuge are not subject to the requirement of § 22(g) of ANCSA that uses on Native lands chosen under that Act comply with the regulations of the Refuge.

Therefore, the uses that an allotted might make of these lands or permit to be made of these lands could have significant impacts on the Refuge – if oil development were allowed, allotments could be used for staging areas, port development, or refuse storage. Therefore, the size and location of allotments is relevant to assessing the possible overall effects of oil development on the coastal plain and the Refuge. As noted above, some patented allotments are located on the coast and in the Sadlerochit Spring area. BLM advises that 9,797 allotment acres have been conveyed in the Refuge and another 1,720 acres have been approved.

Other statutes relating to the management of environmentally sensitive federal conservation units have provided for regulation of valid existing rights and inholdings. For example, the Wilderness Act authorizes mineral leasing under "such reasonable stipulations as may be prescribed by the Secretary of Agriculture for the protection of the wilderness character of the land consistent with the use of the land for the purposes for which they are leased..."[62] Congress also subjected existing mining rights in national parks to "such regulations prescribed by the Secretary of the Interior as he deems necessary or desirable for the preservation and management of those areas."[63]

Neither bill addresses individual allotments within the Refuge – e.g., by providing for regulated access and use, or for buying them out, etc.

(6). Timing

Both bills would repeal the § 1003 prohibition against oil and gas development in the Refuge, thereby allowing such development. Neither bill currently contains any time limitations on activities on Native lands leading to development or production, even though leasing regulations for the federal lands are not to be finalized for either 14 or 15 months. As discussed above, neither bill expressly addresses the provisions of the 1983 Agreement and which of its provisions are expressly superseded. Therefore, it is not clear that ASRC must wait until the federal leasing regulations are completed before moving forward in accordance

---

[61] 50 C.F.R. § 25.21 at 65 Fed. Reg. 62481-62482.
[62] 16 U.S.C. § 1133(d).
[63] 16 U.S.C. § 1902.

with the terms of the 1983 Agreement. It will be recalled that an exploratory well was already drilled on KIC lands and some oil companies could be ready to move forward immediately on the Native lands. Express provisions addressing this issue of timing could ensure a fair start under the same rules.

III. Access, Rights of Way, and Exports

Title XI of ANILCA provides for rights of way across federal conservation areas for transportation and utility systems. Section 6509(a) of H.R. 4 provides that Title XI of ANILCA "shall not apply to the issuance by the Secretary under section 28 of the Mineral Leasing Act ... of rights-of-way and easements across the Coastal Plain for the transportation of oil an gas." Because the House bill also states that leasing is to be under the MLA, the intent appears to be that rights of way on the Coastal Plain be issued under the MLA.

However, subsection (b) of § 6509 requires that terms and conditions on rights of way or easements to transport oil and gas ensure that such transportation does not result in a significant adverse effect on the fish and wildlife, subsistence resources, their habitat, and the environment of the Coastal Plain. Current 30 U.S.C. § 185(h) requires that the Secretary impose stipulations on the right of way that are "designed to control or prevent (i) damage to the environment (including damage to fish and wildlife habitat), ..." This standard in current law appears to be more protective than that in the House language.

Section 512 of S. 388 directs that "[notwithstanding Title XI of ANILCA, the Secretary is authorized and directed to grant in accordance with parts of § 28 of the MLA rights of way and easement across the 1002 Area for the transportation of oil and gas – again with terms and conditions to avoid significant adverse effects. The same comments can be made about the Senate bill language with respect to the environmental standard, as were made regarding the House language. The leasing regulations required by § 504 of the title are to include provisions on rights of way and easements.

The parts of § 28 of the MLA that the Senate bill states are applicable to rights of way in the Coastal Plain are subsections (c) through (t) and (v) through (y). This choice eliminates subsection (u) that generally prohibits the export of domestically produced oil transported by pipeline over rights of way granted under the MLA unless the President determines it is in the national interest to do so. Subsection (s), which is retained, reverses this policy posture on oil exports with respect to oil transported by pipeline through the TransAlaska Pipeline System (TAPS). Such oil *can* be exported unless the President determines that export is *not* in the national interest. It has generally been assumed that oil from ANWR would be piped over to the TAPS for transport south to the port of Valdez. If so, then under the Senate bill, ANWR oil could be exported unless the procedures set out in 30 U.S.C. § 185(s) are complied with. Section 650(a)(8) of H.R. 4 would direct that leases prohibit the export of oil produced under a lease.

The rights of way language in the House bill addresses only the transportation of oil and gas by pipeline. However, any use of the surface of the federal lands is a "right of way," not just those uses for the transportation of oil and gas. The areas occupied by drilling pads or other oil development structures, for example, would require a right of way or easement, yet the bill does not address these other situations or specify which other law is to govern.

Although the House bill provides that leasing is to be under the MLA, the MLA provisions on rights of way only address pipelines. As discussed in the first section of this report, ambiguities remain as to which agency would otherwise be the managing/permitting authority and with what scope of authority, hence it is not clear under the House bill which laws and regulations would pertain to non-pipeline rights of ways used in connection with leasing activities. Title XI of ANILCA provides a process for obtaining rights of way for transportation and utility systems in federal conservation areas in Alaska (which term includes refuges), and the Refuge Administration Act provides at 16 U.S.C. § 668dd(d)(1)(B) that the Secretary (acting through the FWS) may grant easements across or upon refuge lands. Whether this provision would come into play depends again on how the management division between BLM and FWS is interpreted.

Neither bill expressly addresses access to the Native inholdings in the Refuge. As discussed, there are individual allotments scattered in the Refuge that might be developed once the Refuge is open to oil and gas development. Under § 1110(b) of ANILCA, notwithstanding any other law, the Secretary is to grant access rights to the owner or occupier of inholdings in conservation system units.[64] The access rights are to be:

> as may be necessary to assure adequate and feasible access for economic and other purposes to the concerned land .... Such rights shall be subject to reasonable regulations issued by the Secretary to protect the natural and other values of such lands.[65]

As noted, the Refuge Administration Act provides that the Secretary (acting through the FWS in that instance) may provide permit or grant easements across or upon areas within the Refuge System, but because of the "notwithstanding" language in the ANILCA access provision, arguably this statute would not apply to access easements.[66]

IV. Compliance with NEPA

Some observers questions whether the existing final legislative environmental impact statement (FLEIS), prepared in 1987 to comply with the National Environmental Policy Act (NEPA), is adequate to support development now, or whether an updated or new EIS should be prepared. A court in a declaratory judgment action in 1997[67] held that the COI should have prepared a Supplemental Environmental Impact Statement (SEIS) at that time to encompass new information about the 1002 area in connection with the Department's recommendation that Congress legislate to permit development. Therefore, it seems clear that either an SEIS or a new EIS would have to be prepared before development, unless Congress changes this

---

[64] Under § 1323 of ANILCA, (16 U.S.C. § 3210), the Secretary of the Interior is to provide access to nonfederally owned land surrounded by national forests or public lands managed under the statute that usually governs BLM lands – the Federal Land Policy Management Act (FLPMA). However, because BLM would be administering leasing in the Refuge under the current bill proposals, rather than managing the Refuge lands under FLPMA, this ANILCA access provision appears not to apply.

[65] 16 U.S.C. § 3170(9b).

[66] Congress has at times regulated access to inholdings in other conservation areas. For example, under 16 U.S.C. § 1134(b), access to inholdings in designated wilderness areas is allowed "by reasonable regulations consistent with the preservation of the area as wilderness, ... by means which have been or are customarily enjoyed with respect to other such areas similarly situated."

[67] NRDC v. Lujan, 768 F. Supp. 870 (D.D.C. 1991)

requirement. Both Senate and House bills address the issue of the EIS and future application of NEPA.

Section 505 of S. 388 states that the Congress finds the 1987 EIS adequate to satisfy the legal and procedural requirements of [NEPA] with respect to the actions authorized to be taken by the Secretary of the Interior in developing and promulgating the regulations for the establishment of the leasing program, to conduct the first and subsequent lease sales, and to grant rights-of-way and easements to carry out the title. This language appears to eliminate the need to redo or update an EIS for the leasing program and regulations. Yet, at the same time, under § 503(a), the Secretary is directed to impose terms and conditions on leases to ensure that oil exploration and development in the 1002 area will result in no significant adverse effect on fish and wildlife, their habitat, subsistence resources, and the environment. If knowledge of environmental conditions has changed since 1987, developing lease terms and conditions adequate to avoid significant adverse effects might be difficult without more current studies. The bill language does not prohibit completion of such studies; it eliminates any legal requirement to do so for lease sales and with respect to grants of rights of way and easements. For example, even as to the granting of rights of way regarding which NEPA documents need not be prepared, the Secretary, under § 512 of S. 388 is to "impose such terms and conditions as may be necessary so as not to result in a significant adverse effect on the fish and wildlife, subsistence resources, their habitat, and the environment of the 1002 area." However, it could be difficult to develop terms and conditions for particular rights of way without the benefit of site-specific studies of the environmental effects of various alternatives.

It is not clear whether the necessity to prepare NEPA documents for decisions other than the issuance of leasing regulations, lease sales, or grants of rights of way is eliminated. (For example, are new terms and conditions for leases to be viewed as a part of "lease sale?" Some level of NEPA documents may still be required for other types of decisions and for consideration of site specific impacts of particular decisions. Under current NEPA regulations, an agency should prepare an Environmental Assessment to determine if an EIS is necessary, or merely to guide agency decisions.[68]

Section 6503(c)(92) of H.R. 4 deems the 1987 EIS adequate with respect to actions authorized to be taken by the Secretary to develop and promulgate the regulations for the establishment of a leasing program. Yet § 6503 (c)(3) requires the Secretary to prepare a full EIS with respect to other actions authorized by the title. This is noteworthy because only the smaller document, an environmental assessment, might normally be sufficient, depending on the magnitude of the action involved. The section goes on to say that the Secretary is to identify only a preferred action for leasing and a single alternative and analyze only those two choices, and to consider public comment only on the preferred alternative. Public comments must be submitted within 20 days of publication of the analysis. The first analysis on the first lease sale is to be completed within 18 months of enactment. Compliance with paragraph (3) is stated as satisfying all requirements for consideration and analysis of environmental effects. However, paragraph (3) both directs the preparation of an EIS for all actions authorized by the title, yet also speaks as though it is only meant to address proposals for lease sales, so the intended import is not clear.

---

[68] 40 C.F.R. Part 1500.

V. Judicial Review

The current bills contemplate prompt action to put a leasing program in place. Toward that end, both S. 388 and H.R. 4 have a section on expedited judicial review. Section 511 of the Senate bill and § 6508 of H.R. 4 are alike in several respects; they both require that judicial review be sought within 90 days from the date of the action being challenged or the date the complainant knew or reasonably should have known of the grounds for the complaint. Section 6508 (9a)(1) and (a)(2) as currently written contradict each other in that one states that suits challenging any action of the Secretary under the title must be filed in the appropriate district court of the United States [subsection (a)(1)] and in the United States Court of Appeals for the District of Columbia [subsection (a)(2)]. Section 511 of the Senate bill provides for suits generally to be filed in any appropriate district court of the United States except that a complaint seeking judicial review of an action of the Secretary *in promulgating regulations* under the Act may only be filed in the United States Court of Appeals for the District of Columbia. Possibly this same distinction between the two courts is what was intended in the House bill.

Both bills provide that actions of the Secretary that could have been reviewed under the section on judicial review may not be reviewed as part of a civil or criminal enforcement proceeding.

In addition, H.R. 4 also limits the scope of review by stating that review of a Secretarial decision to conduct a lease sale, including the environmental analysis thereof, shall be limited to whether the Secretary complied with the terms of Division F of the leasing statute and shall be based upon the administrative record of that decision. Furthermore, under § 6508(a)(3), the Secretary's identification of a preferred course of leasing action and the Secretary's analysis of environmental effects is "presumed to be correct unless shown otherwise by clear and convincing evidence to the contrary." The requirement of clear and convincing evidence in this context differs from the usual standards for proof and may be confusing,[69] but appears to be intended to make overturning a decision difficult.

VI. Disposition of Leasing Revenues

Another issue that has arisen during debates over leasing in the ANWR is that of disposition of possible revenues – whether Congress may validly provide for a disposition of revenues other than the 90/10 percent split mentioned in the Alaska Statehood Act.

Under § 35 of the Mineral Leasing Act (MLA),[70] an act that applies to the leasing of oil and gas and certain other minerals from federal public lands, certain western states receive directly 50% of revenues. An additional 40% goes to those states indirectly through the construction and maintenance of irrigation projects under the Reclamation Act of 1902. These percentages previously were 37 ½% share of federal leasing revenues. Before enactment of the Alaska Statehood Act, Congress amended the MLA to provide that the territory of Alaska would receive an additional 52 ½% share, thereby putting Alaska on the same footing as the

---

[69] See Charles H. Koch, ADMINISTRATIVE LAW AND PRACTICE, § 10.8 (2d. Ed. 1997).
[70] Act of February 25, 1920, ch. 85, 41 Stat. 450, 30 U.S.C. § 191.

other states, receiving a total of 90% of revenues from leasing under the MLA.[71] Section 28(b) of the Alaska Statehood Act again amended the MLA to change the references from the territory of Alaska to State of Alaska.[72]

Section 317 of the Federal Land Policy Management Act of 1976 again amended the revenues section of MLA to direct payment of 90% to Alaska, rather than the separate percentages previously stated.[73] The committee report accompanying the 1976 change states, under a heading regarding changes to distribution of revenues from MLA operations, that the action was intended to clarify that Alaska was to continue to receive 90% of the mineral revenues taken in from lands in Alaska.[74]

Alaska has asserted that the 90% total referenced in the Statehood Act cannot be changed and must always be paid to the state because the Statehood Act is a compact between the prospective state and the federal government. Others assert that the Statehood Act provision was a technical one, meant to recognize that Alaska should receive a share comparable to that of other states sharing revenues *under the MLA*, but does not preclude the Congress from changing the MLA or at times making special provision for leasing certain areas under a different regime.

Alaska sued in the U.S. Court of Federal Claims, asserting that because the United States had an obligation under the Statehood Act both to maximize mineral leasing in Alaska and to always pay a 90% share of *gross* receipts to Alaska, the United States had either breached the contract established by the Statehood Act, or "taken" property of Alaska by withdrawing some lands in Alaska from leasing (notably ANWR), and by deducting administrative costs prior to the disbursement of the 90% revenues to the State. The court found that the Statehood Act and the previous statute providing the territory of Alaska with the same shares as the other states "simply plugged [Alaska] into the MLA, along with the other States."[75] Therefore, Congress could amend the MLA, *e.g.*, to provide a different way of calculating receipts, and the changes would lawfully pertain to Alaska. Furthermore, the court concluded that the United States did not promise in the Statehood Act to make federal mineral lands productive of royalty revenues for the State, and that the United States therefore retained discretion over leasing decisions.[76] Because of these findings, the court also granted the government's motion for summary judgment on the takings claim. Although this case was in the context of the power of the United States to pay administrative costs before dividing MLA revenues with Alaska, arguably the same analysis of the provision in question would apply to a direct challenge to the authority of Congress to change the revenue shares under a particular statutory leasing regime as opposed to paying 90% as stated in the Statehood Act.

If the Statehood Act simply means that Alaska will be treated like other states under the MLA, the question may be asked whether Congress may legislate specially as to ANWR and prescribe different revenue-sharing provisions in that particular leasing context. Congress has directed a different split in the past, e.g., with respect the National Petroleum Reserves, in

---

[71] Pub. L. No. 85-88, 71 Stat. 282 (1957). 37 ½ % was to be spent for the construction and maintenance of public roads or for the support of public schools or other public educational institutions as the legislature of the territory may direct. The 52 ½% was to be paid to the territory to be disposed of as the legislature directed.
[72] Pub. L. No. 85-508, 71 Stat. 339, 351.
[73] Pub. L. No. 94-579, 90 Stat. 2743, 2770-2771.
[74] H.R. Rep. No. 94-1724 at 62 (1976).
[75] Alaska v. United States, 35 Fed. Cl. 685, 701 (1996).
[76] *Id.*, at 706.

which situation all of the revenues go into the federal Treasury,[77] except for the National Petroleum Reserve in Alaska in which instance the revenue sharing is 50/50.[78] Therefore, arguably Congress has flexibility regarding revenue sharing in special legislation regarding oil and gas leasing in the Refuge. Absent new provisions, revenues might either be divided as currently provided under the MLA – if leasing in ANWR is under that statute – or go to the U.S. Treasury as miscellaneous receipts under 31 U.S.C. § 3302. Issues may remain, however, because of the wording of the current bills.

Section 6512 of H.R. 4 states that notwithstanding § 6504 of the bill (which addresses lease sale procedures), the Mineral Leasing Act, or "any other law," 50 percent of all "adjusted" (meaning, the bill states, adjusted for previous overpayments or refunds, etc.) Bonus, rental, and royalty revenues from the oil and gas leasing and operations authorized by the title is to be paid to Alaska. Then a new Fund is created to spend the remaining share of *bonus* revenues and a second new Fund is created to spend the remaining of *rent and royalty* revenues.

This language presents several issues. First, under § 6503(a), the Secretary is to establish and implement a leasing program "under the Mineral Leasing Act," yet § 6512, notwithstanding the Mineral Leasing Act, directs a revenue-sharing program different from that in that Act. Possibly the § 6503(a) language was included to ensure that BLM not the FWS would administer the ANWR leasing program. However, establishing the ANWR leasing program under the Mineral Leasing Act, as opposed to a new, entirely separate statutory program, while also requiring a revenue split different from that pledged to Alaska in its Statehood Act regarding revenues received from leasing under the Mineral Leasing Act, arguably could raise new questions as to the validity of this approach. If a court were to find the alternative disposition of revenues invalid, then quite possibly 90% of the revenues could go to Alaska and 10% to the federal Treasury – with no funds applied to conservation purposes or for renewable energy research.

Also, under § 6512, fifty percent of revenues from *bonus* payments for ANWR leases is to be deposited into the Renewable Energy Technology Investment Fund. Under § 6512(c)(2), fifty percent of revenues from rents and royalty payments from ANWR leases is to be deposited into the "Royalties Conservation Fund." It is not stated whether the base for revenue sharing is to be gross or net receipts, an issue that has been litigated in the past.

However, § 6511 of the bill provides for up to $10,000,000 of the "amounts received by the United States" as revenues derived from rents, bonuses, and royalties to go into a new fund to alleviate coastal impacts. It is not clear how this $10,000,000 is to relate to the 50% share of the United States that is to go into the other two new Funds. Perhaps, the $10,000,000 comes off the top and the remainder is then divided 50% to Alaska and 50% into the other two Funds, or perhaps this is an inadvertent mistake that will be resolved.

Under § 514 of S. 388, "all revenues received" by the federal government from competitive bids, sales, bonuses, royalties, rents, fees, or interest are to be deposited into the Treasury, then Alaska's share is to be paid and the Secretary of the Treasury is to "deposit the balance of all such revenues as miscellaneous receipts in the Treasury." However, the Secretary is directed to deposit amounts received as bonus bids into a special fund known as the Renewable Energy Research and Development Fund. It is not clear whether bonus bids go

---

[77] 10 U.S.C. § 7433.
[78] Pub. L. No. 96-514, 94 Stat. 2964.

into this Fund before the state share is taken out or afterwards, or how the amount received as bonus bids is to be earmarked during the process.

Under § 514(a) of S. 388, Alaska is to receive the same percentage as paid for exploration of the National Petroleum Reserve-Alaska under Pub. L. No. 96-514, which is 50%.

INDEX

A

Agreement on the Conservation of Polar Bears, 107, 128
Agreement on the Conservation of the Porcupine Caribou Herd, 76
air pollution, 6, 54, 55, 56
aircraft, 14, 26, 53, 68, 78, 84, 88, 108, 134
airstrips, 6, 28, 29, 53, 54, 58, 66, 81, 106, 108, 126, 129
Alaska Department of Environmental Conservation (ADEC), 55, 56, 60, 62, 63, 87
Alaska Department of Fish and Game (ADF&G), 52, 88
Alaska Department of Natural Resources (ADNR), 4, 36, 88
Alaska Federation of Natives (AFN), 72, 88
Alaska National Interest Lands Conservation Act (ANILCA), vii, 1, 8, 9, 13-15, 20, 23, 72, 75, 83, 87, 88, 91, 92, 102, 103, 109, 118, 119, 121-123, 129-132, 136, 138, 139
Alaska Native Claims Settlement Act (ANCSA), 15, 71, 73-76, 88, 89, 92, 94, 96, 98, 102, 109, 118, 121, 130-133, 135, 137
Alaska Natives, 7, 15, 30, 69-74, 78, 88, 92, 94
Alaska Natural Gas Transportation System (ANGTS), 38, 88
Alaska Oil and Gas Conservation Commission (AOGCC), 61, 88, 97
Alaska Statehood Act, viii, 12, 85, 109, 118, 141
Alaska v. United States, 86, 109, 142
Alaskan economy, 46
Alaska's North Slope (ANS), 19, 31, 32, 36, 52, 94, 104, 105, 111
Aleuts, 70, 88
allotments, 54, 75, 76, 109, 119, 132, 133, 137, 139
Alpine Corporation Oil Field, 88

American Indians, 70, 74, 88
Angun Plains, 54, 88
animal populations, 8, 79
Arab-Israeli War, 16
ARCO Alaska, 27, 63, 78, 88, 89
Arctic Circle, 12
arctic ecosystem(s), vii, 1, 3, 5, 9, 12, 48, 106
arctic haze, 57
Arctic National Wildlife Range, 9, 12, 47, 96, 102, 118, 121
Arctic National Wildlife Refuge (ANWR), vii, viii, 1-16, 20-24, 26, 27, 29, 31-37, 40-47, 51, 53, 55-57, 59-62, 64, 67, 69-76, 80-82, 84-93, 95, 96, 99, 101-104, 106, 107, 109-112, 114-119, 122, 123, 126, 128, 129-131, 133, 135, 138, 141-143
Arctic Power, 28, 66, 89
Arctic Slope Regional Corporation (ASRC), viii, 7, 32, 70, 72, 73, 75, 76, 89, 90, 93, 109, 119, 126, 131-135, 137
Army Corps of Engineers, 24

B

Barter Island, 7, 69, 89, 92, 93
Beaufort Lagoon, 54, 69, 89, 94
Beaufort Sea, 38, 51, 57, 80, 87, 89, 95, 118
Best Available Control Technology (BACT), 55, 56, 89
Best Management Practices (BMP), 60, 90
bidding, 5, 22, 34, 82, 113
bills, vii, viii, 10, 14, 15, 18, 21-23, 84, 87, 103, 104, 111, 112, 117, 119, 121-126, 129, 132-135, 137, 140, 141, 143
biological resources, vii, 6, 13, 54, 102, 107
bird populations, 17, 68
Borough Acts, 71
British Petroleum (BP), 20, 27, 55, 58, 59, 62, 63, 90, 92, 94, 96

Brooks Range, 3, 9, 11, 48, 49, 50, 54, 73, 87, 90, 91, 95, 106, 107
Bureau of Economic Analysis (BEA), 46, 89
Bureau of Labor Statistics (BLS), 44, 89
Bureau of Land Management (BLM), viii, 13, 14, 20-24, 30-33, 67, 75, 90, 116, 120-122, 131, 132, 134, 137, 139, 143
Bush, President George W., vii, 85
Bush, President George, 85

C

California, 18, 19, 31, 38, 47, 111
caribou, 1, 6, 7, 9, 12, 47, 48-51, 64, 70, 72, 73, 76, 90, 96, 101, 106, 118, 125
Center for Economic and Policy Research (CEPR), 45, 90, 99
Central Arctic Herd (CAH), 48, 49-51, 64, 72, 90, 96
Chandler Lake Agreement, 75, 90, 131, 132
Clean Air Act, 55, 56, 89, 96, 127
Clean Water Act (CWA), 59-61, 91, 124
Clinton Administration, 18
Clinton, President Bill, 85
coastal plain, viii, 1, 3, 4, 7-9, 11-14, 20, 31, 32, 34, 36, 48, 49, 50, 53, 63, 67, 69, 70, 72, 74,- 76, 82, 83, 87, 89, 91, 95, 101, 102, 104, 107, 108, 109, 112-115, 116-119, 121-126, 130-135, 137, 138
Coastal Zone Management Act (CZMA), 59, 61, 91
Committee on Environment and Natural Resources, 15
Committee on Environment and Public Works, 15, 115
compatibility policy, 83, 121
compatible use, 91
Corps of Engineers (COE), 91, 95
corps, 59, 61, 64, 67, 91
crude oil, 14, 16, 18, 20, 34, 36, 38, 39, 42, 45, 46, 60, 63, 92, 111

D

deadhorse, 7, 65, 91
Department of Energy (DOE), 18, 20, 39, 92, 115
Department of Justice (DOJ), 20
Department of Labor (DOL), 3
Department of the Interior (DOI), 2, 4, 9, 19-21, 83, 90, 92, 93, 95-98, 101, 116, 120
Department of Transportation (DOT), 2, 19
development bills, 14, 15, 22, 23
development phase, 26, 27

development rates, 34, 35, 36, 105
DEWLine, 3, 7, 69, 89, 91, 93
Distant Early Warning Line, 7, 69, 91
domestic wastes, 6, 54
Doyon, Ltd., 71, 74, 92
drill pads, 3, 6, 26, 28, 50, 51, 54, 58, 65, 79, 84
drilling waste(s), 62, 106
drilling, viii, 3, 4, 6, 19, 22, 25, 26, 28-30, 50, 54, 57, 58, 59, 60, 62, 64, 67, 74, 76, 80, 81, 93, 105, 109, 117-120, 122, 124- 126, 129, 133, 138

E

economically recoverable oil, 5, 13, 14, 32-36, 40, 41, 46, 92, 95, 98, 101
ecosystems, 3, 98
electric power generation, 37, 38
elevated pipelines, 28
employment, 4, 26, 43-46, 71, 73, 74, 78
Endangered Species Act (ESA), 53, 92, 124
Endicott (oil field), 32, 92
energy companies, 3, 5, 8
energy costs, 43
energy development, vii, 2, 4, 6, 9-12, 15, 16, 24, 28, 30, 46, 48, 53, 72, 77, 81, 82, 87-93, 101, 103, 107, 113, 114
Energy Information Administration (EIA), 5, 34-37, 41-43, 45, 92, 105
energy leasing, 8, 23, 115
energy prices, 9, 43, 44, 81
energy production, 11, 30, 78, 97
Enhanced Oil Recovery (EOR), 62, 92
environmental controls, 4, 76, 132, 134
environmental impact statement (EIS), 19, 20, 23, 83, 111, 112, 139, 140
environmental impacts, 3, 4, 9, 11, 26, 65, 106, 108
Environmental Protection Agency (EPA), 56, 59-63, 89, 91, 92, 94, 96, 97
environmental protection, 4, 6, 22, 55, 77, 84, 108, 120
environmental regulations, viii, 38
erosion, 57, 63, 79, 80, 82
Eskimos, 70, 88, 131
exploration, 4, 6, 13, 19, 20, 22, 23, 25, 26, 29, 30, 34, 40, 46, 47, 49, 51, 54, 57-65, 70, 72, 73, 76, 77, 80, 82, 84, 91, 94, 96, 97, 103, 105, 107, 108, 111, 113, 123, 125, 127, 131, 133, 134, 140, 144
export restrictions, 17, 18, 107, 111
extended reach drilling, 28
extraction technology, 34

Exxon Valdez, 15, 17
Exxon-Mobil, 92

F

facility removal, 81
Federal Land Policy Management Act, 86, 139, 142
federal lands, viii, 9, 16, 17, 20-22, 32, 33, 48, 59, 86, 88, 90, 93, 94, 96, 98, 104, 109, 110, 126, 135, 137, 138
Federal Trade Commission, 20, 63
federal waters, 18
Final Legislative Environmental Impact Statement (FLEIS), 8, 11-13, 15, 21, 23, 26-28, 35, 45, 48, 49, 51-58, 65-68, 72, 73, 77, 78, 81, 83, 84, 87, 88, 92, 95, 98, 103, 106, 113-115, 126, 139
financial resources, 30, 60
Fish and Wildlife Service (FWS), viii, 2, 13, 24, 30, 52, 53, 58, 67, 69, 92, 93, 101, 116, 118, 120-122, 124, 126-129, 134, 139, 143
fly populations, 49, 51
footprint, 64, 93, 108
foreign oil, 17
full employment, 44, 45

G

gas pipeline, 38, 39, 40, 76
gas resources, 2, 37, 38
General Accounting Office (GAO), 24, 116
global warming, 77
goods and services, 40, 43, 45, 46
gravel mines, 28, 29, 65, 66, 84, 93
gravel roads, 26-28, 58, 59, 78
gravel structures, 63, 79, 80, 84
grizzly bears, 1, 9, 50, 101
Gross Domestic Product (GDP), 43, 45, 93
Gross National Product (GNP), 45, 93
Gulf Coast, 18, 111
Gwich'in, 70-74, 76, 93

H

hazardous wastes, 6, 62, 96
human habitation, 6, 54, 89
human population levels, 78
hunting, 52, 53, 72, 74, 79, 107, 128, 130

I

ice pad melts, 59

ice roads, 7, 25-28, 54, 57-60, 67, 68, 84, 127
industrial activity, 30, 77
industrial phase, 30
infrastructure, 4, 6, 8, 26, 28, 31, 37, 41, 42, 47, 93, 98, 101, 105, 114, 126
INGAA Foundation, 39, 93
inholdings, 24, 32, 81, 93, 135, 137, 139
Inuit, 70, 88, 93
Inupiat, 69-73, 75, 93, 109, 130, 131

J

Jago River, 54, 59
Japan, 16, 18
judicial review, 4, 84, 108, 112, 115, 120, 124, 129, 135, 141

K

Kaktovik Inupiat Corporation (KIC), 7, 32, 69, 70, 72, 73, 75, 76, 89, 90, 93, 94, 102, 109, 119, 130-133, 135, 137, 138
Kaktovik, 6, 7, 9, 15, 28, 32, 52, 54, 69-75, 78, 89, 92-94, 102, 109, 119, 124, 130
Kongakut River, 54, 94
Korea, 16
Kuparuk, 7, 31, 65, 88, 94, 106

L

labor market, 44
land management, 21, 88
leasing process, 20, 21, 23
leasing regulations, 112, 120-122, 125, 127, 129, 134, 135, 137, 138, 140
liquefied natural gas (LNG), 5, 38, 94, 98

M

Mackenzie Delta, 38
macroeconomic effects, 43, 44
Marine Mammal Protection Act (MMPA), 51, 127, 128, 129
Marine Protection Research and Sanctuaries Act, 61, 95
migratory birds, 48, 52, 101, 106, 118
Milne Point, 94
Mineral Leasing Act (MLA), 16, 18, 21, 22, 24, 85, 86, 94, 97, 109-111, 120-122, 127, 129, 138, 139, 141-143
mineral leasing laws, 83, 121
mining, 6, 40, 46, 54, 58, 63, 83, 96, 121, 123, 129, 137

mosquito populations, 49, 51
multilateral drilling, 106
musk oxen, 1, 7, 48, 52, 59, 106, 118

N

National Ambient Air Quality Standards (NAAQS), 55, 56, 94, 96
National Congress of American Indians (NCAI), 72, 95
national economy, 1, 44
national energy goals, vii
National Environmental Policy Act (NEPA), 4, 19, 21, 23, 83, 95, 107, 111, 114, 115, 123, 125, 126, 139, 140
national parks, 56, 123, 137
National Petroleum Reserve-Alaska (NPRA), 4, 19, 20, 23, 26, 31, 48, 75, 80, 89, 94-96, 104, 109, 123, 131, 144
National Petroleum Reserves, 86, 142
national security, 3, 91, 101
National Wildlife Refuge System Improvement Act, 24
National Wildlife Refuge System, 23, 75, 83, 91, 102, 120, 121, 136
National Wildlife Refuges, 23, 24, 75, 102, 130
Native Corporation, 94
Native groups, 3, 118
Native Lands, viii, 4, 7, 14, 15, 22, 28, 29, 66, 73, 79, 109, 119, 123, 126, 129, 133, 135, 136, 138
Native Village, 70, 73, 74, 89, 93, 94, 98, 118, 129
Native, viii, 6, 7, 11, 13-15, 20, 22, 24, 29, 34, 39, 48, 54, 66, 68-76, 79, 81, 82, 87-89, 91-94, 96, 98, 102, 103, 106-109, 113, 118, 119, 121, 122, 126, 128-135, 137, 139
natural gas, vii, 1, 5, 8, 30, 33, 34, 36-40, 47, 55, 76, 77, 93, 97, 98, 104, 105, 117, 118
natural-gas-fired turbines, 55
non-OPEC producers, 43
North Slope Borough, 60, 70-74, 78, 93, 95, 124
North Slope, viii, 4-6, 9, 11, 16-21, 23, 25, 26, 29, 31, 32, 34, 36-39, 41, 45, 52, 54-63, 65, 70-74, 76, 78, 80, 89, 90, 92, 93, 95-97, 99, 104, 105, 110, 111, 124
Northern Gas Pipeline Project, 38

O

Ocean Dumping Ac, 59, 61, 95

oil and gas development, viii, 5, 15, 31, 36, 41, 46, 47, 70, 72-77, 81, 85, 102, 103, 109, 117, 119, 128, 129, 131, 132, 134, 137, 139
oil and gas leasing, 19, 83, 86, 112, 114, 115, 120-122, 137, 143
oil and gas reserves, 104
oil companies, 3, 40, 41, 59, 61, 84, 138
oil development, viii, 2, 3, 6, 7, 20, 30, 44, 45, 56, 63, 64, 71, 73-76, 82, 93, 95, 117, 119, 125, 126, 132, 134, 135, 137, 138
oil discovery, 4, 45, 59
oil fields, 8, 36, 38, 41, 48, 50, 58, 64, 66, 67, 78, 92
oil imports, 31, 42
oil industry, 1, 34, 44, 45, 46, 59, 60
oil operations, 4, 7
oil potential, 2, 5, 9, 31, 102, 104
oil prices, 9, 18, 21, 32, 34-36, 40, 42-46, 67, 78, 92, 94, 111
oil production, viii, 5, 8, 18, 30, 31, 42, 45, 61, 65, 76, 81, 87, 133
oil prospects, 9, 44, 46
oil reserves, 4, 8, 31, 33
oil spills, 16
Organization for Economic Cooperation and Development (OECD), 43, 95
Organization of Petroleum Exporting Countries (OPEC), 42, 45, 95

P

Panama Canal, 18, 111
Persian Gulf War, 8
petroleum consumption, 31, 105
Phillips Petroleum, 63, 88, 89, 94, 96
physical environment, 6, 54
pipeline construction, 38, 105
pipeline extension, 46
pipeline routes, 16
pipelines, 4, 6, 16, 19, 26, 28-30, 37, 51, 58, 66, 84, 93, 98, 108, 111, 126, 139
Polar Bear Agreement, 127, 128, 129
polar bears, 1, 9, 48, 51, 52, 102, 106, 107, 118, 128, 129
pollutants, 6, 55, 56, 60, 89, 95
pollution control, 56, 78
Porcupine Caribou Herd (PCH), 14, 48-51, 64, 72-74, 76, 87, 90, 96, 106, 114
port development, 68, 137
preservation, 3, 123, 137, 139
Prevention of Significant Deterioration (PSD), 55, 56, 89, 96
production levels, 34, 105

production phase, 29
project labor agreements (PLAs), 85, 96, 110
Prudhoe Bay, vii, 1, 3-5, 7-9, 12, 16, 19, 27, 31, 36, 38, 48, 50, 52, 55, 56, 59, 67, 78, 79, 89-92, 94, 96, 98, 101, 104-106, 118
Public Land Order (PLO), 12, 83, 96, 102, 118, 121, 131, 132

R

Reclamation Act of 1902, 85, 141
reclamation, 4, 20, 22, 30, 84, 108, 115, 125, 129
recreational visits, 69
recycling programs, 62
Refuge Administration Act, 120-122, 124, 127, 139
refuge management, 74, 83
Refuge System, 23, 24, 112, 120, 122, 139
Regional Corporations, 71, 73, 75, 96, 102, 109, 118, 129, 130
regulation, 61, 63, 68, 81, 84, 88, 121, 127, 137
regulatory authorities, 59
regulatory controls, 8
rehabilitation/restoration, 78
Renewable Energy Research and Development Fund, 109, 143
Renewable Energy Technology Investment Fund, 110, 143
rental payments, 22
Resource Conservation and Recovery Act (RCRA), 62, 96
revegetation, 8, 79, 80
revenues, viii, 11, 13, 15, 40, 43, 47, 71-73, 78, 85, 86, 87, 103, 107, 109, 110, 115, 141-143
rights of way, 79, 111, 138, 140
Rivers and Harbors Act, 59, 61
road removal, 79
Royalties Conservation Fund, 110, 143
royalties, 19, 40, 47, 110, 143

S

Sadlerochit Spring, 7, 53, 76, 84, 97, 124, 132, 137
Safe Drinking Water Act (SDWA), 59, 61, 89, 97
Secretary of Agriculture, 123, 137
Secretary of the Interior, 12, 19, 24, 47, 75, 96, 102, 107, 118, 120, 121, 123, 131, 134, 137, 139, 140
seismic exploration, 25, 51
site restoration, 4
Statehood Act, 86, 109, 142, 143

Supplemental Environmental Impact Statement (SEIS), 83, 95, 97, 139
Supreme Court, 12, 118
surface rights, 15, 75, 130, 131

T

Tanana Valley (Alaska) Sportsmen's Association, 102
technically recoverable oil, 98
technological improvements, 58, 66, 124
telecommunications, 46, 91
terrorism, 9
terrorist attacks, vii, 82
tourism, 78, 79
TransAlaska Gas System (TAGS), 38, 98
Trans-Alaska Pipeline Authorization Act, 17, 98, 111
TransAlaska Pipeline System (TAPS), viii, 3, 5, 10, 16-18, 26, 29, 33, 38, 40, 41, 65, 82, 98, 138
Trans-Alaska Pipeline, ix, 17-19, 90, 93, 98, 111, 138
transportation market, 82
Tundra, 67, 68, 98

U

U.S. Army Corps of Engineers, 27, 29, 59, 61, 67, 91
U.S. Geological Survey (USGS), 5, 10, 13, 33-35, 37, 38, 40, 41, 69, 80, 98, 104, 116, 122
U.S. Treasury, 19, 143
underground sources of drinking water (USDWs), 61, 97
unemployment, 44, 46
University of Alaska, 50

V

vegetation, 12, 30, 47, 48, 54, 59, 63, 67, 68, 78-80
Venetie Tribal Government, 70, 74
village corporation(s), 71, 74, 75, 88, 94, 98, 102, 109, 118, 119, 130

W

waste disposal, 26, 62, 63, 84, 93
waste management, 3
water pollution, 59, 84
water reservoirs, 59
WEFA Group, 44, 45, 99

Wellhead Price, 99
wetlands, 12, 57, 61, 79, 91
Wilderness Act of 1964, 123
wilderness bills, 15
wilderness boundaries, 12, 87, 114
wildlife, viii, 1-3, 5, 7, 8, 12-14, 17, 19, 20, 22, 47, 48, 52, 54, 61, 73, 75-77, 79, 83, 84, 91, 93, 97, 98, 102, 106, 108, 111, 112, 117-127, 129, 130, 132-134, 136, 138, 140
world oil supply, 43, 45

Y

Yupik, 70, 88